HOW TO WRITE AND SELL YOUR FIRST NOVEL

TAKING THE FEAR OUT OF WRITING YOUR FIRST NOVEL

A Note to the Reader:

Nobody was a famous writer before writing that first novel. Some of the most famous weren't even noticed before the second, third, or fourth. But they did it, struggled, bungled along somehow—and got the job done.

Everyone has to start somewhere. And that's what you're doing now—starting at this point in your life. The whole purpose of this book is to take the fear out of writing your first novel. We will be with you every step of the way, and when you close the book, you'll be ready and confident. You'll know you can do it.

May the fates be with you.

Oscar Collier
Frances Spatz Leighton

Contents

Introduction

During twenty-five years in book publishing one of my greatest satis-factions has been helping first novelists on the path to seeing their books in print—and sharing that pleasure with others in publishing who felt the same way. The thought that I was helping these new nov-elists add to the body of living American literature has been a power-ful motivator.

I remember when, as an agent, I sent over a promising first-novel manuscript to Donald I. Fine, a publisher with many years' ex-perience. He liked it, and published it. "Published it" might seem like a simple phrase until you remember what it really means. It means he read it, had others read it, negotiated a contract for it, paid money for advance royalties, as well as for the services of a typesetter, design-er, paper manufacturer, printer, and binder, and that he devoted time personally and passionately to editing it, announcing it, and advertis-ing it.

Finally bound copies were available, and he sent me one of the first copies. When I called to thank him, he asked, "How does it look?"

"Great," I replied. "It's a real first novel."

With deep satisfaction in his voice, he said, "That is what pub-lishing is all about."

Why do Don Fine and hundreds of others in book publishing bother to read countless queries, study thousands of sample chapters and outlines, and read dozens of complete manuscripts of unpub-lished novelists each year? Wouldn't it be easier, and more business-like, to concentrate on the plentiful supply of new works by already-published, proven writers, as some agents, editors, and publishers do?

There are two compelling reasons to pursue new talent. I truly relish the prospect of being the *first* reader to recognize a gifted new writer—whether a genre novelist or a new writer of literary works. Reading a promising new work puts me ahead of all other readers in the world in enjoying it. And in helping get it published, I share with the author something that makes us both feel good—*being first.*

If I can get such a charge from merely *discovering* a new novelist, think how much more you can benefit from *becoming* one. After all, it is you, not the agent or publisher, who are communicating with all those readers out there.

That said, I must immediately add that in this book, my coauthor and I have tried to write about the current realities of the contemporary scene in American publishing. You won't find many references to works of the far past, nor frequent quotations from *Aspects of the Novel*, by E.M. Forster, or *The Art of the Novel*, by Henry James, useful as those books are. We have tried to assimilate the actual experiences of modern novelists as they worked and fought their separate ways to publication, and winnow down the vast amount of material written about novelists in the popular and trade press to the most helpful and interesting information for fledgling novelists.

I have to admit that I've dredged up a few anecdotes from my experience simply because they entertain, and I wanted to share them.

In 1984, according to *Publishers Weekly*, a little over five thousand books of fiction were published in the United States. No actual figure I know of tells how many of these were by new novelists, because many mass-market paperbacks are first novels, and their publishers make no fuss over this fact.

Ann Burns, who collects information about first novels for *Library Journal*, learns of "two hundred to three hundred first novels each year" from those publishers who respond to the *LJ*'s semiannual questionnaire. But she says that some don't respond, particularly paperback publishers of genre novels. She only sends the questionnaire to a list of publishers she thinks might publish first novels because she knows they have done so in the past.

Disregarding self-published novels and "vanity press" novels (because this is a book on how to write and *sell* your first novel), even if 10 percent of all works of fiction published in 1984 were first novels, only five hundred new novelists would have seen their works in print.

An article in *The New York Times Book Review* estimated that thirty thousand unsolicited novels are submitted annually to book publishers, while *Books: The Culture and Commerce of Publishing* reports that 60 percent of trade book editors receive more than a thousand "over the transom" submissions each year. Such figures prove there are certainly a lot of novelists out there writing—many more than get published. Taking the thirty-thousand figure, and assuming that many of these were duplicate submissions, let's say five thousand actual first novels are completed and submitted each year. Then, if my five hundred estimate of how many are published is near the mark, you have a one in ten chance of getting published. Clearly, it's a highly competitive field.

Who are these budding first novelists? My experience as agent, editor, and publisher tells me that they come from practically every walk of life. They are bookkeepers, full-time homemakers, millionaires, lawyers, screen writers, reporters, criminals in prison, doctors, professors, students, casually employed drifters, computer programmers, policemen, soldiers, senators, spies, editors, college presidents, and other people with something to say in fictional form. They are people with a drive to communicate. They are men and women, old and young, diverse in every way.

How do you make the transition from aspiring scribbler to published novelist? This book will tell you how writers—both famous and still on their way—did it, and offer hints from their histories that may help you. Some of their strategies may be well worth imitating.

One of the lessons my years in book publishing taught me is that good craftsmanship alone won't necessarily get you published. Naturally, you must strive to meet certain requirements—show a storytelling flair, offer a feeling for characterization, have a passable plot, use an interesting and well-detailed setting, time frame, and set of circumstances; and display a sense of spoken and written language. But a number of other elements enter the picture also, and we'll try to point them out as we go along in this book.

How often have I heard the anguished cry, "But my novel is better than ones I see published!" And how often it was true! This truth is illustrated by the fact that first novels with many rejections have been later accepted by publishers, and succeed with the public—even to selling a million copies. If such a novel had had just one less submission, or never found the right publisher who needed an additional work of fiction at just that time, it would never have seen print. It would have been just as good as before, but who would know?

In the true success stories of this book, you will learn how first novelists evolved work methods that won publication. You will see threads that weave through their success stories: doggedness, the will to succeed, attention to detail, knowledge of subject matter, willingness to solicit the help of friends and professionals, and inventiveness in overcoming everyday obstacles, such as finding the time to work undisturbed. A subplot in the lives of some of these writers was seeing or creating an opportunity and being bold or bluff enough to grab it.

Through experience, I have learned of many common errors and problems of first novelists. So my coauthor and I will not only suggest things you can do, but also will focus on other things you should avoid doing. It is a sad fact that in book publishing sometimes a new work is published only because the publisher cannot find enough reasons *not* to publish it. When your editor or agent is pushing for you, he must overcome at least one devil's advocate—and sometimes it may be the president or editor-in-chief, who is trying to preserve the capital resources of the company. This person asks people to *prove* that he needs your manuscript. So every fault you can remove from your first novel brings it one step closer to publication.

There are several ways to define a "first novel." Some would narrowly restrict the term to books from authors who have published a novel before they have any other kind of book (such as a biography or textbook) published. Others think that the first completed manuscript of a novelist is his first novel, regardless of whether it is published or unpublished, or published later in the novelist's career. Then there are those who would stretch the term a little more, and define it as the author's first "mainstream" novel, or the author's first book published under his or her real name, and would overlook earlier "romance books" or other genre titles published, not counting them as real novels.

I regard category or genre novels as novels first, and category second. "Romances" are not just books, they are novels, and so are the pulp books of the past called "penny dreadfuls" and "dime novels," in the days when a dime bought a big meal.

In this book, the term "first novel" simply refers to the first novel an author has had published and offered for sale to the public, even if the author has had other kinds of books published before. Whether it is mainstream, romance, or any other genre does not matter, nor does whether an author may have used some pen name on past novels—just using his/her real name for the first time does not make a writer a first-time novelist. And I do not count any other manuscripts the author may have lying in the drawer or even under contract for publication at the time. The first published is the first novel.

The reason I have used this definition is that this is a book about *breaking into print as a novelist*. For me, your first novel will be the first one that actually makes it to a bookstore.

So be warned that what you are about to read is not a guideline on how to write "the great American novel." My coauthor and I take the most unpretentious romance novel as seriously as a work of great literary ambition. This is not a work of criticism, but one on how to write and sell your first novel. Good luck!

Oscar Collier

Part One

HOW TO WRITE AND SELL YOUR FIRST NOVEL

1.

The Heart of It

If you don't write it you can't get it published. Simple truth.

Other people much like you join the ranks of novelists every year Simple truth.

"Ha!" you say. "But I'm just ordinary."

"Ha!" I say. "So were they—except nobody's really ordinary."

Let me tell you about a few of the more recent ones.

Jay McInerney was a part-time liquor store salesman who started writing a novel about Japan, where he had lived for several years as an English teacher. It was hard going. Then he had an idea for a different novel. He felt rather guilty deserting his first novel, but he switched anyway and wrote what was uppermost on his mind.

What emerged was *Bright Lights, Big City,* which was sold as an original trade paperback to Vintage and quickly became a best seller with 125,000 copies in print and a movie sale. Then in a reverse twist, hardback publishing companies expressed interest in bringing out a hardback edition of the paperback.

And what happened to the novel he left behind? Nothing sells like success. He finished it and had no trouble placing it with a publisher. At this writing, the book will be titled *Ransom*, the hero's name.

Not bad for a twenty-nine-year-old.

Now let me tell you about someone a little older. Tom Clancy, thirty-seven. He had never been on a submarine. He had never been in the Navy, or any other branch of the service, because of poor eyesight. He was an insurance salesman, and a good one. Today he is the darling of the military and a best-selling author with his *The Hunt for Red October*.

What happened?

What happened is that Clancy, back in 1975, became fascinated by newspaper reports of a Russian destroyer whose crew attempted to defect to Sweden. The ship was the *Storozhevoy* and the defection attempt was led by the ship's political officer, Valery Sablin. Unfortunately Sablin failed, was captured by the Soviets and executed.

Clancy couldn't get the case out of his mind. It struck him that if the ship had been a nuclear-powered sub, it would be harder to find. He thought of writing a book. He had thought of writing a book before but hadn't gotten far before giving up. This time he meant business. He started researching for the thousands of things he would need to know to make such a book sound authentic. Books like *Guide to the Soviet Navy* and *Combat Fleets of the World* became his favorite reading. Before he was finished he had read or skimmed some three hundred books and had dared to call numerous naval brass hats and civilian experts on submarines and missiles for answers to questions which stumped him.

Along the way he learned the naval jargon—both American and Russian—that he would need for authentic dialogue. By 1982, he was ready to write. By 1985, he finished his manuscript and had turned it over to the Naval Institute Press, which had helped him a great deal with his research and was interested in publishing it as their first work of fiction.

In Clancy's high-tech international thriller, the captain of the Soviet Union's most advanced ballistic missile submarine tries to defect to the United States and the White House learns of it. The race is on between the Russians trying to find and destroy their own sub before it can get to American waters and the Americans who are trying to save it.

"I never considered giving it to any other publisher," Clancy told my coauthor, Fran Leighton. "They had been very good to me and besides, I wasn't sure that any other publisher would be interested. But I did make a mild protest when they offered me a $3,000 advance. I said, 'I have to have at least $5,000.' They agreed immediately and I didn't try to get any more."

But all's well that ends well. The paperback rights to what became a great best seller were sold for $49,500 and Clancy started sifting through movie offers. Finally, he was escorted through his first submarine with VIP treatment.

The wonderful thing is that age and sex have nothing to do with your chances when your manuscript gets to the publisher. Helen Hooven Santmyer was eighty-eight years old and in a nursing home when fame finally caught up with her in January 1984. She was unable to go on a promotion tour around the country, but G.P. Putnam's Sons was not worried about the lack of a promotional tour when they grabbed the book and put a $250,000 floor on what they would accept for the paperback rights for her novel . . . *And Ladies of the Club*.

It took Santmyer fifty years to finish her book. We'll talk more about her later, but the point I want to make now is that you won't have to wait that long if you follow a few simple suggestions I've culled from my years as a literary agent dealing with authors, other agents, and book publishers. I was, at various times, an agent, an editor and senior editor myself in one publishing house, and president of another. I have seen the problems of writing and getting a book published from all angles. So maybe I can give you some new perspectives on your situation.

Let's consider the question of what it takes to become a novelist—the question uppermost in the minds of beginners. "Do I have the right stuff?"

John Gardner, winner of the National Book Critics Circle Award for *October Light*, and a well-known teacher of writing, said it best: You need "an almost demonic compulsiveness." He added that it also helped if a person was suffering a bit from some psychological wound or was driven to try to change the world or himself.

That takes in about all of us. And so, now let's see how *you* are going to change the world or your life—not by grabbing a gun or going on a wild shopping spree, but by building your own little world—on paper.

Don't panic. I don't expect the impossible. You are going to get all set. You don't just sit down at the typewriter and say, "Here we go. Page One," though if you want to try that plan, I have nothing against it. But if you follow my plan instead, by the time you do sit down to write Page One, you will feel right at home—you will almost feel that it's *not* your first novel.

First, let's walk around the problem and get a view of it. A few questions are in order.

WHAT DOES THE READER
WANT FROM ME?

A story. A reader wants you to tell him a story. He's saying, "Let me have a new adventure—let me escape from danger." Or, "Give me a new, sexy life. Make me rich." Or, "I'm feeling hemmed in with all this city life. Take me out west and let me see blue skies, high mountains, and let me be on the side of the good guys." Or, "Let me escape to another century [backwards or forwards], I'm tired of the 20th."

Your reader is going to identify with someone in your book. And it doesn't have to be someone exemplary. He may, for a brief moment in time—the length of time it takes to read your book—become a master computer bank criminal or head of a crime syndicate. Or he may become a child again—but this time joining a gang that is planning to knock off the local video games arcade.

Whatever you choose to write about, you have to assure the reader in the first sentence that you are going to introduce him to his new identity. Take Somerset Maugham's opening line in *The Moon and Sixpence:* "I confess that when first I made acquaintance with Charles Strickland I never for a moment discerned that there was in him anything out of the ordinary."

Aha, the reader knows he is going to delve into someone else's life, through the narrator telling the story in first person, and he's going to be witness to something strange. Curiosity turns pages, and your opening is there to arouse curiosity.

But that's only the opening line, you say. That's not scary. It's the thought of tackling a whole novel that's terrifying.

It shouldn't be.

WHAT IS A NOVEL?

A novel is a story. It's just a story. It has a beginning, a middle, and an end. That's all there is and you can handle it.

A short story has the same things, you say. Right. And sometimes a group of short stories centering around the same locale or people are strung together in a book and then you have something like James Michener's *Tales of the South Pacific* or Sherwood Anderson's *Winesburg, Ohio*.

Short stories are making a comeback and are being collected in book form again after a long period of unpopularity with publishers. So if that is your bent, try a short story. Or a novella, which is longer than a short story but shorter than a novel. It's harder to get a novella published and harder to get reviewed but writing one may have its rewards. Tobias Wolff managed to get his 101-page book, *The Barracks Thief*, published by Ecco Press and though it was not reviewed by a single book reviewer, its quality was such that he received the PEN/Faulkner Award for Fiction in 1985, and the $5,000 that goes with it.

What makes a novel different from a short story is its length and plot complexity. A short story usually centers around a single incident which shows the character of the hero or villain or which changes that person's life.

A novel, on the other hand, is a string of incidents that builds to a climax and at the end also shows the true character of the heroes and their antagonists—the villains, opponents, or spoilers—or changes their lives. A novel can, but doesn't need to, have many more characters than a short story. A novel can span any amount of time. Tom Clancy, in his *The Hunt for Red October*, covers just eighteen days. James Michener, in his sagas like *Poland* or *Hawaii*, spans many generations.

And there is one more difference. A short story often makes just one point. A novel may, but doesn't need to, have one or more subplots if it has a lot of characters. The main character is working toward his goal and the minor character or secondary character is working toward his own goal. But the secondary character must have some reason to be in the novel, some connection with the main character even if he or the main character is not aware of it. If he's not needed in that story, sweep him out or cut him out and give him his own story in another book.

My personal definition of a novel is that it is a long work of fiction that transports you into a particular culture, or "world." The culture may be the narrow world of a black ex-cop on West 72nd Street in New York, as in J.F. Burke's "Sam Kelly" novels, or the vast panorama of Tolstoy's *War and Peace*, which tells you everything about Napoleon's invasion of Russia.

It can be the world of bohemians, as in *South Wind* by Norman Douglas, or an examination of a group of people on a trip, as in Thornton Wilder's *The Bridge of San Luis Rey.*

It can be everything connected with a particular problem, such as the shipwreck in *Robinson Crusoe.* It can be all the ramifications of a particular imaginary world, as in Niel Hancock's *Circle of Light.*

But in each novel that's been successful with me—that is, one I enjoyed reading—the novelist has decided exactly what and how he will tell you about a particular set of characters in a particular place or set of places, who live in a particular span of time, and to do this efficiently, has created a set of rules and limitations within which the characters must live.

That's it. He has told you no more—not one word or sentence more. A good novel is exactly long enough to tell you everything you need to know to understand the story the writer wants to communicate. When the reader finishes a good novel, he or she sighs, says, "That was good, but I wish there was a little more of it," and regretfully closes the book.

It is the telling-you-everything part that makes it a novel, rather than a short story or novella.

To illustrate further the important point that you must create a set of rules and limitations within which to depict the world of your novel, think of an artist preparing to paint. He chooses a canvas of a certain size to suit his subject or idea—say two feet by four feet. He decides what colors to use—maybe only green and brown. He decides whether to paint with brushes, a palette knife, or to drip the paint. He elects to use fine lines or coarse ones, or perhaps just blocks of color. These and other decisions set the rules and limitations within which he must create his painting. If his first choices of size, technique, and color prove inadequate for his subject, he might come to regard his first effort as a study, and start over with a new set of dimensions, colors, and painting techniques for his final version.

So you must decide what elements to use to build the world of your novel, and stick with them, or start over with a new set of rules and limitations.

Ernest Hemingway built a world in which man had to survive in spite of hostility and brutality around him, had to kill sometimes, had to be as brutal as his environment. And even when man won sometimes, he still lost. For example, in *The Old Man and the Sea*, the old man finally succeeds in his exhausting, fanatical struggle with the great fish, and it is the triumph of his life. And then what happens? The sharks get it.

What is the world you like to think about? Faulkner thought about the world of the South, of its post-Civil War sadness, of its old families still trying to dig out from the ash heap of war and slavery and guilt and fortunes lost. He built it—someone said he "rebuilt" it—and he gave it a sardonic yet poetic quality.

Hemingway liked to think about safaris in Africa, bullfight rings in Spain, and battlefields where brave men died, and he wrote about all these things with starkness.

Some science fiction writers like to think about the world of the future and that's why they write about it. They are surely not writing about the world they know. And when a writing teacher or writer-friend tells you you *must* write about what you know, you can either reply that, like Faulkner, that is exactly what you are doing—"rebuilding" what you know into a novel, or you can say that like Hemingway, you prefer to create a world in your own image.

Writing about what you know is fine, and writing what you only dream about in your mind is fine too. If you choose the winged horse of your imagination, you can take your readers for as fine a ride as Louis L'Amour does in his westerns—and maybe, like him, you can ride right up the best-seller list.

You can *learn* what you need to know—the books to read, places to travel to, people to interview—specialists of every kind, from convicts, junkies, and pregnant teenagers to priests, judges, and bankers, who have actually lived through the kinds of experience you want to novelize. Your own life can be the background that helps you know what they must think and feel. However, beware of too much research!

Nancy Hale, author of such books as *The Empress's Ring*, *The Young Die Good*, and *Dear Beast*, was lucky enough to have Maxwell Perkins as her editor at Scribner's and told him she needed to go to Paris to research a book she planned. To her surprise, Perkins was not enthusiastic.

"You don't want to know too much about it," the legendary editor told her. Writing about the incident in her own book on writing, *The Realities of Fiction*, Nancy Hale adds, "The dead hand of research lies heavy on too many novels." She says she learned that Perkins was right when he told her that what a writer must do is "make it up out of your head."

While I think Perkins put it too strongly, it is possible for too much knowledge of a subject to inhibit your imagination. Remember, you can "rebuild" the world you know into a new one in your novel if you want to.

SHOULD YOU WRITE
FOR MONEY?

Without exception, the writers I have represented as agent, or whose books I have edited or published, have been writing to express themselves. They wanted to get paid, of course, because their royalties were tangible proof that the public valued their message. As "Adam Smith" (who uses a pen name) says in *The Money Game*, money is a way of keeping score. But money is second, not first.

Let me give you a striking example. When Norman Mailer completed *The Deer Park*, my favorite of his novels, the publisher that had it under contract required that he change six lines which it considered salacious. He refused and kept refusing even though his refusal threatened publication of his novel. The publisher *did* cancel the contract and it was not easy to get another publisher. Bennett Cerf, for example, is quoted as having commented, when his firm, Random House, turned it down, "This novel will set publishing back twenty-five years."

At that time in book publishing history, the freedom of authors to express their observations about sexual reality was the cutting edge of liberty.

Eventually Mailer was able to make a publishing agreement with G.P. Putnam's Sons, the novel was published, and he experienced the triumph of having his integrity vindicated.

This example is inspiring, but it wasn't Mailer's first book. With his first book, *The Naked and the Dead*, he debated with his advisers and publisher how to treat a certain well-known expletive often used by soldiers. It came out in that book of World War II as "fug." So on a first novel, you may have to make some compromises of a practical nature.

Though the issues are rarely as explicit as the one Mailer faced with *The Deer Park*, you may have to listen to your editor's suggestions, and make some changes. Just remember the publisher wants a best seller as much as you and has guided many books to success. Publishers make mistakes, of course, turning down books they bitterly wish they hadn't, or censoring books that later are published unexpurgated. So it doesn't hurt to argue a little with your editor!

But certainly until the book is done, you are boss. Now, following some general guidelines from me, write it *your* way.

SHOULD YOU TALK
ABOUT YOUR WORK?

Some beginning novelists do better if no one knows what they are writing or even that they are writing at all. In my experience with writers, almost all are better off if they do not tell their plots or ask advice of friends and relatives.

Here is a true story. While working on a manuscript, an editor would ask a writer to rewrite a scene, and having done so, the author would invariably show it to his wife. He would then report to the editor, "She said it was awful!" The editor noticed that consistently the better a scene was, the less the wife liked it. So the editor got smart. He would say, "What does your wife think of *this* scene?" and if the wife liked it, he would ask for a rewrite.

The anecdote serves as a good commentary on the value of an outsider's or amateur's advice. Other writers find that if they tell their stories to friends, writing them down becomes boring, so they don't. My advice to you is to be mysterious.

DO YOU HAVE THE TIME TO WRITE A
NOVEL? THE FAVORITE DODGE . . .

Don't tell me you wish you could but you just don't have the time. You may even have a great plot you've been toying around with, or an "idea for a novel" in some incident you saw, or a main character—what a story you could build around him! But you guess you'll never get it done. "No time," you say.

That's nonsense, and the experiences of busy careerists who also write books proves it.

I'm going to tell you in a later chapter a sane and sensible way you can write your novel in the course of three months—ninety days!—without having to do anything dramatic like giving up your job, driving your family crazy, or going through the agony of loneliness.

But first, let me tell you that Voltaire is said to have written *Candide* in three days. Ken Kesey supposedly wrote *One Flew Over the*

Cuckoo's Nest in four. It doesn't really matter—except to the *Guinness Book of Records*. When a book is great, nobody cares how long it took to write.

Nor do you have to follow the example of these two writers, although maybe you could. Have you heard of the three-day novel contest that originated in Canada? The story goes that while drinking a few beers in a Vancouver pub, Steve Osborne, founder of Pulp Press, and book dealer Bill Hoffer made a bet that each could write a novel in three days. The best novel would win. Neither succeeded in finishing, but a contest was born.

Now each year since 1978, adventurous writers from Canada and the U.S. try to come up with a winner in the seventy-two-hour mara ' thon, called the Pulp Press International Three-Day Novel Contest. The winner gets his/her novel published by Pulp Press. And in 1984, some four hundred otherwise sane novelists competed.

Of the four hundred, not just the winner got lucky. The runner-up was Fatima Shaik, who wrote so well that she received an offer to have a collection of short pieces published. Another loser succeeded in selling her three-day novel as a subject for a Hollywood movie.

The winner, incidentally, was a postal worker from Calgary, Jim Curry, who reworked his winning plot, *Nothing So Natural*, into a successful play.

I only tell you all this to spur you on, to give you confidence, to show that you *do* have time.

If you are still not convinced that you have time enough to write a novel, read some of the interviews with first novelists that are in Part II of this book. Steven Linakis worked full time as a bookkeeper, commuted long hours on the Long Island Railroad, and still managed to write a first novel that earned him more than $200,000.

Okay, we have faced your doubts and gained some new perspectives on your situation, answering some preliminary questions. It's time to become more specific.

2.
Mainstream? Crime? Literary? Science Fiction? What Kind of Novel Do *You* Want to Write?

Many would-be writers are put off by the often-repeated advice I mentioned earlier, "Write about what you know." This hoary dictum can be a killjoy for an imaginative person.

So should only murderers write about murder? Women write about women only? Only men write about men? Should we wait for extra-terrestrials to come down to Earth before writing about them? Whatever you write about, the real problem is to make it believable—and you can do that through research and imagination as well as through living.

I'm reminded of the science-fiction editor's story: A Martian youngster got tired of living underground on Mars and crashed the spaceship he had stolen to joy-ride. He landed on Earth. He hadn't the faintest idea of how to fix the ship, or how to build a device to communicate with Mars—he had been studying ancient literature in his Martian school. Wandering around New York City, after stealing some clothes off a clothesline, he spotted some books in a drugstore with pictures of all sorts of strange and fascinating creatures on them. Making himself temporarily invisible, he grabbed several, went to a quiet park, and decoded the language. With his Martian intellect, he quickly read them. "Ah!" he cried. "I know how I'll be able to make a living on this queer planet. I'll write the history of Mars and sell it as science fiction!"

Easily solving the problems of getting a typewriter and paper, he wrote his first story, and sent it in to a science-fiction book editor. Right away it came back with a letter. "This is the most unbelievable stuff I've ever read," the editor wrote.

The Martian was outraged. He rushed to the editor's office, pushed aside the receptionist and secretary, and in the editor's office, tore off his shirt and brandished all four of his arms.

"How can you say this is unbelievable! I really am a Martian. This is the true history of Mars!"

The editor replied, "You writers are all alike. You always offer the same tired excuses. When somebody criticizes your work, you claim it really happened!"

The editor's point is a good one. It's not what you know that counts—it's whether *the reader believes* you know something. This effect is also called "suspension of disbelief." You achieve this by being so convincing in your details and surprising as a storyteller, by evoking such strong emotion, or by making your characters so fascinating that the reader is hooked and wants to read on and learn more. But your fiction must be largely as plausible as what the ordinary reader regards as fact, or accepts as a convention of your genre.

So widen your horizons. Find out what you need to know to convince a reader in any field that turns you on. And you don't always find the information you need in books. Author Kelly Cherry solved her problem with great aplomb when her publisher, Viking, liked her first novel, *Sick and Full of Burning*, but said she needed to flesh out the character and life of the medical student in it. She walked right up to a medical student at Mt. Sinai Hospital's library in New York.

As Cherry tells the story in *The Writer*, she said, "I'll buy you a cup of coffee if you'll tell me what it's like to be a med student." What he told her extended the book by fifty pages. It was as though Cherry's fictional medical student got a transfusion of living blood from a real medical student. These pages must have helped round out the book, as it was highly acclaimed.

Whether you want to write a story about what you already know, or invent a story based on your imagination or research—and often you will do both—you will still have to examine your potential material, and think further about what *kind* of novel you want to write to express your story. So let's examine some familiar types of novels.

MAINSTREAM NOVELS

Is your life a shambles in your well-tended suburban house? Do the neighbors think you have the perfect marriage while your wife is packing your clothes and demanding a divorce? Maybe at least a novel can be salvaged from the situation.

This kind of book, about marriage problems, falls into the very broad classification called "mainstream," or general interest, by publishers. Mainstream novels aim at the wide audience—men, women, and young adults. They tell us about problems many people can identify with. In the list of labels publishers use to identify different kinds of novels, given at the end of this chapter, I'll define this category further. But first let's look at some examples.

To see how a famous writer handled marriage problems, read Philip Roth's *When She Was Good*. In an article in *Book Week*, Josh Greenfield said that Roth's engrossing themes of family life were "essentially devastating renderings of the eternal bitch coupled with classic castration candidates—sensitive, well-intentioned, weak men."

The mainstream theme of family or ethnic background has absorbed many writers. The same Philip Roth attacked it with bitter humor in *The Ghost Writer*. Mario Puzo capitalized on the myths and facts about being Italian in America and wrote *The Godfather*. James Baldwin turned the suffering of his black childhood into *Go Tell It on the Mountain*.

Other mainstream writers look at the world about them, ponder man's journey through life, and ask the question: Can we be happy?

John Updike, who published his first novel in 1959—*The Poorhouse Fair*—wrote of life in a home for the elderly. The book has a message in it, an ominous hint that this is life in the world of the future. Loneliness, the emptiness men feel inside, the search for fulfillment continue in his later and more famous books: *Rabbit, Run; The Centaur; Rabbit Redux*.

Carson McCullers was dealing with a mainstream theme—the problems of a person who is different from others—when she wrote the book that made her an immediate celebrity, *The Heart Is a Lonely Hunter*. It is about a deaf mute who eventually commits suicide. She had a particular sympathy for those who could not help their handicaps. Crossed eyes in one novel, a hunchback in another. Even in her best-known book, *Member of the Wedding*, pathos is always present and the emphasis is on the pain of childhood and not the happiness—a familiar mainstream subject.

Grace Metalious picked another kind of subject that has a broad appeal—the outrageous goings-on in a small town. What if someone assembled the secrets of a town and a cast of town leaders—a schoolteacher, a beautiful, sensitive young girl, her beautiful, ambitious mother. . . . *She* did and became a household word with that first book, *Peyton Place*. The book became a movie and then a long-running TV series.

Though the book was clearly about a mainstream subject, Metalious stretched the definition of acceptable subject matter, and *Peyton Place* found its publisher almost by accident. Editor Leona Nevler mentioned the manuscript when she went job hunting at the Messner publishing house. She had seen it at Lippincott, where it had received several readings and been rejected. Nevler had read it and liked it and she urged Kitty Messner to get hold of it. Though Nevler did not end up working at Messner, she did get the assignment of editing the best seller after Messner contracted for it through its agent, Jacques Chambrun.

Leona Nevler, who became an editor at Fawcett and rose to the top of that company, told me that in the original manuscript, the stepfather who rapes the heroine was really the girl's father. But incest was a taboo subject of that period and so she persuaded Metalious to make the change. This is the sort of decision a mainstream author often faces—how much can the broad audience take and remain fascinated, rather than be repelled?

So you can see that in writing for the mainstream novel's very broad audience, you will have to pick a subject vital enough to be of wide interest—but keep society's conventions and taboos in mind in deciding how much to reveal about it. Probably like Grace Metalious, you will want to tell it your way and not worry about whether you have gone too far.

GENRE NOVELS

In choosing what kind of novel you want to write, don't feel shy if you want to aim at a narrower audience. "Genre" novels appeal to readers interested in a particular subject, and often follow a successful formula that is pleasing to that audience.

So if you have a favorite kind of novel—say you buy every new historical novel about kings and queens—then you have a good starting point. In choosing what kind of novel you want to write, remember that other novelists' books can be your textbooks, though of course you won't want to copy them too closely.

You probably have unconsciously studied many techniques of fiction writing, and know many formulas used in genre writing, just by the normal reading you have done in school and for pleasure. And if you haven't done much reading, you'd better start now. One of the questions I ask people who tell me they want to write a novel is, "What are some of the recent novels you liked?" If they can't think of any, I stop taking them seriously as potential clients for my literary agency.

Genre novels can be a good place to get your feet wet as a writer. "Vanessa James," who got her start writing romances, was recently revealed to be the same person as Sally Beauman, who received a million dollars from Bantam for hard and soft cover rights to her "first" mainstream novel, *Destiny*. Stephen Rubin, editorial director of adult books at Bantam, called it, in *The New York Times*, "a mainstream commercial novel written at a high level," a good example of editors' jargon.

Let's look at some of the better-known genres in detail, before tackling a whole list of them.

CRIME, SUSPENSE, AND INTRIGUE

Are you engrossed in the crime news in your newspaper? So was Lawrence Sanders, who worked for *Popular Mechanics* and wrote pulp magazine stories on the side for $75 apiece. Bugging devices were much in the news. He played the "What if?" game. What if there were a robbery and for some reason someone had a tape recorder under a bench and happened to record two men talking about it? What if. . . . He toyed with the idea and started writing official-sounding reports and memos. The result was *The Anderson Tapes*, a book that gave him a new career, led him to wealth, and allowed him to live where he pleased—in Florida, overlooking the water.

Many new mystery novels are published every year. In my own small agency, we have introduced the "Brandstetter" series by Joseph Hansen, the "Sam Kelly" and "Joe Streeter" series by J.F. Burke, and the paperback mysteries of Margot Arnold. My associate, Oliver Swan, sold more than a dozen "Apple" mysteries by Marc Lovell to Doubleday's Crime Club, among others—and all this because we like to read mysteries.

Mystery stories take the fear out of death by turning it into a problem of *who* done it. We get acclimated to dead bodies by shifting attention to the search for the criminal.

In building a mystery, some writers start with locale. Patricia Moyes used a ski slope and came up with *Dead Men Don't Ski*, with the current theme of drug smuggling. She turned to Paris and its fashion industry and wrote *Murder a la Mode*.

Readers are interested in the thrill of danger they can identify with. Read the opening of Graham Greene's *Brighton Rock:* "Hale knew before he had been in Brighton three hours that they intended to murder him." Now who could put *that* down? How are they planning to murder him? The reader feels a little chill, a little fear . . . and, important in selling books, an instant identification and sympathy for the intended victim.

Do you devour the international news and every spy story you can find? Maybe it's time for you to work out your own cloak-and-dagger plot. However, in this highly competitive field, just remember you will be competing with professionals, past and present, who used to be in the intelligence world—Ian Fleming, John LeCarre, Howard Hunt, and many more, so do your homework carefully.

I am one who enjoys novels that give an insider's view of a particular field and have handled some good first novels of this kind—ex-FBI agent Bernard F. Conners's story about the FBI, *Don't Embarrass the Bureau*, and ex-CIA intelligence officer George O'Toole's novel about the CIA, *An Agent on the Other Side*.

But even these two experts in their fields wanted to try other subjects, too. Conners's second novel was *Dancehall*, a suspense novel about a long-forgotten murder that suddenly surfaces, while George O'Toole's second book was a historical novel about the assassination of President Lincoln—*The Cosgrove Report*.

So if you love a mystery and can see something sinister in what is going on next door, or on the boat where you are vacationing, or in a hotel, on a bus, a train, a subway, you may have your career laid out for you. Though this is a specialized kind of fiction, it has a wide audience of devoted fans.

ADVENTURE NOVELS

Would you choose a life of adventure—at least in your mind? Several hundred pages from now, your daydream could end up as a book that goes on to be filmed for TV or big screen. The adventure story involves the hero proving himself, proving his manhood or his cleverness or superiority in some way. He must overcome a great obstacle to gain his prize. And he must best a clever, mean, cunning villain.

The action usually takes place in some far-off or exotic place—at the bottom of the sea, the north pole, in the desert, or the mountains.

The prize (which the villain is also after) can be gold, a lost treasure, national secrets. The hero has to get there first and then maybe still have to fight for it. Not till the end is it clear that the hero will make it. Maybe when the hero gets to the treasure, the villain is already hovering over it. Or has hidden it.

The reward for winning does not have to be personal wealth, but it can be. The search may be undertaken to help some good guy, or a woman, or somebody's victimized mother. But the reader wants the good guy to win. And in this day of "upward mobility," the hero may win the reader's sympathy by just being the kind of man who refuses to be tied down to a 9-to-5 job. He can be the kind who cares nothing for money and just asks enough of a fee to get along. He simply happens to live for adventure and challenge. Or he is adventure prone: someone is always seeking him out for help.

To write your adventure story, it is wise to have reference books around with the proper terminology for authenticity of dialogue, description of action, and locale. The public library is the best place to start your quest, unless you want to undertake an adventure yourself!

A book that analyzes heroes of adventure stories from the beginning of history is *The Hero With a Thousand Faces*, by mythologist Joseph Campbell. Campbell shows that the mythic hero receives a summons to adventure, which often he initially resists, just as Odysseus did not want to go conquer Troy. Someone, a god, or father or mother figure, urges him on and gives him aid. He is beset by trials and temptations, and has setbacks. Like Christian in *Pilgrim's Progress*, he may become bogged in the "Slough of Despond." But he overcomes knotty problems—just as Alexander cut the Gordian Knot—with wit, ingenuity, trickery, and bravery. He is often aided by a woman. He achieves his objective, such as killing the life-destroying Minotaur, and gets his reward, such as the Golden Fleece, and thus aids the world and becomes a larger man.

The James Bond novels of Ian Fleming closely follow this mythic formula. The hero, Agent 007—a symbol the psychoanalyst might see as standing for Everyman, because the lucky number seven stands for the seven openings of the human body, and the "00" adds the eyes James Bond uses so well—usually is called away from a life of childish pleasure. His "father and mother," the characters "M" and Moneypenny, must urge him on, and practically force him to accept better weapons (symbols of sexual maturity) in preparation for his mission. He confronts, in exotic places, an organization with monstrous forces, headed by a figure with mythic powers engaged in life-destroying evil. Bond (representing the cement that holds civilization together) must face trials and obstacles. Some he wins easily, but he usually suffers at least one terrible setback. Through wit, trickery, and life-enhancing sexual vigor, he defeats his opponent, often with the help of a woman, and in the end destroys the evil monster and saves the world. And the reader is satisfyingly entertained by an ancient story in modern dress.

WESTERNS

A western is a special kind of adventure story which often is a historical novel as well. One of literary agent Lisa Collier Cool's clients who writes westerns is in a penitentiary. He can write about tough hombres with real authority. To see mean characters, he has only to look around. Dalton Loyd Williams, author of *Bullet For Gold*, may be in prison, but he has had a pleasure only a few modern American authors have experienced—his novel has been translated into Greek and published in Greece, where few modern American novels are welcome.

The western formula has many variations. A cowboy story might center around cattle rustling, or rancher vs. farmer. Fred Grove's westerns, published by Doubleday, often center around quarter-horse racing, as in his *Match Race*.

King of the westerns, whom I mentioned earlier, is Louis L'Amour. The number of his titles has passed the ninety mark and one of his latest, *Jubal Sackett*, was on the best-seller list, as many before it had been. It doesn't hurt that a president reads your books: President Reagan let it be known that L'Amour was one of his favorite authors.

SCIENCE FICTION

If you daydream of other worlds, have an interest in space travel, space medicine, astronomy, terrestrial navigation, and are fascinated by the mysteries of time and space, you have a pseudopod up on science-fiction writing.

Science fiction often deals with aliens from other worlds, or man on other worlds, in the near or distant future. But it doesn't have to. The key word is "science," and the effect of science on man.

Books published in this field can vary from modestly distributed mass-market paperbacks to super best sellers in hard cover and paperback alike.

One of the stars of this genre, Kurt Vonnegut, writes in a new novel about a world in the year 1,001,986 in which a ghost looks back on what happened in 1986-2016. The size and dominance of man's brain is the theme.

But an earlier work, *Flowers for Algernon*, by Daniel Keyes, dealt with the same theme in a simpler way. Keyes's short story, later developed into a novel, then an Academy Award-winning movie, *Charly*, came up with a fictional operation that temporarily turned a moron into a genius. The story, though science fiction, was set in the present.

This is a fascinating, but rather specialized genre, and you might want to join a s/f fan club, or attend a convention of science-fiction fans, before going too far in deciding to write in this form. Also, it is one of the few forms left with some good magazines which buy stories. If you want to start out with shorter works, a market for them exists.

HORROR NOVELS

Horror stories dwell on man's primitive fears—of being buried alive, of being captured by monsters. Fear of the supernatural. Fear of madness. Coffins. Corpses. The strange powers of ghosts. Supernatural animals. Dr. Frankenstein and Count Dracula live forever to do their work.

If you want to see how a modern horror story is constructed, read one of Stephen King's books, such as *Pet Sematary*, or Peter Straub's *Ghost Story*.

Horror can be found anywhere—it can come from the reversal of the usual view of life. Ken Greenhall in his 1977 novel *Hell Hound* (published under its original title, *Baxter*, in England), tells of a *very* bad dog, Baxter, and his effect on the lives of his owners and their children. A few years later, Stephen King also tackled the subject of a dog in his horror story, *Cujo*.

If you want to try a horror novel, keep in mind that they demand strong, sensitive craftsmanship.

COMIC NOVELS

Humor looks so easy. It isn't. It just reads easy. Actress-writer Elaine May may have said it best, "Never let them catch you trying to be funny." Humor must seem accidental, must catch the reader off guard. Things happen, and somehow the reader finds himself smiling or chuckling. The teller of the story—the author—seems serious, but the situation is so ludicrous or the character so uncomfortable, the reader must laugh, involuntarily.

As someone once said, "One man's misfortune is another man's joke." Humor is perverse. Humans are perverse. Even if they sympathize, they find it funny. Of course, the discomfort must not be too profound or it will no longer seem funny. Most people, though they appreciate the perverse, are not overtly sadistic.

Humorous effects are achieved by saying the outrageous. For example, Jean Kerr describes her son in *Please don't eat the daisies*, as "a slightly used eight-year-old."

Unlike Jean Kerr, Herman Wouk in his very funny novel, *Don't Stop the Carnival*, gets his humorous effects, not from clever retorts, but from outrageous situations. A mildly wealthy New Yorker plows all his money into a small Caribbean island resort in order to get away from it all and enjoy life. But everything turns into an emergency followed by a disaster. He must keep the guests from knowing the resort is out of water. He has a handyman who isn't very handy.

Eventually, our suffering hero finds a bright spot, as it appears that he is about to have his sexual fantasies realized. He has enticed the girl who inspires his lust to sail with him on a boat, along with a picnic basket. Before the festivities with her can begin, the heavens begin first. By the time the couple come dragging back to shore, choppy water, searing sun, wind, and a boom that keeps hitting her on the head and throwing her to the deck, have rendered the would-be playmate, Iris, into a wet, hungry, cursing madwoman.

IT'S ALL RIGHT TO BE ORIGINAL

You are not locked into writing anyone else's kind of book. Some of the best writers in the world would be lost if they had to turn out a romance novel to earn a living, or if they had to write a detective story. So go along with your own bent of mind. It's easier when you are just beginning to pick the type of book you like and then start with one in that style or category, or as close to it as you can get.

But if you don't know a single book that does what you have in mind, write your book anyway and you may find you have come up with a new category, or a new variation on one. Just be sure you still give it a beginning, a middle that is moving in some direction, and finally an ending and resolution that make the reader smile, cry, or pause to ponder your message.

Novels may be categorized in many ways. Some entertain, others express a message, and still others do both. Some are "women's interest," some "men's interest," and others "juveniles" or "young adult" works.

You will see references to Southern novelists, Jewish novelists, black novelists, Irish novelists. Such labels can have meaning to the experienced reader.

Academic commentators and critics might use periods of time for their designations: the early American novel, 1800-1900; the American novel, 1900-1960; the contemporary American novel.

But you wouldn't want to call a publisher and say you have just finished a contemporary American novel. He would laugh and say, "What *kind* of contemporary American novel?"

Publishers and agents have their own shorthand ways of labeling the kind of book you have. Though not everyone uses exactly the same terms, and their jargon is constantly evolving, I have put together below a list of labels and categories editors, publishers, and agents use. If you study and learn these terms, it will help you communicate with members of the publishing industry.

The list is not organized entirely by logic—it also reflects a "feel" for how publishers think. For example, though a war novel is surely a kind of action adventure novel in most cases, so many major works have been war novels that I give them their own separate heading, confident that if I call an editor and say I have a good war novel, he/she will understand immediately what I mean.

For simplicity, I've kept the list to just twenty main headings. But when you start dealing with publishers and agents, you'll often hear combinations of these terms, such as "medical thriller" or "comic spy caper."

1. MAINSTREAM NOVELS. This large category includes all works with twentieth-century settings intended for the general public, rather than some special audience with a particular interest. Subject matter includes coming of age, some love stories, initiation into career and the search for professional or business success, family life, works about problems of ethnic groups, making it socially, coping with milestones of life. Also, courtroom dramas, dealing with physical and psychological problems, some religious novels, feminist novels, and other works that aim at a serious and profound treatment of their subjects for the general audience. Many of these are called *COMMERCIAL NOVELS*, particularly if they aim for very large audiences and deal with "dreams made plausible," with "larger than life" characters, as in some of the novels of Harold Robbins, Irving Wallace, and Jackie Collins.

2. LITERARY NOVELS. Though good literature turns up in every category, editors use this term to describe some novels, so I do too. It includes avant-garde and experimental novels, fiction by writers best known for their styles, re-creations of classic styles, and the "faction" or "nonfiction novel" such as *In Cold Blood* by Truman Capote. Most of the work of novelists like Philip Roth, Bernard Malamud, Saul Bellow, Mary McCarthy, and Joan Didion I would describe as "mainstream literary novels."

3. WAR NOVELS. Major works like *The Red Badge of Courage*, *The Killer Angels*, *All Quiet on the Western Front*, *From Here to Eternity*, and *Catch-22* shape our thought on this subject.

4. COMIC NOVELS. Some of these are *HUMOR*, such as the works of Peter De Vries; some *SATIRE*, as *The Magic Christian*, by Terry Southern; and many simply show wonderful high spirits, like the "Jeeves" novels of P. G. Wodehouse.

5. PHILOSOPHICAL NOVELS. These are written to make a point about life's meaning. They can be by philosophers, as *The Last Puritan*, by George Santayana; be *UTOPIAN* or *ANTI-UTOPIAN*, like *Animal Farm*, by George Orwell, or otherwise express political ideas, as in *Darkness at Noon*, by Arthur Koestler. Allegories fit here also—*The Book of Daniel*, by E. L. Doctorow. Of still another sort is *Siddhartha*, by Hermann Hesse.

6. MESSAGE NOVELS. These deal with pressing social concerns of their period. *Nana* is an old one; Upton Sinclair's *The Jungle* is a later one; *The Grapes of Wrath* by John Steinbeck is a more recent one.

7. RELIGIOUS NOVELS. Except for mainstream examples, such as *The Devil's Advocate*, by Morris West, these are mostly brought out by religious publishing houses. Some religious spokesmen, like C. S. Lewis, prefer fantasy novels to express their views of the universe.

8. EROTIC AND PORNOGRAPHIC NOVELS. These are about sex. They can be divided according to their intended audiences— heterosexual (men, women, and both); homosexual (men, women, and both); and those with wilder tastes. Erotic novels, sometimes penned by famous authors, have sexual love as their main subject matter and can be quite varied in style. Pornographic novels are usually more programmatic in their treatments of sex acts, and can be divided into hard- or soft-core.

9. ACTION/ADVENTURE/THRILLER. These emphasize fast-paced action, often exotic locale, and setting usually in the present or recent past. *SUSPENSE* is another term used for some of them. Other labels that fit into this category are *SEA STORIES, DISASTER NOVELS, MEN'S ACTION ADVENTURE* (including some war stories), some mysteries, some westerns, and some horror/occult (where the main emphasis is on action). The word "thriller" is often combined with another label, as in "spy thriller."

10. ROMANCES. The emphasis used to be mainly on courtship, but now courtship often includes sex. These novels, geared primarily to women readers, may be *CONTEMPORARY*, or set in some period of history, such as *REGENCY ROMANCES. GOTHICS* follow the formula of a young, inexperienced girl in an old house or castle, courted or menaced by a sinister man, and usually saved by another man. Some are *HISTORICAL ROMANCES*.

A sub-genre of these is the *BODICE-RIPPER*, in which the courtship gets rough. Many paperback romance lines of books follow strict (but frequently changing) formulas, and other romances, often in hard cover, such as the works of Daphne Du-Maurier, are as individual in treatment as mainstream books.

11. HISTORICAL NOVELS. These include some *FAMILY SAGAS* and *FICTIONALIZED BIOGRAPHIES* (such as Irving Stone's *Lust For Life* or Mary Renault's *Fire From Heaven*); some picaresque adventure stories set in the past, such as Gary Jennings's *Aztec*, and such old standbys as *PIRATE TALES*. Some westerns are really historical novels. Also part of this category are the sweeping panoramas of a great historical period or event, such as *Gone With the Wind* or *War and Peace*.

12. WESTERNS. Most of these are set in the post-Civil War period in the West, Southwest or in northern Mexico, but there are *MODERN WESTERNS*, too. Typically, they involve conflict between ranchers, cowboys, Indians, farmers, outlaws, lawmen, townspeople, the military, prospectors, miners, mine owners, and sometimes dude or tenderfoot Easterners, rich or poor. A few are "comic westerns."

13. SCIENCE FICTION AND FANTASY. Science fiction is about the effects of science, technology, and social and psychological theories on people in the far or near future. A *SPACE OPERA* is an adventure story with science fiction elements. S/f sometimes involves imaginary "aliens" from other worlds. Fantasy is usually about magic, or is set in "alternate worlds" with or without dragons and witches. *SWORD AND SORCERY* tales are set in an imaginary Earth past, and may have armed conflict as well as witches and warlocks.

14. HORROR/OCCULT NOVELS. These use creepy menaces such as ghosts, witches, Satan worshippers, revived mummies and other cadavers, and monsters like werewolves, vampires, and persons with occult powers to scare us.

15. CRIME NOVELS. These include *MYSTERIES, DETECTIVE STORIES, CAPER NOVELS* (describing an elaborate crime in detail), *NOVELS WITH A MURDER IN THEM*, and sometimes just a novel mainly about crime. Mysteries and detective stories may be puzzles, hard-boiled action stories, or romances with a detective and a crime. But usually the emphasis is on solving a crime, most often murder. Some *SPY STORIES* and novels

of *INTRIGUE* are mainly mystery stories.

16. ANIMAL STORIES. One or more of the main characters of these are usually animals. Sheila Burnford's *The Incredible Journey* is a good example. *Watership Down* by Richard Adams is a good but very different kind of example.

17. MEDICAL AND NURSE NOVELS. *M*A*S*H*, by Richard Hooker, is a famous example; another is *Coma*, by Robin Cook.

18. INTERACTIVE NOVELS. This is a new category, referring to novels that contain alternate endings and situations the reader can construct.

19. DIDACTIC NOVELS. Both editors and academics use this label for novels that are mainly intended to teach, or drive home a lesson. *A Piano For Mrs. Cimino* by Robert Oliphant, for example, teaches the elderly how to deal with their situation.

20. JUVENILE/YOUNG ADULT. Virtually any other kind of novel, except erotic (juveniles seem to prefer adult works in this area) can be written for younger readers, usually featuring a protagonist who is of the age group for whom the novel is intended.

Some books don't fit readily into any category, and publishers call these "offbeat works," which freelance editor Ann Hukill Yeager defines "as practically a genre—it means 'I don't know if I can sell this, but I'm going to try.' " Franz Kafka's *Metamorphosis*, in which a man turns into a giant insect, is an example of a work that defies classification: Is it literary, science fiction, an animal story, black humor, or what? Maybe it fits into another informal category, "quirky," or possibly it could be called a fable.

With such an elaborate menu to choose from, surely by now you have found a type of novel that suits your taste—or decided to create your own new kind of novel. Probably you knew in your heart all along what it was. But if this list gives you courage to *announce* to yourself the kind of fiction you like to read and write best, it will have served its purpose.

3.

Do I Start with the Characters, or the Plot?

There is disagreement on which is more important, the plot or the characters of the novel. Ellis Amburn, the former editorial director at Putnam's, says the plot is more important. You have to have plot to make the reader turn pages.

William Sloane, Holt editor and independent publisher, lectured students at Bread Loaf, Vermont, writers' conferences during his lifetime that it was character. "People," he said, "are the story, and the whole story."

The debate will continue. You would not remember Scarlett O'Hara if she were only beautiful. The action of the novel makes her unforgettable. If someone mentions *Gone With the Wind* by Margaret Mitchell, we think immediately of Scarlett, but we immediately *see* her in the actions which made her so memorable—clawing the bare earth with her hands to find a few stray radishes to keep from starving, driving the team of horses through the burning city of Atlanta.

But where would plot *or* action *or* characters be without dialogue? Who can forget the confrontation on the grand staircase when Scarlett finally insults Rhett Butler to the point where he is walking out on her? She suddenly realizes she *does* love him, realizes the results of her own actions, and wails, "Oh my darling, if you go, what shall I do?" And then comes Rhett's memorable line, by which the novel lives on in the minds of its readers, "Frankly, my dear, I don't give a damn."

And so, let's consider all three as you prepare to start your first novel—your characters, your plot, and the dialogue your people will use.

Let's take characters and dialogue—how your characters talk—first. Great characters become part of the language. We think of Camille and what she stands for—a beautiful woman wasting away, full of suffering. We talk of Captain Queeg when we are describing an irascible, cruel man, abusing his power. We speak about Sir Galahad, so kind to women. Or the memorable villain, like Dr. Fu Manchu, created by Sax Rohmer.

WHAT MAKES A CHARACTER MEMORABLE?

Character traits make a character interesting and memorable. Traits that reveal themselves. Captain Queeg constantly clicked those little metal balls in his hand in *The Caine Mutiny*, by Herman Wouk. You didn't have to say he was nervous, driven, and a little strange. The balls said it.

You didn't have to say Sherlock Holmes was brilliant in Arthur Conan Doyle's tales about him. It was enough that he was *shown* as being brilliant while at work. What makes him memorable is the fullness of his characterization—his eccentric mode of dress, his violin playing, his use of cocaine when he is bored, his joy when "The game's afoot!", the sort of acquaintances he had, the kind of clients who brought him their problems.

SHOULD WE WRITE ABOUT THE PEOPLE WE KNOW?

We don't even know ourselves fully, so how can we write about what goes on inside another person's mind? If you are talking about physical appearance and things that have happened to another person, be careful about "borrowing" too much from real life. Tell someone's deepest secrets—*she* was a secret alcoholic or *he* swindled his next door neighbor, Mr. Soandso—and you may end up in court.

The rule is you cannot invade someone's privacy or hold him/her up to ridicule.

So what do you do? You mix up characteristics as you'd shuffle cards. You take a trait you find in one person and a few from another, and one from yourself. You change the appearance and make sure the person who once was a swindler looks nothing at all like the man you know. You make it someone other than his neighbor that he cheated. You leave out the real story of how his fiancee found out about it and killed herself on their wedding day because she feared he was marrying her for her money. That has to be shuffled too, and the details removed from your version.

You write fiction, not fact. But even then there is sometimes no way to keep people from seeing themselves.

After the success of her book, *Hollywood Wives*, Jackie Collins found that dozens of people in the movie colony identified with one or another of her characters with varying reactions. She had just arrived at a Beverly Hills restaurant with her sister, actress Joan Collins of *Dynasty*, and had ordered a drink. A producer who thought he had been portrayed in the book came storming over and threw a glass of champagne in her face.

Keeping her cool, Jackie Collins said, "Hmm, tastes good. Let's order some more."

William Styron, whose memorable book, *Sophie's Choice*, also became a memorable movie, admits that his character Sophie was indeed rooted in reality to a certain extent, or at least inspired by a woman he met. As he told students at George Mason University, in Fairfax, Virginia, he was introduced to a "beautiful Polish survivor of Auschwitz. Sophie didn't speak English very well and I was ten years younger than she. . . . Though I was infatuated with her there was clearly no way we could bridge the gap."

But Styron's imagination did bridge the gap, weaving a fictional story of an awful and agonizing secret Sophie was hiding, set against her passionate romance with an emotionally unbalanced biologist.

Judith Krantz, author of *Scruples*, told *Los Angeles Times* reporter Pat Nation, "A novelist has to be schizophrenic without being mentally ill. You draw on a lot of facets of your life for characters and then fictionalize." She added that "a sliver of myself" was in all her characters.

HOW DO YOU BUILD A CHARACTER?

You build a character by asking yourself questions about the person to which only you know the answers.

"Is she tall?" Yes. She's six feet tall. She *hates* it. A little guy is in love with her and keeps following her around. He owns a fabulous resort. She says, "He's taller when he's standing on his money." She can't get rid of him, she says.

Maybe that's the start of a humorous novel about the making of a showgirl who is the top attraction at his resort's nightly show. Or maybe she is rich and he is poor and she says, "He's taller when he's standing on *my* money." Maybe she becomes a stand-up comic in night clubs and this fellow seems to be following her all around the country. At first it seems kind of funny and she starts making quips about size the moment she spots him in the audience. But eventually a sinister note creeps in and she is terrified. It develops into a horror story in which he is a psycho and wants to lock her up and possess her all by himself—no more men looking at her in a night club. Or he has been sent to kill her so that someone else will inherit a fortune.

As you see, the plot can grow out of the character, and the character and plot are locked together.

But back to character development. Suppose you're writing a serious novel about a young divorcee involved in a custody fight over a set of twins. Her husband has played Solomon and said, "Let's separate them, share and share alike." The court case is about to begin.

You will need to know a lot about the husband, the wife, and even about the judge who handles the case and the wife's best friend, to whom she has confided many things.

Let's take just the wife and write down the answers to all the questions about her so that you can read them until you know her inside out and she is alive in your mind:

How old is she?

What are her bad habits? Her good ones?

Is she pretty? Is she conceited?

What about her disposition?

Does she really love those children? How do you know? (Maybe she once stood in the rain for an hour to buy them a treat.)

Does she have a job? Is money a problem?

What are her hobbies?

Is she a good housekeeper? Does she have a maid?

What kind of education did she have? Did she get good grades?

What was her earliest ambition? Was it achieved?

Is she artistic in any way?

How did she happen to marry this man? Did they have an affair or live together first? What irritates her about him?

What was her background like? Did her parents get along with each other? Did they show her love? Is there some secret in her family? Does she know it?

Start having conversations with her in your mind. What does she say? What is her speech pattern? Suddenly she tells you the twins aren't even his. She doesn't know whether to tell the court. She has never told her husband.

If you are writing the novel from the standpoint of the husband, you might find out different things about her. He says what irritated him most was her attitude toward personal grooming, which he took as a studied insult. "If she had taken a bath now and then I might have stayed around longer." It galled him that she had only two pairs of panties in spite of all the money he gave her, and wore stockings with snags in them.

It's earthy but we are building real people with real quirks. Truth within the boundary of the book is what you are looking for. No man is an island but each book *is*. And you are placing every character who lives on that island and will live there forever. When your reader closes the book, he/she can hop to the next island, but your characters remain on the island to intrigue the next person who picks up the book.

You, as the author, are building a world. *You* make the ground rules. You decide the rewards and punishments of life. Is goodness rewarded? Is goodness even at issue? Does a murderer in some instances deserve to go free and does the heroine help him escape? Only you have the answer.

To get to the answer, you have to know that heroine by asking all kinds of questions. Is she afraid to open her front door? How does she say hello to people? Is she really evil inside and pretending to be sweet and kind? Or is she so kind that people take advantage of her, saddle her with their dirty work? Is she capable of suicide? Would she slap someone or run to her room and cry and hide her hurt? Would she raise her voice? What *would* make her raise her voice? What do the neighbors say about her? How do they treat her and she, them?

You may not use all these facts in your novel but you need to know them so *you will know* how she would react when good things and bad happen in your plot.

Your characters have to be compelling and powerful to keep you and the reader interested. But that doesn't mean they are necessarily physically or morally or mentally strong. Walter Mitty, the invention of James Thurber, in *The Secret Life of Walter Mitty*, could not stand up to his wife, the parking lot attendant, or even the man selling him dog biscuits. But in his dream world, he was a giant—a bomber pilot, a surgeon, a condemned martyr, among others.

If some character is weak, make him a fascinating case of weakness. If he is evil, let the evil shine through. Let it flow until the reader is filled with it and understands it or accepts the truth of it. Or if the evil man masquerades as virtuous, let there be signs of it so that the reader suspects he is a snake. An exception would be if you're writing a murder mystery and the snake is the least likely suspect until the very end. But even there, you still give the reader clues—subtle, hidden ones.

Remember that nobody is all one thing or the other. To be believable, the evil man must have some goodness in him, no matter how slight. Perhaps on the way to kill someone, he stops to feed a hungry alley cat. And the good guy is not all that good. He flirts with another man's wife or borrows money and doesn't care if he pays it back or not.

The clothes your characters wear are important because they make a statement about their wearers. If the great Gatsby had not worn the clothes he did, he wouldn't have been *The Great Gatsby* who cared so much about his facade that he built his whole life around impressing the girl who got away. F. Scott Fitzgerald's Gatsby, as well as Thurber's Mitty, have become a part of the English language.

HOW DO YOU MAKE A CHARACTER SYMPATHETIC?

Editors frequently tell first-time novelists their characters are not sympathetic enough, giving them the kiss of death with the comment, "Who cares!" Well, the reader had better care or you don't have a sale.

So how do you make a character sympathetic? In many ways. If he's put upon by wife, salesmen, and other intimidating people as Walter Mitty is, you want him to enjoy his dreams, at least. "Please win," the reader tells him. If the *reader* also feels put upon, the reader becomes the hero in the fantasies, as well. The great Gatsby wins your sympathy because you want him to succeed in getting the attention of his love, Daisy. Almost everyone can identify with someone seeking to regain a lost love.

Having a noble goal for which someone scorns him makes a character sympathetic. A young man works hard to perfect himself at his sport instead of going after money and a good job. It is his secret dream to be in the Olympics. Someone important to him and "successful"—maybe a relative—treats him as if he were a bum and says condescendingly, "What do you want to be?"

Eagerly the young man says, "A champion." The smug one looks at him without a flicker of expression and says, "They're a dime a dozen." The young man may not have the sympathy of the successful man, but he has ours.

If the character has a strong goal, the reader will be eager for him/her to achieve it. If the character is in any kind of danger, the reader is immediately on his side. And the same goes for a character beset by problems, held up to ridicule or scorn or made to look foolish. But you, the author, have to be careful. If the hero goes too far in retaliation by maiming or killing the tormentor, sympathy may turn to contempt or disgust.

YOUR CHARACTER MUST GROW

To be real and interesting, your character must change and advance, or regress, or somehow be different at the end of the novel than he was at the beginning. Characters cannot remain static and neither can real live people unless they are in a catatonic state—and even then they may come out of it!

Think of Scrooge in Dickens's *A Christmas Carol*. He seems so mean and despicable that the reader is almost ready to give up on him but Dickens makes something happen—a dream—that changes him into a wonderful man at last. You don't have to go that far in your character change—only a Dickens could pull off such a switch—but there can be a less drastic turnabout. Perhaps your character learns a lesson that makes him suffer a bit in silence instead of berating his wife, whose mannerisms annoy him.

Or perhaps he learns that the only way to handle a bullying wife is to confront her right away, not wait and make excuses. Or he makes a decision—to give up his empty dream of starting a new life and settle down to live life now, where he is, with his family.

Whatever he chooses, something vital must hang on it. The decision must matter. And if it matters to your character, it will matter to your reader and he'll care how it all comes out in the end.

YOUR CHARACTERS CAN GROW
FROM THEME, OR VICE VERSA

Maybe you know what your book is about, but have to decide how to make the meaning come alive. Harriet Beecher Stowe had her theme first—slavery and how vicious it was—and her plot in *Uncle Tom's Cabin* arose from her knowledge of slave stories. But until she came up with her characters, Uncle Tom, Little Eva, Topsy, and Simon Legree, she could not realize her theme with full force. She wrote a story, not a sermon, and made her characters spring to life so well the resulting novel helped change the history of a nation.

Evan Hunter is a contemporary "thematic" sort of novelist. He started with the theme of fear in the schools—danger resulting from a lack of discipline. How did he know about it? He was a substitute teacher for a short while. He came up with *The Blackboard Jungle*, a novel so successful it not only brought his message to the public as a book, but also again when it was made into a compelling movie. Hunter has said that only after he knew the point he wanted to make did he pick characters and actions to express it. For such a work, a novel is a train of thought pulled by a "theme" engine.

Now let's take a case where the character came first. This legendary story of the book trade tells how Somerset Maugham, the commercially successful British novelist, got the idea for "Rain," a story that became part of his book, *The Trembling of a Leaf*, set in the tropical islands of the Pacific.

Maugham was traveling in the Pacific with a male secretary-companion and happened to be in Honolulu when the respectable wives of the community were trying to close down the Iwilei red light district.

Maugham went to see what all the fuss was about and even had an interview with a lady of the night who made him pay double because talk took longer than sex. He also went to court after a police raid to listen to what the judge had to say.

Some of the women opted to leave the island, and it was Maugham's fortune to have a stateroom near one of them who almost drove him crazy by playing her gramophone at all hours of the night and doing a lot of late entertaining with laughter and liquor much in evidence. The woman, whose name was Miss Sadie Thompson, became an object of obsession and fury.

Maugham was much relieved when they docked in Pago Pago because that would be the end of Miss Thompson and her eternal noise machine. His companion, Gerald Haxton, who was not as shy as Maugham, had found out that she planned to get a job in a bar.

Fate stepped in in the form of a quarantine. Maugham found himself in Pago Pago hemmed in by mountains drenched by torrential rains that alternated daily with horrible heat. He quickly developed a fungus on his body and had to spend days in his room, nursing the rash. Fate struck again when Miss Sadie Thompson got a room right across from his in the little *pensione* where he had found pathetic lodging.

Now, he had to listen not only to her gramophone but to the squeaking of the bedsprings. Miss Thompson had taken a Samoan lover.

Bored and miserable, Maugham played the game of "What If?" to while away the time. He had had a single encounter with a missionary's wife before the onset of his affliction. She had bragged about all the souls her husband was saving as he made the rounds by boat from island to island, and how, when they had arrived on the islands, they had found not one single *good* girl, so depraved was the life of the natives.

What if, he wondered, the missionary saved Sadie Thompson's soul? What if he became obsessed with Sadie, persecuted and pursued her, preached at her—the man who raised Maugham was a vicar—offered her pure love instead of the wicked love she was enjoying with the native boy, hammered and hammered at her until she broke down? Then what if, after she is brought to her knees and confesses her sins and seeks repentence, the missionary cannot resist her himself? Well, that's a twist. What happens then?

Maugham had plenty of time to think about it as he listened to the rain and tried not to feel the rash. He made a note about his resolution of the plot: the missionary is found dead—he has slit his own throat. And Sadie? She's the old Sadie again with the gramophone going full blast. Maugham even wrote down the last line. Sadie looks at a passing group of men and spits out the words, "Dirty pigs."

DIALOGUE BRINGS YOUR CHARACTERS TO LIFE

What brings the plot to life is the characters. What brings the characters to life is dialogue—with each character having his own way of talking. Someone once said that if you can't tell which character is talking, if they all sound alike, none of them is talking, it's the author who is talking.

If that happens with your characters, you're in trouble. Try to keep your own speaking pattern out of it. Give each character his pet expressions, even if you hate those expressions yourself. Give each his/her favorite words and each a different cadence.

Each speaker has his characteristic pattern, his "speech tune." For fun, try imitating someone's speech without using words—just nonsense syllables. Usually you'll find that you can do a good imitation, even get across emotion, without a single recognizable word. Each character will sound a little different from all others. Some will use long words, some short, but usually in a characteristic mixture. Once you have identified the rhythm, the speech tune, of a character, it will be easier to hear this character speak in his own voice in your mind, or when you say his words aloud.

SHOULD YOU USE FOREIGN ACCENTS OR DIALECTS?

It's most difficult to copy a foreign accent throughout a novel and very hard to read if you do. You can use just a garbled word now and then to suggest the accent but better yet, you can show by the speech pattern—the order of the words in the sentence—that a different sound exists.

You can also solve the problem by saying something like, "... she said in her thick Irish brogue." Or, "He spoke with a heavy German accent." Or a "slight shadow of a Swedish accent still remained." Or, "She seemed warmer, more approachable than her staid Yankee neighbors, maybe because of the way her voice still reflected the warm sunshine on the vineyards of her native Italy. Her hands, too, conveyed her message of hospitality."

Once in a while there is a book that depends almost totally on a heavy dialect. Such is the case with the hilarious *The One Hundred Dollar Misunderstanding*. It's the story of a white and not too bright adolescent who falls into the hands of a young, streetwise black hooker. The hero has a hundred dollars and is very happy about it. The misunderstanding comes when *she* thinks the money is for her and *he* thinks she likes him for himself. The whole book, by Robert Gover, revolves around the hooker's desperate efforts to separate the money from the teenager.

Much of the humor comes from the difference in their thinking and their speech patterns—his earnest, simple "whitey" speech against her black gutter talk. Her vocabulary abounds in raunchy insults and endearments which neither he nor the average reader has heard before. Without dialect, without the hooker's unique speech pattern, which gives a glimpse into a strange, colorful subculture, there would be a weak story and no book.

HOW DO YOU MAKE PEOPLE SOUND NATURAL IN A NOVEL?

How do real people talk? They talk like you. They talk like me. They don't always finish sentences. They speak in fragments of sentences. They seldom make long statements. It's usually short comments with dangling participles and dangling emotions tossed back and forth that is the real stuff of dialogue between two people. And if one seems to be launching into a long speech, the other is apt to say, "Shut up, darling. I've heard that before." That's in a happy kind of conversation. If they are angry, the comments are tossed much faster and collide in midair, overlapping each other.

How your characters talk will also depend on the part of the country or way of life they come from. A western rancher is apt to be taciturn. A Southern girl might be bubbly, a Hollywood matron openly materialistic.

Here's how Joseph Hansen renders light sexual banter between two gay men in his detective novel, *Gravedigger*.

"Look at that," Cecil said, and poked at the omelet with his fork. "What is *in* there, man?"

"Avocado," Dave said, "Cheese."

"Oh, wow." Cecil took a mouthful. His eyes widened. He opened his mouth and panted. "Hot!" he gasped.

"You wouldn't like it cold," Dave said. He pushed the basket of corn bread at him. "You want to play detective with me today? Or have you things to do?"

"Only thing I have to do is you," Cecil said. "Forever. From now on. All right?"

"All right." Dave smiled. "But I won't hold you to it."

"Hold me," Cecil said, "any way you want. Only the last time I played detective with you, you nearly got killed . . ."

DO YOU NEED MUCH DIALOGUE?

Yes, you need a lot of dialogue in most novels. It can become dull to read that someone did this and then he did that. It's interesting, on the other hand, to listen in on his conversation—say, one in which he is bragging to a buddy about how he handled that blind date who was trying to wreck his finances at their first dinner together. "I told her, 'Listen, stupid, if you think . . .' "

You don't just *recite* what happened, you show it happening. You talk it through with someone who, in effect, is speaking for the reader by asking the right questions. "But Sam, why did you have to lie to him?" Or, "But Muffie, I thought you hated Jim after the rotten things he said about you to the judge. How come you let him come in the door, let alone stay the night?" The reader's sentiments exactly.

Or this one: "Quick. Behind you!" How much better than: "He shouted to his friend to turn around quickly."

In a normal conversation between two people, it is distracting to read "He said" or "She said" with every line of dialogue. You know who is speaking most of the time, so just an occasional "He said" or "she replied" will keep the reader on track. It is also distracting to read dialogue in which the author has reached for every variation of "said"—asserted, breathed, exclaimed, stated, averred, and on and on. Unless the character really hisses or bellows out the words, don't bother to say so. It's the mark of the amateur to use elaborate variations on "said" just to seem erudite.

You must consider several things in writing dialogue. One is that people talk differently when talking to their peers and when talking to someone who makes them nervous or on guard, such as a boss, parent, or social superior. The dialogue must reflect this difference. The vocabulary is different. Sinclair Lewis uses this effect brilliantly in his novel *Babbitt*. When Babbitt visits a pillar of the community, he becomes tongue-tied, embarrassed, and overly formal. But when he entertains one of his subordinates, he is jolly, voluble, and at ease. As the scenes follow one another, the contrast is easily visible to the reader and reveals much about Babbitt's character and his failure as a social climber.

As part of your building of an adolescent male character in your novel, take a sheet of paper and write down that character's favorite words in talking to his gang members, his father, his mother, his kid sister, his teacher. Maybe with a person he feels safe around—his little sister, perhaps—he rambles on with a lot of "like"s and "Right?"s thrown in. With a particular teacher he might be taciturn, sullen, only answering in monosyllables. The reader gets to know that when the boy starts "sir"ing his father, he is going to ask for money or some favor.

Do the same with each of the other major characters. Not only the words but also the tone of voice you choose for your characters convey their emotions—whether love or contempt.

WHAT ARE THE FUNCTIONS OF CHARACTER AND DIALOGUE?

Why have we been discussing the people in your novel, and how they talk? Let's go back to the disagreement between the editors at the beginning of this chapter, over whether character or plot was more important to the novel. I'm now ready to take a stand.

I believe the plot is more important, because the plot has the entertainment value that pulls the reader along. The characters are your vehicle, the tools through which you tell your story. If they are strong, they strengthen the plot and the hold on the reader.

But when readers buy a book, they are saying, "Tell me a story."

4.

Four Steps Are All It Takes

By now you are starting to get comfortable with the idea of your own novel. You have some characters, maybe you even have some snatches of dialogue. You may have a message or theme you want to express. But to use these elements, you need to decide how to express your story with action.

WHAT YOUR NOVEL IS ABOUT

Maybe you are worried about finding a good plot. So before getting into a detailed discussion about the structure of your novel, I would like to suggest a plotting aid that arrives fresh every day and costs little to buy—the daily newspaper.

Every issue has material for a dozen plots: A teacher is arrested for sexually abusing a child. The plot thickens—the police raid his home and find pornographic pictures and proof that he belongs to a ring that sells such pictures.

Or, from the same paper: A new journey into space is about to begin. Astronauts are going to have to leave their ship to correct something in another orbiting satellite. What if something were to go wrong, threatening their lives, and another spacecraft must try to save them within a certain length of time?

Or another news story: A sunken treasure is being hauled up from the bottom of the sea. The salvagers must keep the exact location of the sunken ship secret. What if they don't, and a modern pirate arrives?

The Ann Landers or Dear Abby columns: Just one week's letters have enough plots to keep writers going for a lifetime. The anguish of a woman who knew of an incestuous relationship between her husband and daughter and said nothing. The secretary who says she is having an affair with her married boss and is not sorry, because, from what he tells her, his wife, the mother of six, has let herself go.

Or, you can reuse one of the oldest, strongest, and simplest plots: Boy meets girl, boy loses girl, boy finds girl. That's the plot of *Rebecca*, and every other happy love story. If boy *doesn't* find the girl again, you have *Love Story*, Erich Segal's super best seller, and hundreds more. But in each story, the characters and details, the opening and ending, are individual inventions of the author.

Let's take a closer look at the structure of a novel. An easy way to think of it is as having three parts: the beginning, the middle, and the end.

Suspense writer Graham Greene, speaking at Georgetown University, said, "I generally have a character, a beginning, and an end. In between, the middle develops in a way I don't foresee." That's his way. You'll see others. Look at each part of a novel and you'll see what other famous novelists have done with them.

THE JOB OF OPENING LINES

The beginning of your novel must grab the reader and also give a hint of what to expect. If it's a cowboy story, start with your hero moving through the outdoors, or with a confrontation. If it's an adventure or mystery, let a little shadow of danger or some clue appear in the first paragraph—or a suspect or some portent or some concern the main character has about his own safety or the fate or safety of someone he knows or is told about.

If it's the genre of book that publishers call "Romance," let there be assurance right from page one or sentence one that this is going to be about the ins and outs of romance and courtship. Let it be clear that this will be a woman's or girl's mighty struggle to achieve happiness—which in this case translates into finding the right man and falling in love.

Books which cater to females no longer have to be peopled with heroines who only learn about sex on their wedding night. Look at the opening of a Jackie Collins book. She has developed a following of millions of women across the country and a good share of men as well. In *The World is Full of Divorced Women,* the first sentence finds the heroine's lover asking her, "Are you bored with sex?" And immediately you learn that she is not bored with sex but bored with him.

In using this first line, Jackie Collins shows she realizes the importance of putting the subject of her novel, sex, right up front. Another writer, Stephen Shadegg, author of a first novel about politics, *The Remnant,* and of a number of nonfiction books, told me how he learned this same lesson early in his career when he was writing for pulp magazines. He sent a story to his editor, and it came back with the notation, "Not enough sex in it."

Shadegg telephoned the editor and said, "What do you mean there's not enough sex in it? There's sex on the first page."

The editor replied, "Yes, but it's near the bottom of the page."

Now let's see how a master of international intrigue, John LeCarre, opens his best seller, *The Little Drummer Girl,* how he catches the reader's curiosity in the first sentence while setting the stage in the proper location: "It was the Bodesberg incident that gave the proof, though the German authorities had no earthly means of knowing this." And before you finish the first paragraph, you know a poorly made bomb is involved and that there are clues in the way a bomb is made that give away the identity of the maker, that in effect he leaves his signature on it.

Some editors say that they can almost be sure, when they read that opening sentence or paragraph, if a book will be well written and exciting enough to publish. Ellis Amburn of Putnam's says, "The beginning novelist is apt to dally around till he gets in gear, or put another way, he meanders until he gets his bearings. In a play it's called 'the horrible scene' where the playwright tries to explain who everyone is and all the relationships. It isn't good in a play and it wrecks a novel." Move quickly into action or conflict.

THE ENDING TELLS YOU
WHERE YOU ARE GOING TO GO

Endings are equally important. Editors prefer a happy ending because readers prefer a happy ending, but happy or not, the ending should tell what happens and *not leave the reader dangling*. Let the reader have the satisfaction that comes with at least knowing the outcome on all the problems and issues that have kept him/her turning pages all through your book.

Inga Dean couldn't decide how to end her first contracted novel dealing with a woman's unhappy marriage to a Washington, D.C. psychiatrist, and so left the ending of *Memory and Desire* hazy, hoping the reader would decide. But Viking insisted Dean make up her mind how her plot was resolved, and she did finally rewrite the ending with what she calls a "semihappy ending."

Happy endings are not necessarily *happy* endings. A happy ending can be justice done. A crime solved. A mean relative finally kicked out of the house. A battle over and done with and the hero still alive. You don't have to look for a dancing-in-the-street kind of happy ending or a kissy-kissy one, though those kinds are good, too, once in a while.

Let's look at the endings of two novels, familiar to everyone. In the first, Charles Dickens's *A Tale of Two Cities*, the "happy" ending is peace of mind, even though the hero, Sydney Carton, gives his life in place of his lookalike, the husband of the woman he loves. His happiness is that he has saved her happiness, and his last words, spoken on the guillotine, are the last lines of the book: "It is a far, far better thing I do, than I have ever done; it is a far, far better rest that I go to, than I have ever known." His words live on forever.

The second ending, that of Charlotte Bronte's *Jane Eyre*, is also one of bittersweet happiness because of Rochester, the strange, brooding, self-indulgent hero who almost made Jane a bigamous wife. At the end, he is laid low, ruined and made blind. But Jane still loves him and now he can be hers at last—after 403 pages.

The final paragraph shows the new relationship and her quiet joy at being near him and needed: "Then he stretched his hand out to be led. I took that dear hand, held it a moment to my lips, then let it pass round my shoulder . . . I served both for his prop and guide. We . . . wended homeward."

But don't think you have to spell everything out, spend a whole chapter telling what happened to each of the characters for the next thirty years. Rather, you merely have to come to a conclusive stop, with all major action resolved, all loose plot threads tied up neatly. If you have a lot of subplots with threads to keep track of—in a mystery, for instance—you may find you want to knit them up as you go, one by one, along the way, so that only the strongest major strand is left to be knotted at the end.

A conclusion can bog down in a huge mass of exposition—static description—just as a beginning can. Don't let that happen in your book. Say just enough to let the reader know how the major climax was resolved, and then stop before you write another word.

GETTING FROM HERE TO THERE—THE PLOT THAT DOMINATES THE MIDDLE

Your novel is going to tell how you get from *here* to *there*. It's called plotting. The whole trick of the game is that only *you* know where the character is going and how he/she is going to get there—and *what* waits for him/her at the end. The reader keeps thinking he's going one place but aha, you, the author, know better. *What* you "know better" is the story—the *middle*.

And you, the author, are not telling. If the reader wants to know where the hero is going, let the reader read the book. All the way through. Make him know there's no way of knowing how it comes out for sure until the last page.

FORESHADOWING

You may foreshadow and prepare the reader subtly for events still in the distance. But do it lightly, and don't tell very much. If you foreshadow heavily—"but little did he know that later he would marry her"—an editor will write in the margin: "Don't send the reader a telegram." Better to say, if you need to say anything, "He wondered if he dared ask her for a date." Don't close doors until you actually reach them. Show the reader they're temptingly ajar, that there are lots of possibilities, then guide him to that one door and shove him through. When he discovers what's on the other side, he may find another array of doors, all temptingly ajar, until he finally reaches that last door.

FLASHBACKS

You may find that your story needs flashbacks to tell the story in a more interesting way. Use them discreetly. Joyce Engelson, editor-in-chief of E.P. Dutton, and editor of Richard Congdon's *Prizzi's Honor* when she was associated with the Putnam Publishing Group, says, "Each flashback should result in bringing the reader a little further along in the story." In other words, at the end of a flashback the reader is wiser, knowing something not known before—a murder hidden for years. The death of a child never talked about.

You can also start your novel with a small flash forward—taken from near a high point of action in the middle of the book. The flash forward grabs your attention, after which the whole book can be told in chronological order. The flash forward tells the reader the essential nature of your story right away; it really is a kind of hook, a variation on strong opening lines.

Flashbacks are one way of giving your reader important information, but you don't have to use them. You can have someone tell the reader what happened. Two people are talking, and one says, "I guess you didn't know her father beat her. I was their neighbor." Or you can have a woman character on trial thinking she knows it would get the jury's sympathy if she told them her mother locked her in the closet as a child but she isn't going to do it. She'll tell them anything but that—she doesn't want to look pitiful. After all, she is a socialite envied by her friends.

Be careful not to use too many flashbacks. The reader can become confused, and may finally say, "Who cares?" and close the book. Use them selectively; otherwise, reading your novel may be like watching a Ping-Pong game.

BUILDING YOUR PLOT

However you tell the story, it is the plot, the "how they get from here to there" that is the middle. It's what the reader really wants from the book—experience, entertainment, exercise of his emotions and intellect, vicarious living, enlightenment, edification, a lesson, wit, elegance of language, an adventure, insight—something new that you have created for him, and that he will like enough to tell his friends about.

How do you achieve this?

Plotting is simply playing the game of "What If?"

If you are going to write science fiction, the sky *really* is the limit. What if an ugly/cute creature comes down from another planet and is marooned on earth? And what if a normal family finds him—or, rather, the kids do—and they protect him, afraid of what their parents will do?

Well, you get the picture. You have the plot that captured the imagination of the nation. *ET* became a household word for "extraterrestrial."

But plotting is more than simply a premise that sets up what the story is about. You need complications that continue along the way so it isn't too easy for the hero to reach his goal. In fact, the reader is sometimes in despair, wondering if the hero can overcome all the misfortunes that befall him. Just when he has solved one problem, another, even tougher, comes along. You can approach each of these complications with the "What If?" game. What if, after he escapes from the muggers and runs to the end of the street, he is relieved to see a familiar face? But what if he suddenly realizes that the nice guy he sees is the leader of the gang?

ANOTHER WAY TO PLOT

Say you don't like the "What If?" game. Then look at a plot as a staircase with a chute at the top—like a playground slide.

You have your premise, your opening lines which make an intriguing first step that entices you to want to keep climbing. The reader is curious. What's up there? Now you keep luring him along, adding dangers or complications that threaten the mental or physical well-being of the main character. The reader has to continue climbing to find out what happens. And just as one problem is solved, a worse one pops up on the next step.

Toward the top of the stairs, the reader is almost panting, sharing the character's fear that he'll never escape or reach his goal. It's a fiasco with no way out. Only disaster lies ahead and the villain will surely win. Maybe he has already won. The reader must find out. He gets up to the climax, the top of the steps, and zoom, down the chute he goes to the fast ending.

In quick succession all things are revealed, all problems solved or justice is done or undone. Something happens which has its roots back in the plot.

The reader picks himself up and says, "I should have known it all along." He walks away still mulling it over and ready to go to the bookstore to find your next book.

WHAT TURNS PAGES?

Curiosity and suspense turn pages. Until the very end of a book there must be left questions unanswered. The reader keeps on turning pages to find out what happens. You answer a few questions or solve a few problems along the way, perhaps, and give some true or misleading hints, but the big questions hang there until the end.

Suspense is not the province only of the adventure book. Think of *The Graduate*, by Richard C. Webb, where the suspense builds up in the graduate's race against the clock. He is running, running. He must stop the wedding.

So pressure of *time* is a great page-turner. Every kind of chase and race. Who will get to the finish line first? To the rescue of anyone anywhere. A boiler is going to explode. The men are locked in. They must either get out or keep the explosion from happening.

Anger over injustice turns pages. The big lie. Someone tells a terrible lie and an innocent man is made to suffer and it takes the whole book to resolve it.

I sometimes think of novel-reading as a sort of addiction. The novelist—the pusher—grabs your attention with line one, hooks you with a little sniff of his product, and holds you to the end of the paragraph. But the end of the paragraph makes you want to go on to the next paragraph, eager for more of his stuff, to the end of the page. The end of the page makes you want to turn to the next one. Fascinated, you demand more, and read on to the end of the chapter. But is it enough? No—now you're addicted—your attention is so engaged that you have to read to the next chapter, and so on until the end of the book. So each part has a hook that pulls you forward. That's why successful works are sometimes called "page-turners," or, to use the more formal phrase I first heard from publisher Bernard Geis, they have "narrative drive."

A SAMPLE OF A PLOT

Let's take a very simple plot from Rose Wilder Lane's *Young Pioneers*, a short novel published in many editions throughout the world, then made into a TV movie and reprinted in several textbooks.

It opens in the 1850s with the teenage David and Molly marrying and going West in a wagon to find a home. They homestead a claim in the Dakotas and settle in a sod shanty. Molly is just seventeen and David nineteen when their baby, David John, is born. They plant wheat and potatoes on the prairie. Things are going well, when David, anticipating a fine harvest, recklessly buys a load of lumber on credit to start building a house. But calamity strikes—hordes of grasshoppers destroy the growing wheat and potato vines.

They settle on a desperate plan—Molly and the baby will stay and defend the claim, and David will go to Iowa to work and pay their debts. Eventually a neighbor brings a letter—David has a job in a lumbermill. Then another letter—he has had an accident, and may not be able to return until winter. At the end of summer, the neighbors give up and leave. Molly tries to get a job in town, but can't find one, and buys barely enough supplies to keep herself and her child alive through the winter on the homestead claim.

A great blizzard comes. Molly copes at first, but the supply of twisted hay she uses as fuel is getting low. The sod shanty is completely covered with snow, except for its smokestack. She realizes she might die, and lies in bed with the baby, dreaming.

But David is on his way back. Though left with a limp from the accident, he has recovered and has cash. He sets out through the blizzard and finds the shanty. Molly hears him bump against the smokestack and guides him to safety. The novel ends when the baby says "Blablub," which Molly translates as "Papa."

That's a plot. It is a simple one, but it makes us cry when the grasshoppers eat the wheat, and laugh at the end when all turns out well. The genius of Rose Wilder Lane, and other successful writers, is evident in their creation of wonderful details to make the plot pleasurable to follow. You can learn a lot about how to handle such details by studying other novels, but then you must create your own details from your life or knowledge.

TAKE A CLOSER LOOK AT
A NOVEL YOU ADMIRE

The best way to understand the structure of a novel is to take one you have read and liked and make notes as you scan it again. On which page—how far into the action—is each character introduced? How are they introduced? Is something said about them by another character—something derogatory, perhaps?

Note where flashbacks occur and what purposes they serve. How are they introduced? Note any subplot and how it is resolved. Note where the middle crises of the story occur and how the major problem is resolved. How many pages does it take after the main climax for all things to be solved and all things revealed?

Now, go back and study both the opening lines and the final paragraph. How did the author arouse your interest and curiosity and how does he leave you at the finish?

Don't be afraid that some reviewers may say you're a copy of Isaac Asimov or Stephen King. The basic methods of storytelling are as old as language itself. Start with whatever style you like—you won't be stuck with it—you can change to another style in your next book if you like. That's what Truman Capote did. His first short stories were heavily influenced by the writing of his fellow Southerner, William Faulkner. To me, his first novel, *Breakfast at Tiffany's*, is practically an American version of Christopher Isherwood's *Berlin Stories*. But Capote kept evolving. His *In Cold Blood* was very original, opening a new field, "faction" or the nonfiction novel, which itself influenced other novelists.

Now you are practically ready to plan your first novel, step by step, but you must first make an important preliminary decision:

FROM WHOSE VIEWPOINT ARE YOU TELLING THE STORY?

All stories have to be told from some point of view. Though technicians of fiction can describe many possible points of view, to my mind there are three major ones. The simplest and easiest to understand is the *FIRST PERSON*, using the word "I" as though you were telling a friend something you did yourself, or watched someone else do something and now were describing it. G.J.A. O'Toole, in *The Cosgrove Report*, begins, "I find myself in a strange world." Immediately on reading this, we realize that a character in the story will be its narrator, and the story will be told from this first person narrator's point of view. We don't yet know whether the narrator is the main character, or a secondary character who somehow learned the story—two different ways of using the first-person point of view.

With that sentence, the author committed himself to the first-person approach and to solving its particular problems—which means he may have to use things like letters, telegrams, or documents to get certain information across, or have the narrator eavesdrop on conversations of others to learn certain facts. The narrator is peeping at the world through a peephole we know well: our own eyes.

Joyce Engelson, when she was editor-in-chief of St. Martin's/Marek, told my coauthor that one of the worst mistakes beginning novelists make is to put a story in the first person when it has too large a cast of characters.

First person looks simple. It isn't. It requires a special light touch, and the "I" must not get in the way of the story. "I" can become boring, and can make it difficult to include things that are far away.

But the most important difficulty—one that beginning novelists often don't take into consideration when they start in the first person—is the difficulty of characterization. If your story is told from a first-person narrator's point of view, all characters are seen through that narrator's eyes only. A male narrator may have a character that makes him oblivious to the thoughts and feelings of women. A female narrator may have some blind spots about men. So it may take a lot of effort to get across the most basic facts about the characters—how they dress (does the narrator see himself in a mirror?), how they feel, their mannerisms.

But that said, I have to admit some great and small novels have been effective in the first-person viewpoint. *Robinson Crusoe*, a pioneer piece of fiction in the modern novel form, was written in 1719 in the first person. Daniel Defoe wanted his readers to think his adventure story of being shipwrecked and marooned for four years on an island really happened. And they did. Even today, it seems very real.

So first person is a good way to tell a relatively simple story. In a detective or police story it gives greater believability.

If the narrator is not the central character, a slight story can be enhanced by the emotional involvement of the narrator as an interested bystander. Truman Capote in *Breakfast at Tiffany's*, mentioned earlier, strikes just the right note when he tells the story of Holly Golightly:

I didn't trust my voice to tell the news . . . I thrust the letter at her . . . her eyes squinty with sleep . . .

Or this bit of intimacy when Holly and "I" are wandering about New York arm in arm and pass a Woolworth's:

" 'Let's steal something,' she said, pulling me into the
store. . . ."

First-person writing makes it even more of a lark when Holly
puts a Halloween mask on her own face and then puts one on "I" and
leads him out of the store by the hand. "Outside, we ran a few blocks."
And "I" makes the reader feel the exhilaration he discovers in "successful theft."

There are two other main ways to tell a story, each in the *third
person*, using the pronouns "he," "she," "they," and "it," rather than
"I." First, there is the *OMNISCIENT OBSERVER* who sees and
knows all. Using this method, the author can hop, skip, and jump
from Rome to Berlin to Tucumcari from paragraph to paragraph if he
is daring enough. He can have the reader look in and share the feelings, thoughts, and actions of opposing generals, as Tolstoy does in
War and Peace. He can view a battle panoramically, and then swoop
down to watch an individual soldier. This godlike point of view was a
favorite of writers of the past, and best-selling authors of today sometimes use it too. It is very tempting when you have a large cast of
characters. But this method is probably too permissive for a beginning novelist. It is only successful when the story is told so brilliantly,
in such an absorbing manner, or with such story-telling skill that the
reader suspends disbelief and comes to accept that the novelist really
does know that much about the action and characters. If this technique is poorly done, the reader finds it improbable and cannot buy
the idea of the writer knowing the inmost thoughts and most secret
actions of his many characters.

Between first person and omniscient observer lies an easier way.
It could be called *RESTRICTED THIRD PERSON*. You tell the story in the third person—"he," "she," "they," "it" does this and does
that. But instead of having an all-seeing observer, you limit what can
be seen to what one person, or two people, or at most, a small group of
people, can see.

For example, in the Henry James novel, *The Ambassadors*, we
watch the main character come to Europe and try to carry out a mission. As "he" learns things, the reader learns them too. Focusing on
one character's actions, the story is unified. But Henry James, the
author, is not as limited as the main character—James gets a chance
to describe things, his main character, the settings, and the other
characters, so he is able to include much more detail than if he used
first-person narration.

If you wanted to write a story about a group of travelers who are hijacked, you might want to switch to the point of view of each character to tell some part of the story. You will have several points of view—but still not have an omniscient observer. The story can be as credible as you make your characters and their actions. If such shifts make you nervous, you could adopt some unifying device such as having a journalist interview each one.

To avoid confusion, most writers try not to shift points of view within a chapter. It is important to clearly identify which character is viewing what in each part of the book.

Critics, writers, editors, even agents, have opinions, often annunciated as divine wisdom, about the best point of view to use in telling a story. My own opinion was expressed by the famous bridge teacher and player, Charles Goren: "I never quarrel with success." If it works, use it. And if it doesn't work, even if you have written half your novel, abandon it and switch to a fresh point of view.

So, with preliminaries out of the way, let's go on to a concrete plan.

WRITING YOUR NOVEL

Step One: The Premise

The first step in writing your novel is simply to tell yourself, "I want to write a novel about . . ." and then state the premise in just a paragraph. Or even a sentence. Just for starters, I'll give you one:

> I want to write a story about a man who is planning to kill his wife. She's the obstruction to his happiness.

I see that doesn't explain enough and so I add:

> He has developed a passion for a girl half his age and is afraid he will lose her if he doesn't marry her soon. He's afraid to get a divorce because then he will be penniless. His wife is the fabulously wealthy benefactor who gave him the money for his business, a business which is now failing. He has led the girl to believe he is the one with the money. He must make sure he inherits his wife's fortune.

Now I have a strong premise that can go in many directions. It really could be—and maybe should be—told from the wife's viewpoint. She would get more sympathy. The reader will hope she is somehow saved. Maybe she finds out in some interesting way that he is playing around and slowly she gets the feeling that she is not safe.

It might be more unusual to tell it from the young girl's viewpoint. Marian isn't really an exploitative person. She was just lonely and he was so tender and attentive. She needed comfort. Her boyfriend of three years had sent her a "Dear Marian" letter and she found out he had moved in with her closest girlfriend. So, she did need sympathy and the dependability of an older man.

He has said he's divorcing his wife. Why shouldn't she plan to marry him? She might even invite her ex-boyfriend and her ex-girlfriend to the wedding—let them turn green with jealousy.

In working out the premise and the viewpoint of your novel, it's good to take a look at it from the viewpoint of each of your major characters. Take your time. Just let it percolate in your mind until you suddenly know how you want to handle it, until it feels right to you.

Let's say I have decided to go ahead with my first impulse, which was to tell the story from the man's viewpoint. Now comes the next step.

Step Two: The Opening Line or Lines

I've thought of two. I'll put them both down.

Greg told himself he would be perfectly justified in bumping off the irritable, tired harridan in his bed. He was sure it would not bother him in the least—it was the best solution.

That gives it the suggestion of a psychological study. Will he have the guts for the evil deed?
The second way:

Kurt looked over the medicines in his wife's flesh-pink bathroom. What combination, he pondered, might be lethal to a 200-pound woman? There was only one problem. It had to look like suicide.

Now we have the start of a detective story. I can almost see the arrival of the detectives at the big mansion to ask a few friendly questions. Will he be able to outwit them?

Step Three: The Ending

If you know where you are going, it's easier to get there. It some-times happens that a writer changes his mind about an ending, or a publisher says a different ending would improve the story, but gener-ally the original ending stays.

For the psychological study, I end on an ironic twist:

> Greg turned and found himself looking into a gun. With a sick feeling he saw that his wife and Marian were standing to-gether like old friends. Where had Marian come from? And quietly, a policeman opened the door.

For the detective story:

> As they led Kurt away, he turned and saw that Marian's old boyfriend was back, with his arm around her. It was the final blow.

Step Four: The Middle

The middle is simply a matter of getting from here to there—from your opening line, which hints what's going to happen, to the ending, which shows how it turns out.

The middle is the *megillah*, the monster, the whole schmeer. But you can handle it. You take it one incident or action at a time. You talk out loud, or to yourself, and say, What if they do this or that to him, how will he react? And then what happens if he tries to solve his prob-lem this way, but someone turns against him? The false friend gets him in deeper trouble in order to grab off the prize himself—the prize being money, a woman, or prestige.

Many writers, such as Joyce Carol Oates, say they let a plot sim-mer for as long as necessary in the mind without writing it down and then sit down and write it fast and furiously. That's fine if that's the way your mind works, but others work better by being methodical and writing it down as it comes to them.

An easy way to start a loose outline of your novel is to take a sheet of paper for each chapter and write the action that takes place there. If you come up with sixteen flows of action, then you have six-teen chapters. Keep each chapter in its own folder—sixteen chap-ters, sixteen folders. Each chapter can be as long or short as you like, but it has to have a beginning and an end. Or at least a resting place or a new question raised. Though one small crisis is over at the end of the chapter, the reader must never doubt that there will be more trouble ahead. Or perhaps a note of hope ends a chapter and the reader wonders if the fortunes of the hero are indeed going to change.

If your novel is going to be 270 to 300 pages, the average chapter might be sixteen to twenty pages, some longer, some shorter.

Don't be afraid to waste paper. Use separate sheets to throw into the appropriate folder anything that helps your plot. Eventually, some folders may grow fat. It's all right to overwrite. Editing will take care of it. But that comes much later.

Just as you now have a basic outline of your novel you can now, if you wish, write an individual outline of each separate chapter, adding a page or more to the material in each chapter folder. You might want to indicate where major crises will arise, making sure to space them out in the book. You might want to say where each major character will be introduced and note it in the file folder for the right chapter.

If you have a subplot or several subplots, sketch in each chapter folder how that theme or concurrently running story moves along and how it is resolved. The hero's buddy may be feuding with a cattle baron. But this action must have some effect on the novel you are writing, or else the feud is a different story and belongs in some different novel. Everything in your novel must relate somehow and influence the main character or action of your plot. Your main character also may be involved in a subplot in which he has a secondary goal. It, too, must be resolved or explained somehow before the end of the book. The reader may care a lot that the hero is saving a little boy buried in a mine explosion, but they read on to find out what happens in the major plot—his courtship of a girl whose parents have thrown him off the property and even had him arrested.

YOUR CHARACTERS CAN HELP YOU WITH YOUR PLOT: THE FREE-FORM WAY

Many novelists, like Graham Greene, object to writing outlines of their novels because of the pleasure they get in letting the characters "take over" and dictate the story.

Joseph Wambaugh, former policeman and author of *The Blue Knight* and other best sellers, frankly admits plotting is the hard part for him. He told *Writer's Digest*, "Interaction between characters is what I do best. I have to rewrite, rewrite again and again."

Maybe, like Amelia Walden, author of *To Catch a Spy* and other novels, you'll feel that when you've fleshed out your characters so that they come to life in your mind as real people, they take over and write the novel. Walden says she's found plotting is easy, even effortless, in the hands of the right characters—maybe with an occasional small nudge from the author to keep them headed in the right direction.

If you're that sort of writer, a full-scale outline may be the worst possible way for you to start working on your novel. It may kill all the joy of discovery, even if the lack of a detailed overall plan leads you into a blind alley or two along the way. What you got into, you can get out of. Just go back and take a different turning, once you realize some character, intent on his own troubles, has pulled you off course.

But I still maintain that if you're a beginning writer, you'll find it helpful to outline as much as you can your first time out. It is your security and will keep you from going adrift. Later, you can become more casual about plotting.

So there you have it—the elements you need to consider—and maybe write down—in four steps to planning your first novel:

1. You know what your novel is about.
2. You write an opening.
3. You plan and write the ending.
4. *Then*, you devise a plot and characters to take you from here to there. Ideally, you start an outline consisting of pages or folders for each of the flows of action, or chapters.

You have actually started writing!

5

Curses, Sex Scenes, and Other Puzzlers

We have covered a lot of ground, but I'm sure you have some pressing questions. Here are the ones first-time novelists ask me most frequently.

WHAT'S IN A NAME?

The answer is, in a story, a lot. Dickens's use of "Scrooge" in *A Christmas Carol* is perfect. You can almost see the mean, scrunched-up old fellow. When William Thackeray called one of the characters of *Vanity Fair* "Becky Sharp," it wasn't hard for him to complete her characterization. But you probably will not want to go as far as Emily Post did in her nonfiction book, *Etiquette*, and use names like "Mr. Newly," "Clubwin Doe," and "Mrs. Worldly." Still, the name has to sound and feel right for the character.

A novelist who writes under the pen name "Richard Owen" used to sit in the glass-enclosed office next to mine at his 8:45-4:30 editorial job, and often would be pounding away at the typewriter. From time to time he would pause and pick my brain, asking "What's a good last name for an elderly Texan?" or "Give me a first name for the wife of a young New York artist." He must have had his characters clearly in mind—he would look off into space at his mental picture before accepting or rejecting my suggestions.

You will probably want to use dictionaries of names to help you find a name that conveys the right picture of your character if you don't have me around.

You still have a problem, however, and that is picking a name that no actual person in your plot's location has. You don't want someone with the name you use to rise up and claim you are writing about him/her and that he/she has been damaged by your characterization. When you have your character's name picked out, consult the phone book of that locale to be sure no one has quite the same name, or even one similar if the name is unusual.

Bonnie Golightly, a New York writer originally from the South, was so annoyed at Truman Capote's use of the name "*Holly* Golightly" for the main character of *Breakfast at Tiffany's* that she started a lawsuit against Capote and his publishers. (No verdict was rendered.) Her name is an unusual one for New York, and she knew socially many of the members of the New York gay community that Capote knew also.

If you think hers was a special case, consider what recently happened to Carolyn Chute, a new novelist, writing a completely fictitious book about an incestuous family in Maine. She used the family name "Bean" because it is an interesting name and a very common one in Maine. Everyone knows it's safe to use a name like "John Smith"—there are so many of them no one could say that he was the character intended. So Bean seemed safe. For the town, Chute came up with the name of Egypt. A check of an atlas showed no town in Maine by that name.

The book was published as *The Beans of Egypt, Maine*, and it was a success, but what Chute had not foreseen was the anger of Bean families of Maine and the verbal abuse that would result. Nor did Ticknor & Fields, her publishers who put out 235,000 copies in hard cover and paperback simultaneously. It turned out that though there was no town of Egypt, sections in several towns were called by that name.

It is also a sensible precaution to change the location of your novel. You might try to pick a different state, one with similar physical characteristics to the one of your setting. But you must research the new location to avoid embarrassing mistakes.

HOW MANY CHARACTERS DO YOU NEED?

I would answer: as few as you can get away with to tell your story fully. Be cautious before adding additional characters just because they are colorful or interesting to write about—good characters may require their own subplots, and throw your novel off its main course. Each additional character requires the reader to hold more information in his head to understand your story. So the bottom line answer here is "exactly as many as your story needs."

For most plots, you need at the very least a main character, a villain or adversary, and the main character's sidekick, friend, or co-conspirator.

It may turn out later that the friend or sidekick is really on the side of the villain, but that's beside the point. The point is that the main character or hero/heroine needs the sidekick for dialogue. He/she just can't keep talking to him/herself. Everyone tells someone what is on his mind. Someone has to be the sounding board so the main character can voice thoughts in a natural way.

The sidekick is important for another reason. When the main character is acting stupid or irrational, the friend asks the questions the reader wants to know. Or makes the perfectly sensible suggestion that the reader wants to shout at the main character. In other words, the sidekick is standing in for the reader.

Sometimes the sidekick is the one the reader identifies with, as in *The Great Gatsby,* in which the narrator of the story, who is telling what happens in first person, lives next door and sees what goes on. In that case, the narrator gets more and more involved with the characters in the plot because he is invited to the parties and is enlisted by the main character to bring a certain beautiful woman to the party—the object of Gatsby's all-consuming love.

I have gone on at length about the sidekick in order to make the point that you, the author, must flesh out this person so the reader feels the sidekick has a life of his own. He is not just a limp washcloth to be picked up now and then to wipe the face of the hero.

In the same way, the villain or adversary must be credible and well developed—and he/she may have a sidekick too, or at least associates to herald his/her arrival, and to do the less important work.

So, in deciding how many characters to use, keep in mind how many you need to tell your story.

DO YOU NEED PERMISSION TO QUOTE?

If you quote more than a few words of the works of other authors in your novel, and the material you quote is in copyright, you will probably have to get permission from the copyright owner, or the publisher who controls the rights to the work, in order to include it in your novel. Titles of works are not copyrightable, so merely using a title of a song or poem or any work within your novel is no problem. But using songs—even one line—requires permission. That is because a song is such a short work, even quotation of a single line is appropriating a substantial part of it. The same reasoning applies to poems. Usually authors delay seeking permission to quote until their novels are under contract to a publisher, and then inquire of their editor about the publisher's policy on securing permissions to quote. Usually the author ends up paying whatever fees are necessary.

An interesting instance of quotation within a novel involved my agency several years ago, when Little, Brown & Company published *Myra Breckenridge*, by Gore Vidal. When I read the book, I noted that the transsexual hero/heroine, Myron/Myra, was depicted as fascinated by the works of Parker Tyler, a critic whom I represented as literary agent. Vidal had quoted extensively from Parker Tyler's book, *Magic and Myth of the Movies*, without having asked or received permission to do so. At Tyler's suggestion, I queried Little, Brown about this, and suggested that since the quotations made up about 1 percent of the whole book, Tyler should receive 1 percent of *Myra's* earnings.

Little, Brown resisted this suggestion, and Parker Tyler later learned through an acquaintance that Gore Vidal's view was that his quotation of this work, which he admired, helped, not hurt, Parker Tyler. Tyler asked his good friend Charles Boultenhouse, then manager of Brentano's Fifth Avenue bookstore, to check the sales of his books, comparing their sales before and after publication of *Myra Breckenridge*. Boultenhouse reported that indeed, it was true—the sales of his books in general had picked up after Vidal's novel was published. Tyler decided to drop the whole matter.

Not many authors would be as rational about such unauthorized quoting of their work as was Parker Tyler. So you would be on much safer ground, regardless of your publisher's advice, to secure permission to quote any copyrighted material used within your novel, even if it is a quotation from your own work—such as a nonfiction piece published by another house.

CURSES AND LOVE SCENES— HOW DO YOU HANDLE THEM?

Do you find that every character seems to be rapping out profanity in your novel? If so, it's not realistic. Not *everyone* curses. If one character has to curse, let him. But don't throw in obscenities to sound modern or liberated. This is not a novel about *you*. It's about a bunch of other people.

The same goes with sex scenes. They're not obligatory. But if used, should they be explicit or suggested as going on in some other room, out of sight, out of hearing? You can do either, but it must seem natural. Is explicit sex central to your plot? It could be in the case of a rape or of a seduction scene, but even here, different writers would use different methods. Either way, it's not going to stop the sale of your book to a publisher. If your editor wants a sex scene made more or less explicit, you can talk with her/him about it and reach some agreement or compromise.

To see how scenes of sexual passion can be handled with skill and feeling and yet not rely on four-letter words, study Vladimir Nabokov's *Lolita*, the story of a middle-aged man who cannot resist his mad passion for a beautiful nymphet and in order to possess her, runs away with her. Nabokov died in 1977 but the word "Lolita" will be forever in the English language as meaning a child temptress. The scenes are erotic but not obscene, even translating nicely to the movie screen. Yet the pathetic quality of the romance comes about through Nabokov's clever use of contrasts—the girl's petulance set against the aging lover's slavishly eager attempt to please her by putting nail polish on her toes and doing whatever other menial task she assigns him.

By way of contrast, I remember when an editor, after reading a client's work, called me to complain, "I know this is a realistic story about a race riot in a prison. But to use 'motherfucker' eleven times on one page is excessive."

Sex scenes seem to fit very naturally into historical novels. I remember that I learned a lot about sex as a young adolescent from *Anthony Adverse*, by Hervey Allen, and I noticed my twelve- and thirteen-year-old female cousins reading *Gone With the Wind* with avid attention.

As a freshman in college, my more sophisticated taste was satisfied by works such as Henry Miller's *The Tropic of Cancer*, and later, by Edmund Wilson's *Memoirs of Hecate County*. Novels that I remember with affection as part of my education can't be very bad!

Though I don't buy all the novels of Jackie Collins as does my co-author, Frances Spatz Leighton, we agree about Collins's reasoning that there is life under the covers for women as well as men. As Collins puts it, she wants to show that her women are "not sluts and they're not nymphomaniacs—they're just women who like sex as much as men do."

STREAM OF CONSCIOUSNESS— SHOULD YOU USE IT?

Dialogue may be handled in several ways. One is to say only what the characters speak aloud and let the reader guess at the thought behind the words. Many authors prefer that and so do many readers. In a western, it is assumed the good guy says only what he means and his actions show if he is going to play a trick on the bad guy, or he confides his plan to his sidekick.

In the novels of manners mirroring life in our sophisticated, complex society, the author tells not only what the character is saying but what he is saying in his thoughts, which is frequently at odds with his spoken words. The reader feels almost like a psychiatrist or a mind reader.

Past masters of characters' stream of consciousness were James Joyce in *Ulysses* and Virginia Woolf in *Mrs. Dalloway*. Both novels are engrossing literary experiments worth great study, but they are unique—solitary monuments on the road not taken by popular literature—and hence not suitable to imitate.

However, after reading them, you will see better how to use characters' thoughts in your own novel, if you are using stream-of-consciousness techniques.

WHERE DO YOU GET YOUR TITLES?

For some writers it's fun to come up with titles, but for others it's torture. If you find it hard, remember that you don't have to have a title when you begin—or even after you finish your novel. If necessary, you can put a label on it that says something like "Untitled Western." That's better than a title that you think might turn an editor or agent off, like *Here's Mud in Your Eye*. So if you don't have a title yet, don't despair—you can write your novel anyway. Often you will find you have developed what's called a "working title," the name you use for convenience in thinking about your novel, and such a mental label will do until you come up with a better one.

Since the title is the main hook, the very thing that first catches a reader's eye, you will have to think about the problem eventually. But where do you get one? A title can come from anywhere. From the air. From your subconscious. From the name of your main character, or his nickname. That's how John Updike came up with the titles *Rabbit, Run; Rabbit Redux;* and *Rabbit Is Rich*. Rabbit is the nickname of his main character. Open the Bible or a volume of Shakespeare and touch a verse with your eyes closed. The Bible gave William Faulkner *Absalom, Absalom!* just as Shakespeare gave him *The Sound and the Fury*. James Michener's *Covenant* reminds us that the book of Isaiah tells us, "We have made a covenant with death, and with Hell we are at agreement." And Hemingway reminds us that according to Ecclesiastes, *The Sun Also Rises* upon the just and the unjust.

Titles come from a line of poetry, nursery rhymes, and even from children's stories. One of Agatha Christie's most successful mysteries was entitled *Ten Little Indians*. And Hemingway's *For Whom the Bell Tolls* is from a poem by John Donne.

Hemingway spent a great deal of time getting exactly the right title. When he thought of *For Whom the Bell Tolls*, he wrote elatedly to his famous editor, Maxwell Perkins at Scribner's: "I think it has the magic that a title has to have." Hemingway had one reservation about the title, fearing some people might think he was talking about toll charges and the Bell telephone company. "If so, it is out," he wrote Perkins, quite seriously.

Humorous titles are harder to come by, because they require that you give a clue to the light mood of the story. Jean Kerr, whose amusing book about family life was made into a movie, got her title in a perfectly simple way. As she told it, she was having a dinner party and had told her twin sons all the things they were *not* to do, like use the guest towels or leave their bicycles on the front steps—"but I forgot to tell them not to eat the centerpiece on the table." Presto! *Please don't eat the daisies.* To keep it conversational, she capitalized only the first word.

James Thurber twisted the traditional, solemn title of countless autobiographies, *The Life and Times of* ————, to come up with *My Life and Hard Times.* And you know you're going to be getting more than a staid travelog when you pick up a book called *Around the World with Auntie Mame.* Auntie Mame, flitting about the bookstores and movie screens of the world, earned her creator, Patrick Dennis, a fortune. Actually, the fortune was earned by Edward Everett Tanner III, the author's real name. Tanner had the rare pleasure of seeing three of his titles on the best-seller list at the same time.

Since James Clavell's *Tai-Pan* and *Shogun,* novels about the Orient have tended to sport very brief or single-word titles, like Eric Van Lustbader's *The Ninja.* But don't forget Pearl Buck's best seller about China, *The Good Earth.* From a key word and concept in his novel, Robert Skimin found a title for his saga of a noble Japanese family which immigrates to the United States before World War I: *Chikara!,* meaning "strength" or power.

Titles can come from the names of places—islands, cities, states, countries. Michener used many—from *Tales of the South Pacific* to *Texas*—and has said he has plans for more. (A friend who returned from Texas, my home state, while the state was agog at Michener's new book, facetiously told me he was going to write a novel of just ninety-nine pages with a short historical opening paragraph and call it *Rhode Island.*)

If you call your local post office, you'll find no mailing address for a place called Lonesome Dove, Texas. But Lonesome Dove is very real to those reading the recent western epic of Texas native Larry McMurtry, which is set in the area near the Mexican border around the 1800s. And Edna Ferber chose the apt word, *Giant,* for her blockbuster tale of Texas.

Sometimes a character's wistful yearning makes a title that excites the imagination—*The Magic Mountain,* by Thomas Mann; *Lost Horizon* by James Hilton, with its dream of wonderful Shangri-La just beyond the map's boundaries; *Chocolates for Breakfast* by Pamela Moore.

You may think up a strange and mysterious title that's still dramatic enough to make a reader want to find out what it means—like *The Clan of the Cave Bear* by Jean Auel, about a prehistoric tribe, or *Lord of the Flies* by William Golding, about a more modern and sinister tribe made up of castaway boys.

Some authors have been known to send a whole list of suggested titles along with their manuscripts, encouraging the publisher or agent to decide which is best. This isn't a good idea. I always prefer to see *one* strong title. It's taken for granted that the title may be changed after your novel interests a publisher willing to pay for the change (and the book). But you can send a title list *after* the book has been accepted.

Publishers—the editor, the sales manager, or the president—sometimes come up with good titles, and even agents have made suggestions that eventually were accepted. A few of my title ideas have ended up on books, but I won't mention which ones, to protect the privacy of the authors.

Some book buyers pick novels simply and solely by their titles. One woman told me she buys any book which has a woman's name as a title. And in her hand was Erica Jong's novel *Fanny*. She probably missed that author's earlier *Fear of Flying*.

James M. Cain, author of a string of memorably named best sellers and movies such as *The Postman Always Rings Twice* and *Double Indemnity*, lived near Washington, D.C. before his death, and often told my coauthor stories about his career.

Cain's early years were a series of failures and career changes, from singer to reporter, would-be young novelist to professor of journalism, editorial writer to initially unsuccessful Hollywood script writer. He couldn't seem to get a script done, and play-doctor Vincent Lawrence gave him many tips. What Lawrence taught him about plotting, plus the terse, blunt style he had developed as a reporter at last made him sure, in a burst of insight, that he was overripe to write a novel.

He had a theme—murder for profit of a wealthy man by his wife, in league with her lover. But he needed a good title. He consulted Lawrence, his mentor. There followed a conversation Cain firmly believed was most responsible for his whole success. Instead of *giving* him a good title, Lawrence started reminiscing about problems of his own early career. When Lawrence was living in Boston and writing plays, he had been nervous and excited as he awaited an answer through the mail to his submissions to New York producers.

Lawrence described how he had fervently pleaded with the post-man to give the doorbell some extra rings as a signal if he had a letter from a producer or any letter from New York. But the mailman would not be swayed, and solemnly said, "No, we always ring twice so you know it is the postman."

And boom, Cain had his title for his first murder novel, a best seller that found its way eventually to the stage and screen—*The Postman Always Rings Twice*. Suddenly James M. Cain was eating regularly, even growing wealthy, and writers were coming to *him* for advice.

6.

Gearing Up and Writing It

This chapter could also be called "Where to write, when to write, and how much to write each day."

I remember an old print called "The Writer's Inspiration." It shows a man sitting on the edge of a bed, writing at a tiny desk in a small room filled with wife and a swarm of children. The man has paused, quill in hand, to look up at his inspiration mounted on the wall—a painting of a balloon. I often think of this heroic hack when I hear of the great efforts writers make to get out their pages, regardless of the problems they face.

But there is no reason to make it harder than you have to. You have choices, and you can make your work much easier by thinking about the work habits you want to establish, then choosing the best one possible for yourself.

The first question you should ask yourself is, "How much am I expected to write each day?"

THE DAILY QUOTA—
THREE PAGES

From what I have been told by many writers, three pages a day is a sensible quota. It is an amount which should keep you from panicking, because it is not asking too much. You can sit down and write three double-spaced pages—I know people who write letters longer than that.

It would be foolish to pooh-pooh the small amount and say, "Oh, I can write five pages a day. Or six. *That's* my quota." Writers who set themselves too high a quota have been known to throw up their hands and drop the whole project. They become disappointed in themselves. With three pages you will be proud of your steady progress and work more or less serenely, knowing that in just ninety days— three months—you will have the first draft of an average-sized book.

Of course, if certain days you feel really creative and want to write more pages, go to it. But don't think this lets you off the next day from doing your three solid pages.

WHEN SHOULD YOU WRITE—
WHAT TIME OF DAY?

Everyone has a time of day when he/she feels most alert. That's the time you should write. It doesn't matter when, as long as you go to it every day in the same place and at the same time so that it becomes as routine as getting up and putting on your clothes.

Hemingway wrote every morning, either standing at the typewriter, if he was making clean copy, or sitting at a cigar maker's table if he was writing a first draft, which he did in longhand. Then it was off to his boat, *Pilar*, to fish for the afternoon. He chose to stand for two reasons. He liked to pace, and his leg frequently ached from an assortment of wounds. He was apparently accident prone.

James Michener, whom my coauthor, Fran Leighton, met when Michener was a guest at the National Press Club in Washington, confessed that he was a "two-finger typist." But those two fingers had taken him through some twenty-nine manuscripts. He writes every day, seven days a week—just as if he still needed the money.

Michener's routine is simple: up at 7:30 and at the typewriter in something like five minutes, with just a pause to drink a glass of "battery acid"—his name for grapefruit juice. How long does he work?

Like Hemingway, Michener almost never writes in the afternoon.

But there the similarity ends. Hemingway wrote only about five hundred words when working on his first draft, carefully counting them at the end of the work session and keeping a log of his progress. Michener turns out an average of six pages a day, a good clip. It adds up to forty-plus pages a week.

Another morning worker, my client Niel Hancock, the fantasy novelist, says, "When I get up in the morning, I take my .45 off the bedside table and hold it to my temple, and I say to myself, 'Well, are you going to get right to work?' " Near his bed, he keeps the nonelectronic, old-fashioned machine that has never failed him, and which he has named "Manual, the Talking Typewriter." That way he has no excuse not to sit right down and get to work.

Tom Clancy was so used to working odd hours at the office and at home on his insurance business that he wrote *The Hunt for Red October* in both places—at home, "with the noise of children around me," and at the office on his computer, whenever it wasn't being used for business.

Joseph Wambaugh—*The New Centurions*, *The Blue Knight*, and others—takes the physical approach to gearing up for each day's work session. He runs two miles every morning before attacking the four pages—one thousand words—he forces himself to turn out before he will eat a solid meal.

And he works even while running. Wambaugh carries a little note pad wherever he goes, jotting down any good thought that occurs to him.

William Faulkner, before he was famous, once made a wheelbarrow into a desk. He wrote his novel *Mosquitoes* on the makeshift desk while supervising the shoveling of coal to feed the boilers at the University of Mississippi power plant.

Regardless of *where* you write—and you can do it practically anywhere—the key is to turn out pages of copy *each* day, and not deviate from your schedule.

SHOULD YOU WRITE ALONE?

Should you write alone? Not necessarily, though some must, because they cannot stand a whisper of noise. Others get the shakes when faced with isolation while trying to write, even if they live alone. They must seek out a more public place. The New York Public

Library has a room for writers. If the library in your town doesn't, you might get one started. Some novelists rent space in other people's offices. Some have a kindly friend who provides space, family sounds, and kitchen privileges in a private home.

George Sand wrote her novels in the dead of night when the world was still. A new novelist, David Small, author of *Almost Famous*, found he wrote best after dinner and after the problems of the day had faded away—from 9 to 11 P.M. No matter where he was, even on planes or in a hotel room, wherever his business trips for a Pennsylvania medical society took him, he wrote from 9 to 11.

WHERE IS THE BEST PLACE TO WRITE?

For some it's a matter of getting away from children and noise. But others get claustrophobia trying to write in the same place they live—whether surrounded by people or not. Some feel lonely at their typewriters and need the stimulus of knowing others are working on creative projects all around them. They need the sign of people, the sound of typewriters.

If the loneliness of writing gets to you, you might do what writers have been doing in New York for years to solve this problem. Share the cost. Rent a little cubbyhole of an apartment to as many writers as can comfortably fit in. In Greenwich Village there's one called the Writer's Room.

All that can be heard in the Writers' Room is the clicking of a typewriter here and there. Some authors are writing in longhand. All respect the two taboos, which are not to speak to anyone—even to ask for the use of a pencil—and not to make eye contact. Talking is permitted only in the lounge where there is a dictionary and a few other reference books, a coffeemaker, and a refrigerator stocked with cottage cheese. Exercise pads are on the floor for naps or exercise. Writers slip in and out, keeping their own hours, some leaving to go home and others to go to work in offices.

About seventy writers use the place, paying $100 to $150 a month depending on whether they write in the open or have an entirely enclosed space where they can use a word processor or can telephone without disturbing others.

Judith Rossner of *Looking for Mr. Goodbar* fame came with her sleeping bag and stayed for sixteen-hour stretches at a time, working and napping and sometimes crying over her typewriter as she clicked away. Nobody asked what she was working on—that's another taboo.

David Small, mentioned earlier, was unusual in his easy adjustment to different locales for writing, but others have chosen even stranger places to write. A few have written fiction in their parked cars, because they got a feeling of peace and quiet in an enclosed little private world of glass and steel. Marcel Proust used a cork-lined room, a pretty good equivalent to an ivory tower!

When you find the spot where you feel best while writing, the very place will actually help you get in the mood to turn out your daily three pages-plus. One woman wrote at the kitchen pass-through bar. Another writer, after he had earned enough money from writing, thought that he deserved something better than the cramped corner of his house where he had written facing the wall.

He built a new room, a lovely study with a view of trees and flowers. But he found he couldn't concentrate when looking at moving objects like leaves blowing in the wind and children and dogs. He had to move his desk to a corner of the room and face the wall.

ARE YOU READY NOW?

Okay, you feel you are ready now. You have your plot, your characters, your ream of paper, your favorite place to work, and you know the time of day or night you feel most alert. That magic moment is now approaching. Now do you sit down and start writing?

No. Not for just another minute or two. Or five, if that's what it takes. Because you still haven't decided exactly what you are going to write that day—what part of your novel.

Sit down with a cup of coffee and your looseleaf notebook, or pace around with it, glancing at it and imagining the scene you are going to jump into, the dialogue the characters are going to have, or the description of the place where the murder or love scene or act of heroism is going to happen.

Aha, you've found the segment that fits your mood this day? Good.

PSYCHING UP

Some perfectly normal people exist who can hardly wait to start their writing session each day. They, alas, are the rare lucky ones. Harold Robbins, author of *The Carpetbaggers* and *The Betsy*, likes the daily act of writing so much that he once said, "The only time I'm completely selfish is when I write a book." He explained that it was the only time he felt completely free and was in complete charge, having everything his way and not having to be concerned with "the consideration of other people."

The rest of the first- and even tenth-time novelists say, "Oh God, how did I ever get into this? Who told me I can write—I'll fix him." The good news is that if the book makes the best-seller list eventually and you are making the grand tour to promote it, you will forget the pain and pacing of "book-birth" and be spouting about the joys of writing, like Robbins.

The problem is you can't wait for inspiration. I know people who have waited a lifetime for inspiration.

This might be one of your good days, or a day that is not so good. But *you* are going to write words, paragraphs, scenes, out of your imagination *every* day, rising above your mood, if necessary. And why? Because you have made this commitment. You are going to finish a whole novel. You may write a masterpiece—or at least a book a publisher somewhere will praise and want. No, better than that: It may be the next most-talked-about best seller. Anna Lee Waldo did it with *Sacajawea*. James M. Cain did it with *The Postman Always Rings Twice*.

So there's your answer—anything can happen. You may write a big one, too.

So, what you can do to get started? Plenty. You are going to psyche yourself up before each session. If I were doing it, I would tell myself something like this:

> I'm going to get just three pages done today. It's not much. Just three pages. I can hardly wait. I love the plot. I know exactly what I'm going to say in my first line today and after that, I'll just get going. Somehow the rest of the three pages will come to me. I'll look at the notebook and I'll just keep writing. All I have to do is expand what it says on that page. I'm going to think like the female character. I'm going to think like that fool she's trying to impress. I'm going to talk. I'm going to put in that great line I thought of last night. Thank goodness I put it down. I'm clever. I can hardly wait to get started. Here we go. . . .

THE MOMENT OF TRUTH—
HOW DO YOU WRITE
THOSE THREE PAGES A DAY?

You sit down. You don't doodle. You don't dawdle.

You put your fingers on the typewriter or computer keyboard and you go. Or you pick up the pencil or pen if you are writing in longhand, like the old masters, and you write page after page on a yellow legal pad or a spiral bound notebook, or colored paper or white typewriter paper.

You do not stop until you have finished your three pages.

You do not get up to look up a word. Just put a question mark in the margin so you'll know where to find it later.

You don't go to the bathroom unless kidney stones would result.

You don't take phone calls. You can take the phone off the hook and let people get a busy signal. Or you can just let it ring so people think you're not home. Just tell all your friends not to call during this two- or three-hour period plus in which you are unavailable to the phone. Or get an answering service or an answering machine. You don't have to be as extreme as Carolyn Chute, author of *The Beans of Egypt, Maine*. She could not cope with any of the above, and so simply disconnected her phone—permanently.

You don't jump up and pace around trying to decide whether your character says a thing this way or that or reacts this way or that. You simply put both ways down and put that good old question mark in the margin so you can ponder it and decide later.

You just keep writing in a straight line shot at the plot the way you thought it through. You try to go into a trance in which your characters come to life and take over for you and tell you what they want you to write down.

If they won't speak up, do it for them, muttering aloud if you like, writing the dialogue as best you can. You may later be surprised at how good it is. And write all you want. Don't stint yourself. You can always cut out the redundancies and the maudlin notes later.

You work along a while and suddenly you're out of the mood. You want to quit for the day and make up for it tomorrow. Don't. Keep going. You can do it. It's only *three* pages.

The main thing is to keep the rhythm of work going. You will get used to it in a week or so of starting a novel. You will get keyed up and anxious when your set writing time arrives. You will become like a firehorse of old, ready for the signal to run to the fire. Or like the horse who knows the way home and doesn't have to be told what to do. He takes the wagon there—home—a step at a time, just as you are going to take your characters home to the last page.

But you won't get there unless you condition yourself.

Every day will be a triumph if you have managed somehow to keep writing and get those three pages done. Give yourself a little treat of some sort, some reward. Your personal carrot. Some writers relax with a drink afterwards. Some have a sweet. Some get on the phone and have a talk with a friend—on any subject but the book.

WRITER'S BLOCK

Harold Robbins may say he never has writer's block. But most writers do and I can't promise you that it will only happen once.

Say it happens again and this time it's worse. Much worse.

You're sailing along but suddenly you can't think of what to say. You reach in the air and it's not there. You start to get panicky. Don't. I guarantee it will pass if you don't waste time struggling with that particular bit now. Just leave some blank lines and keep going with the next person's dialogue.

You're still stuck. You absolutely cannot continue the scene where you are. You are dry. You have nothing more to say anywhere in this scene and you know it's not finished. Okay, no sweat. Look in your notebook quickly and choose a different situation or scene that is more to your liking today. Make a note on the typed or handwritten page where you are leaving off, that you are switching to Chapter so-and-so "where John is hunting for the body in the woods."

Now take a new sheet of paper, label the top *Chapter so-and-so. John hunting for body.* And now keep those fingers moving. You may get so involved when you are writing about the body search that you write five pages instead of the three required for the day. Good. But that doesn't mean you only have to write one page tomorrow. Keep the count going. It's three plus any extras. Extra pages will make you *feel great!*

You might even want to have a day-by-day calendar or a chart and on it, at the end of every day's session, write the date, which scenes, and the number of pages you did. Example: "April 3, Started argument John with father, Chapter 6. Wrote 1 page. Switched to Chapter 8, Search for body. 2 pages. Total 3 pages."

The accumulation of pages is your reward. The true sign that you are getting there. Progress, like virtue, is its own reward.

Maybe you're stuck because your character isn't motivated strongly enough. Now may be the time for you to reveal why your character's life will be in shambles if she/he fails to stop the villain. Whatever the individual motivations of your characters are, those motivations must be made very clear. If the reader doesn't know, doesn't *feel*, why the fellow wants to climb the mountain or why the girl has centered her romantic fantasies on this one particular man, the reader will lose interest in a hurry. If the *characters* don't care, your reader surely will not care either.

If your characters have no goals, that's even worse, unless you are writing a book like J. D. Salinger's very touching and effective, *The Catcher in the Rye*. Sixteen-year-old Holden Caulfield is simply reacting to life as he wanders around. Oh, he has some vague hope of growing up and watching little kids play in a field, but it is *life* that is in effect the strong character in the story, and *life* is buffeting him about.

Maybe your dissatisfaction is triggered this day by the feeling that not enough is happening in one particular phase of your plot. It's blah. This may be just the time to throw in that extra-awful thing that could happen. Remember, you thought about it on the bus and jotted it in your little note pad? Your heroine makes a sudden, terrible mistake. Novels are like life and life is like a game of Monopoly where, if you land in the wrong square, you are in trouble. But your reader keeps hoping your character will land on the squares marked with the rewards of life. Try tossing your heroine into the wrong square—give her an instant problem.

Dwelling on your mood is a luxury you can't afford. The writing mood will catch up with you once you get absorbed in your plot, action, or the dialogue—what the characters are screaming or cooing or conniving with each other about that day. Yes, when you finally are *in the mood*, you won't want to stop. The time will fly and you may find yourself with an extra page or two. Writers have told me that days that started out most poorly have sometimes ended up most productive.

The great American psychologist and writer William James tells, in his often-quoted *The Varieties of Religious Experience*, of days when he woke up and felt so bad he wondered if he could live through the day. Later, in the midst of a lecture to his students, he would suddenly realize he felt wonderful. His own words cheered him up.

YOU'RE HANGING IN THERE

Your novel is moving right along and you're feeling as well as a first-time novelist can, some days elated and some days wondering if simple torture on a medieval rack wouldn't be easier. You've written a little part of this chapter and all of that chapter. And almost all of a couple others.

It's important to keep track of what is written because sometimes you have lived it in your mind so much you think you already wrote it. This is especially important if you are the kind of writer who does best by writing the part you are in the mood for that day. Those who start at page one and go in a straight line to the final page, always picking up where they left off the day before, will only have to make a notation of the page they are on and the scene they wrote: "April 3, Finished 6th chapter on page 123. Mary Ellen gets blackmail letter. 3½ pages." Aha, you wrote an extra half page. Even that is cause for celebration.

It's a good idea to use a different color folder to hold the pages already written, to distinguish them from the folders that hold your outline.

You've now established a routine. Once you finally sit down at the typewriter, you do not doodle around or wonder what to say. The reason is that you have psyched yourself up before the session. You get the job done a day at a time, telling yourself you don't have to write a whole book, just three pages each day, and you can do it.

In your mind, you play each character's part, saying what you know that person would say. All you have to tell yourself to start the juices flowing is, "I am Evelyn and I am trying to throw myself over the bridge and some man has grabbed my legs. I am screaming at him. So what would I say?" It's the old game of "What If?" "What if he lets go? Then what do I do? Fall toward him or make the plunge?"

When you have gone through your whole list of chapters in this way and have come to the brilliant ending you have been working toward all along, it will be like the great Union Pacific Railroad. Yes, it will be like the moment when the two ends of the long, mighty line of track finally came together and the builders knew they were through. Joy.

FINAL TOUCHES

Now go fill in the gaps, all the places you left blank where you needed to look up a fact or you didn't know which way a certain scene or bit of dialogue went. But that's it. That's all you do. Right then you put the manuscript away to cool. You don't even need to look up those misspelled words yet. Just hide your manuscript in a drawer or closet and relax. You deserve it. You have typed a 270- or 300-page novel. And you did it in ninety days.

And there you have it. You have the *first draft* of what may be a great novel. You are too close to it now, too jaded, too tired of it to know.

COOL IT

Do not, repeat, DO NOT read any of it yet. So what do you do and where do you go from here? You let it rest for a few weeks, at least. Work on something else for a while. Catch up on your reading. Go on a vacation. Do whatever you need to get a fresh viewpoint, and then suddenly you'll be ready for editing.

7.

Editing Your Manuscript

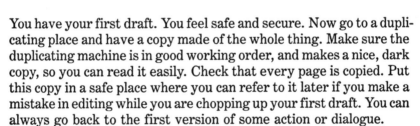

You have your first draft. You feel safe and secure. Now go to a duplicating place and have a copy made of the whole thing. Make sure the
duplicating machine is in good working order, and makes a nice, dark
copy, so you can read it easily. Check that every page is copied. Put
this copy in a safe place where you can refer to it later if you make a
mistake in editing while you are chopping up your first draft. You can
always go back to the first version of some action or dialogue.

    Now read your manuscript pretending you are a reader who
bought it in a bookstore. Keep notepaper beside you. Jot down any
ideas you have for improvement. Mark places in the chapters where
you get bored. Mark the places on the manuscript that you especially
like. If you think some action comes too soon or too late in the story,
make a note about it. Each chapter is still in its folder so put all the
notes about that chapter in the right folder.

    One approach to editing your own work is to do nothing except have it typed. Best-selling detective story writer Lawrence Sanders says he makes few changes once he has his story down. He simply follows his outline and his chapter breakdown, working in longhand, then roughly types it out. The clean, professional-looking draft that goes to the publisher is typed by other hands. "I never rewrite," says Sanders.

On the other hand, Mario Puzo thinks rewriting is everything. He says, "I don't write, I rewrite." James Clavell, whose new novel *Whirlwind* sold at auction for $5,000,000, says, "I've always known the art of writing is rewriting."

An extreme of not rewriting was the method John M. Kimbro used to write his forty-book chronicle for Popular Library, *The Saga of the Phenwick Women*. A former Broadway actor, he dictated each book into a tape recorder, acting out in appropriate voices the dialogue. He then sent the tapes to a manuscript typist, and delivered the typed manuscript to Popular Library.

Romance author Joan Wolf writes her original draft in longhand—and then edits it as she goes along, typing it herself.

But these are the methods of experienced authors. And of them, the Mario Puzo-James Clavell method is probably closest to what you'll be doing yourself when you edit your first draft.

THE MECHANICS OF EDITING

Editing need not be a formidable task. If you have used the same word several times in a paragraph or on the same page, think of another, or consult your thesaurus. Write the new word above the old and draw a line through the old so you can still read it.

If you think you told about something too late in the story, cut that section out with scissors. Keep a lined yellow legal pad beside you and write on it, "Moving bottom page 6, Chapter 12 ax murder scene to Chapter 9." When you decide where it goes in Chapter 9, add that information, " after stranger goes into barn."

Wait, you are not finished yet. Now put the original page number and chapter in the margin of the piece you are moving. In this case, it would be marked, "Ch 12, p 6." This will save endless bother when you are asking yourself, "Now where did I put that murder scene?" Your legal pad will tell you to look in the folder marked Chapter 9 and the writing in the margin will keep you from having to look at all the cut pieces of paper to find the right one.

You may have a lot of scenes moved to different folders and you may not. You may like the way you put the story together the first time.

It may need only a better word, here and there. A little more dialogue. The reason for someone's behavior made more clear.

Read your manuscript for plot, for characters, for action. See if it's so compelling you want to keep going. If you don't, stop. Look again. Is it that it needs action at that point? Is this the time for the cops to barge in with guns drawn—to the wrong house? For the kid to be discovered growing pot in the woods behind the house? Don't be afraid to talk out loud when you are editing.

Sometimes what is needed is some dialogue. Maybe the trouble is too much action and not enough talk. Let the characters speak. Or at least break into the description of what the character is doing to tell what he is thinking. Thoughts can be very juicy. People think about a lot of shocking things they don't dare do. And they analyze people around them with sharp insights that would surprise—if not horrify—the other person. They may act dumb but they know what skullduggery is going on and it's in their thoughts.

If you find parts that are good, compliment yourself in the margin. Write "Great," and run a line along the margin to show how long a passage it is. If it's artificial sounding, write "Sounds fake." If it's boring, write, "Who cares?" I think you get the picture. Be pleased that you can spot strengths and weaknesses because then you can fix whatever needs fixing.

A common fault that makes the action flow bog down is pausing to describe someone. You can fit bits of description into dialogue or action. In *How Green Was My Apple*, a detective story that is part of a series published by Crime Club, author Marc Lovell has to get across the fact that his spy-detective, named Apple, is a sympathetic comic figure because he is too tall to be a good spy. Rather than come out and say it, here's some dialogue that establishes this fact, and also characterizes Apple:

Her voice drawling lazily, she said, "If one may ask, how tall are you?"

"Six feet seven inches," Apple said. He gave a smile of apology.

"In your socks?"

"In my bare feet."

"Good heavens," the woman said.

Apple wondered with discomfort if it was proper to use

the word "bare" to this type of woman, a thought he then swiftly amended to cover women of all types. Yes, he decided. In this day and age, of course.

Having the courage to make cuts in material that, no matter how interesting or well written, does not advance your story line, is an essential part of editing. Steven Linakis, author of *In the Spring the War Ended*, was not afraid to make drastic cuts in his first draft, and discarded almost half of it. But he writes a long first draft.

No matter how you might despair at your first draft, it is essential to have it in order to proceed further. Editor and writer Hugh Rawson put it succinctly. "You must have a framework."

EDITING TO PLEASE YOURSELF

Don't get paranoid about how an editor will react to your subject matter. Write it the way you feel you must. It is impossible to guess which way the publisher would prefer something scandalous or shocking treated. If your manuscript is accepted, the editor assigned to your novel will not be shy about suggesting some different way the scenes or action in your plot could be handled or put together to make a more exciting book, or to tone something down.

Each editor has his pet likes and peeves, as you will learn if you deal with enough of them. So don't be afraid to submit your manuscript with your original thinking. First, please yourself. Remember, *you* are the boss.

However, after you have the plot the way you want it—with or without rearrangement—there are other things to do:

Cut out unnecessary adverbs and adjectives. They slow the action and don't really say anything. Take, "She was very beautiful." She's either beautiful or she's not beautiful. Authors used to say "Her beauty rivaled the sun," or other such comments now considered corny and gushing. The same with, "Her face could stop a clock." Unless it's being said by a real "country boy" type in your manuscript, what might get stopped is your manuscript from being read a moment longer.

Editor Ellis Amburn says the worst mistake beginning novelists can make is to be boring. And one of the ways they can be is by using trite expressions. The same elements used in poetry—figures of speech—can make a description of something a delight to read. Try a comparison of unlike things, never compared to each other before.

Marcel Proust, in *Remembrances of Things Past,* constructs a beautiful metaphor on the effect of time. When one of his characters, Baron Charlus, gets old, and begins to totter, he suggests our years are like a set of stilts, and the older we become, the longer the stilts— until first we totter, then fall.

So if something looks boring in your writing, cross it out and look for a fresh approach, or just leave it out.

If scenes aren't needed after all, leave them out.

If characters are not needed, leave them out.

If part of the conversation isn't needed, cut, cut, cut. Or use your pencil or ballpoint pen to draw a line through it. The problem with using a black marker is that you can no longer read what you had, in case you want to rethink it. Marker pens are too final. If there is a long speech or description you think you want to eliminate, just draw a line around it with a pencil or pen and write in the margin: "Out?"

Go slow with self-criticism. One day you may feel so blue that nothing looks good to you. You have to protect yourself from your own moods. On bad mood days don't cross anything out. Just do something constructive such as using your thesaurus to see if you can find more colorful words for some you have used and overused. Write the new ones in the margin and circle the word in question. But don't try to find a lot of ways to say "said." Leave "said" alone unless the character is screaming or whispering, in which case, say so.

If you use a lot of participles—"ing" endings—get rid of them. Use, "She laughed." "She cried." Editors don't like a lot of "She was laughing"s and "She was crying"s.

It's not the end of the world if you can't edit well. That's why publishing houses hire editors. If they are really impressed with your novel and see there a spark of genius, they will work with you as long as necessary to make suggestions so that you can make the changes. In some cases, the editor will do much of it for you—probably more than you want.

Helen Santmyer, who was mentioned before, is a case in point. Her novel, . . . *And Ladies of the Club,* originally exceeded the length of Tolstoy's *War and Peace,* and the publisher called for cuts.

Fortunately, Helen Santmyer had a friend qualified to help her with the editing that the publisher, Putnam's, was demanding—a former librarian who lived in the same nursing home. By day, the friend, Mildred Sandoe, would make editing suggestions on how to reduce the manuscript by several hundred pages, as was wanted, and Santmyer would agree. But then, in the night, Santmyer would get up and secretly put back most of the deleted material.

"So what happened?" my coauthor asked Mildred Sandoe in a telephone interview.

Miss Sandoe chuckled. "Eventually, I just bundled it all up the way it was and sent it to the publisher for them to shorten. But I don't believe they did very much." And that is why the Santmyer book still rivals Tolstoy's *War and Peace* in length, each being some 600,000 words long. Miss Santmyer's novel fills 1,344 pages in printed form—three normal books.

An even more extreme case of a writer at sea when it came to editing was Thomas Wolfe. He was absolutely helpless. Everything he wrote seemed important to him and some of it did read like deathless prose. He turned in thousands of pages on his first novel, *Look Homeward, Angel.*

The manuscript traveled to various publishers in a crate. One editor said that had he unpacked it, it would have been two feet taller than a grand piano. He stopped reading before he finished the first thousand pages because he still had not found the plot. He added that when the book came out, it did not contain any of the sections the editor had read. Somewhere else in the crate was the great best seller.

The question arises, if his editor at Scribner's, Maxwell Perkins, had not done a superb job editing that crate of manuscript, would the world have heard of Thomas Wolfe? The story went that Perkins took the time to plow through the endless pages because he owed a favor to Wolfe's first literary agent, Madeleine Boyd, wife of a noted literary critic.

PUTTING IT ALL TOGETHER

Now it's time to put the pieces of your manuscript together to see how it looks with your improvements and, even possibly, your new plot structure. You will need a table to spread out your bits of pages and full pages. When you need to put several partial sheets together, staple or tape them to a sheet of paper. Anchor the rearranged sections firmly to prevent loss and make pages easier to handle.

It doesn't matter how the pages look, just so *you* can read them. When you have cut and fastened the first chapter to have everything in the right place, put it back in the folder and spread out Chapter 2.

When the whole book is done in this fashion, read it again and see how you like it. If more surgery is necessary, do it. Again, at this point, rely on your own judgment. Editors in publishing houses will have their comments later.

If you like it the way it is, now is the time to type clean copy and look up every word of questionable spelling. (If you're writing on a computer, you may have a spelling-dictionary program that will do this for you.) If you are weak on grammar, now is the time to use the services of a consultant—maybe a schoolteacher, or college English instructor, or a professional copy editor for a newspaper or magazine. If your typing is not good, you might consider hiring a professional typist who is accustomed to book manuscripts. It can be a good investment—every editor prefers an attractive manuscript.

Of course, if you are using a computer and word processor, you will have your novel stored in the computer. You can make changes on the screen—move around parts of your story at will—and do this general editing work more easily.

If you're typing your manuscript yourself or running it off on your computer's printer, start the first page of every chapter a third to half way down the page to set it off, and be sure to add the number of the chapter—centered two or three lines above the opening line.

HOW SHOULD EACH PAGE LOOK?

The rules are very simple and logical. You want each page (except chapter openings) to be approximately alike in the number of words, so you and a publisher can estimate the total length of the manuscript easily. You don't want too many words on the page, so that when the publisher, or his sales manager, is reading it, he or she will finish each page fast, and think of the novel as a "page-turner." I recommend using pica type, double spaced, on plain white nonerasable typing paper. Have a one-inch margin all around, except for the left-hand margin, which should be at least one and one-half inches, or preferably, one and three-quarter inches. The reason you leave more space on the left is so your editor or copy editor will have room to write comments and suggest corrections if your manuscript is put under contract. Put the page number at the upper right, or upper center—*not* upper left, where it would be covered if pages are paper clipped together. *Never* put page numbers at the bottom of the page, because it's a real nuisance to try to find page numbers at the bottom of a pile of pages in a box.

If you follow these rules and use pica type, you will have approximately 246 words to the page—and can safely round off the total number of words to 250 a page.

You will find you have about fifty-three characters to the average line, counting each letter, each mark of punctuation, and each space between words as a character. Incomplete lines and dialogue are counted as though they were full lines, because they will use up full lines when your book is printed.

You will probably find you get twenty-six lines to the page, using pica type. Multiply fifty-three characters times twenty-six lines, and you get 1,378 characters to the page. Divide this number by 5.6 (the average number of characters, including spaces between words, occupied by each word), and you get 246, the number of words per page.

To adjust for *elite* type, which is smaller, just allow a *two*-inch margin on the left, and set your typewriter for a 55-character line. Allow *two and a half spaces* between each line, and again, you will have a page of about 250 words. And you will again be producing an easy-to-read manuscript—a page-turner.

One of the things most annoying to a publisher is to receive a manuscript typed with a worn-out ribbon. It is almost an affront to be expected to read something that looks faded and tired. Editors read constantly. Don't strain their eyes! Using a nice clean, dark ribbon that makes a manuscript look crisp and fresh is some of the best advice I can give you.

Your name goes only on the title page, which shows the book's title in the center, with your byline under it. At the lower left or right of the title page, print your real name, if you are using a pseudonym, your address, and telephone number.

Don't put anything on the top of each page but the page number. Anything else you might include would have to be crossed off each page by your editor, or the publisher's typesetter might set it into type.

While you are doing your second draft, you can stick to the routine that has seen you through the writing of the first draft. That is, sit down at your typewriter or table at the same time you did for three months. It has now become your habit, and a good one. Type your three pages of clean copy a day, but this time while looking up any words you need to in the dictionary.

Within a reasonable amount of time you will finish your second draft. Now you may stop, or you may want to do a third or fourth draft. But eventually you *are* finished! Congratulations!

Now, how do you present your product? Don't staple each chapter together. Staples rust. Don't paperclip them together. Paperclips rust. *Don't put it in a binder of any kind,* or your editor will never take it home to read because it's too heavy to take all at once.

Don't do anything but put the whole manuscript in a stationery box. That is the *only* professional way to present a manuscript. If you don't have a box from which a ream of paper was taken, you can buy such boxes at stationery stores.

Your novel is born and it's time to let go and send it on its way to a literary agent or publisher.

WHAT IF IT DOESN'T SELL?

What if you do everything you can—give it your best shot and edit and clean copy the manuscript—and nobody wants it? You thought it was good. You couldn't believe how good it was. Your agent liked it, but twenty-two publishers said "no" and the agent doesn't think he ought to submit it any more. The publishers say nobody is reading that particular type of story these days. Or they just don't like it and they don't say why. They may say, "It just isn't quite what we are looking for," or, "It doesn't suit our present needs."

So what do you do? You have several possibilities. The first is to carry on, curse a little, and vow to show them! Then, throw the manuscript in a drawer where you can find it in a few years and for the present, forget it. Start plotting your next novel. Write the next one with the same three-page-a-day routine that got you through the first.

Now you're proving you're made of the right stuff and your chances of making it the next time have increased. Comfort yourself that you are in good company. Irving Stone was turned down by no less than seventeen publishers on his first novel. Several said "Who cares about the life of an artist?" He put the novel away and wrote a second one which was published. Hardly anyone can remember what the first published one was. But the first one he wrote—*Lust for Life*—the one no one would publish, became a big best seller in 1934, when Doubleday finally took a chance.

Today, the book—and Irving Stone—hold a small niche in publishing history for having improved and popularized the genre called *fictionalized biography.* Before Stone wrote his novel based on the life of Vincent van Gogh, that genre had not been used for years.

REWRITING AND
ADDITIONAL WORK

Another possibility is that rejection will cause you to dig in, and try to improve your novel further. When is such additional work justified by the hope of an eventual sale? I would say only when you have some objective reason to think you are on the right track, but not quite there—such as encouragement from an agent, several near-miss rejections, or sincere praise of your work by some obviously qualified person, such as an established professional editor, writer, or critic. Or maybe you are simply very stubborn and determined.

You might, in such circumstances, consider trying to find a "book doctor," a professional freelance editor who works with publishers and agents. One such book doctor in New York is Darrell Husted. He was formerly an editor with Prentice-Hall, Scribner's, and other publishers. He has also had several paperback original and hard cover novels of his own published—his first novel was *A Country Girl*, published by Popular Library. Husted only accepts freelance editorial jobs directly from authors when he believes, on the basis of an agent's or publisher's comments, that the novel has a chance for success after additional work. His services, like those of others who do this type of work, are not cheap. He and other freelance editors are not ghostwriters—they simply provide you with extensive objective criticism, and try to point you in the direction of writing that will be acceptable to a publisher.

Here are some of the comments he made to me about editing your own work:

> What should shape a book is what appeals to an editor who has the power to get it published. Beautiful writing is useless unless you have hooked the reader, and early on. You have to seduce the reader, and neophytes forget the reader doesn't know where you are aiming.
>
> Get all those loose ends tied up. Readers won't pay $16.95 for a slice of life. They want a story. Don't go off on tangents. Take out unnecessary characters, remove events that have no consequences. Characters should not show up, then disappear. If they are supposed to disappear, they should not show up again without explanation. Authors should offer *specifics*—any office clerk can make general pronouncements.

Good books are cohesive. Their authors express their ideas in a well-formed universe. Form is shape: *Form*ula. Fiction explains life better than any medium including history. It makes events comprehensive and interesting, and brings form to events for the reader.

Fiction is *entertainment* and if it isn't, it's nothing. If a novel is entertaining, the sky's the limit for adding other elements—but entertainment is first. Form in the novel is elastic—works by Dostoevsky, Proust, Jacqueline Susann, Sidney Sheldon all have been successful.

Writers should turn on the reader on page one, and put their best writing near the beginning of the manuscript, or they'll never hook book editors, who will simply stop reading. Your characters should be interesting—if they are, you are way ahead of the game—plots can be fixed, but there is not much an editor can do about uninteresting characters.

One device Husted uses to help a writer think in more depth about a character is to ask the author the character's birth date. He then looks up the character's horoscope in *It's All in the Stars, A Sun Sign Horoscope for Every Birthday*, by Zolar, the astrologer. He then poses a question to the author: "Here are your character's qualities according to Zolar's horoscope for that birthday. Is Zolar a good astrologer? Are these the qualities of your character?"

This exercise forces the author to consider how much he knows about the character, and reflecting on the question, to enlarge his knowledge of the people in his novel, or at least bring the knowledge to full consciousness.

An anecdote Husted tells authors in further reinforcing this point is, he says, possibly apocryphal, and he does not remember where he read it. Ibsen was reportedly asked by an admirer of his plays, "Why does Nora in *A Doll's House* have dark hair, when she is Scandinavian, and most Scandinavians are blond?"

Ibsen replied, "Well, Nora's father went to Provençe when he was a young man, and there met Nora's mother, a beautiful French woman with dark hair. They married, and he took her back to Scandinavia, where Nora was born. Nora inherited her mother's dark hair."

"But Mr. Ibsen," the admirer protested, "none of that is in the play!"

Ibsen said, "What difference does that make? A fact is a fact."

Darrell Husted believes it is not too much out of line even to think of a character's grandparents and get to know them as well as their offspring.

So maybe persistence and rewriting can be the answer for you.

My favorite story of why you should hang on is the real-life saga of Inga Dean which has the happy ending of Dean seeing her first book published, *Memory and Desire.*

Well, it wasn't exactly her first book and therein lies the story. Dean, who lived in Washington, D.C., finished her first novel in 1970 and it bounced around to possibly twenty publishers before she stopped submitting it. The fact that she was the daughter of famed journalist William Shirer was of no help, as she would not trade on his name.

Determined to get a novel published, Dean started another one and had gotten to page 700 before she realized it was "out of control."

As she told my coauthor, "There was too much of everything— plot, time span, characters." The writing was interrupted by her husband's retirement and their move to Lenox, Massachusetts. Then, Dean said, "I took the manuscript out of the closet and tried to save it but some months later realized what I now had was a thousand pages of unusable drivel."

This time Dean did not bother to submit her new manuscript. She carved it up and saved some of the action and all of her main character, a character she had been living with in her mind for eight years.

Now she started again. A new plot with only bits of the old. She also changed the occupation of her heroine from "a failed artist to a not-too-good restaurant critic of a third-rate magazine, who used to be a not-too-good painter." Persistence paid off and this time a publisher—Viking—said yes, and asked only that the length be cut from 600 manuscript pages to 350. At this point, she had written three drafts of the manuscript over eight years but she plowed through it again.

"When *Memory and Desire* finally came out in the summer of 1985, I had to laugh at their description of me as 'a talented *new* novelist,' " Inga Dean told Fran. "I had been at it fifteen years, had written not one but three novels and God knows how many manuscript pages." Then she added, "Tell your readers I'd do it again."

TURNING UNUSED RESEARCH INTO
A NONFICTION BOOK

What if you have put a lot of research and energy into your first novel, and it doesn't sell right away? Maybe you can use the same research as the basis of a nonfiction book—and gain writing experience and make some money in the process. Then you can write an improved version of your novel later.

Does this idea startle you? Consider the experiences of Clyde Burleson, who started writing as a forty-year-old Houston, Texas ad agency president. In 1975, newspapers began to publish leaks and fragments of the amazing true story of how the CIA and Howard Hughes secretly built a giant, new kind of ship, sailed it into the Pacific, and had recovered from three miles deep a whole sunken Soviet submarine.

Since Burleson was fascinated by technology, he followed the stories and did some research. He wrote a twenty-one-page outline and sample chapter of a novel to be based on what he learned, entitled *Project Evangeline*. His agent, James Seligmann, showed it to me in my then-new job as a senior editor at Prentice-Hall. I was intrigued by Clyde Burleson's research, but was not prepared to go out on a limb with a contract for an unfinished first novel.

But most *nonfiction books* are sold to publishers from an outline presentation and a statement of the author's qualifications, and only written after the contract is signed. So I asked Burleson to write a presentation for a nonfiction book based on his research. He agreed, and Prentice-Hall signed the book. After a great deal more research including three months of travel and interviews, he wrote a lively nonfiction work, *The Jennifer Project*, filled with previously unpublished information about this unique secret undertaking.

With nonfiction, the key to sales is *quality of information* on an interesting subject. Information rules the field. Good writing helps sell the book, but is not essential as long as the writing is passable. So publishers are willing to speculate on a good book presentation, before the book is written, if the author seems qualified. With fiction, the *quality of writing* is paramount, which is why editors and publishers want to see a whole first novel.

The Jennifer Project sold out its first printing of 20,000 copies, and ultimately around 23,000 copies were sold. It was also published in Spanish, Portuguese, Danish, and Japanese editions. It earned a favorable full-page review in *The New York Times Book Review* and more praise elsewhere. Burleson went on a three-week, eight-city promotion tour, starting in New York with an appearance on the "Today" show.

Maybe you think we're getting a long way from the subject of writing a novel. But we aren't. Clyde Burleson says that when he finished writing his nonfiction book, he returned to his novel, *Project Evangeline*. "The facts were so much more interesting than my original speculations based on a small amount of information that the story got much better."

His agent continued to offer *Project Evangeline* to publishers, and it was sold to Carlyle Books and published as a mass-market paperback in 1979. Seligmann also placed it with Mondadori in Italy, and Lademann in Denmark, where it became a major book club selection circulated throughout Scandinavia. The Carlyle edition earned royalties above the advance, and the foreign editions earned additional money. And Burleson got to see his book "everywhere—in airports, bookstores, drugstores," one of the greatest pleasures of the author of a mass-market paperback.

Burleson now has had two novels and four nonfiction books published, and has more in progress. In 1985, he and his partner sold their ad agency, and he is free, at fifty-one, to work full time as a writer. Asked about his long-range plans, he said, "I'm going to write a major best seller if I have to keep trying until I'm sixty."

8.

Selling, and Contracts, and Money, Oh My!

In *The Wizard of Oz*, Dorothy chants her special refrain based on her fear of coping with unknown dangers, "Lions and tigers and bears, oh my! Lions and tigers and bears. . . ."

The publishing world is indeed a kind of Land of Oz, where anything can happen—like getting a six-figure advance on your first novel. Or $3,000. Or $15,000. Or $30,000. Or being turned away at the door and coming away empty-handed. So much depends on locating the right wizard. And who are the wizards? The agents, of course.

Don't feel too hurt if an agent says he/she is not interested in handling your first novel. Agents have quirks and preferences. They love this kind of book, hate that kind of book. Some agents are sympathetic and will treat budding authors with kindness, even giving a little advice when they refuse to handle someone's work. Others are blunt and almost seem cruel to the sensitive newcomer.

Often the source of their crossness or abruptness is that they are already overloaded with unsold fiction. So if an agent says he or she is overloaded, you can make a note to try again in six months or a year, when the situation may be different.

Keep in mind that different agents have different sales styles. One is to play hard to get—to act as though dealing with anyone so lowly as a potential client is to extend a rare privilege. Such a role requires the agent to act skeptical of your claims. If the agent is playing this role, he acts as though he has such pricey merchandise from other novelists that he doesn't have to deal with anyone but the most elect writers—and hints that even they have to crawl a little to enter his sanctum.

Naturally, if you—a new author—brush against someone of this type, you will get a little seared. Just remember that even in the most tough-guy organizations, there have to be a few nice guys to balance the act, so things can go better *if* you reach the right person.

Publishers respect agents because agents *do* have power—the power to enrich them by giving them major new books. Some superbest sellers are worth more than whole publishing companies. And agents can also impoverish a shaky publisher by selling to it, for a lot of money, a clinker that seems like a good bet, but which in fact will absorb the publisher's limited capital in a futile effort to make the book go.

The thing for you, an author, to remember, whether you are dealing with agents, editors, publishers, or anyone else whose business is supported by books, is that without authors, they would be nowhere. Even if *they* don't keep this central fact in mind, *you* should. Your importance as a budding member of the class that supports the book publishing industry, and entertains and educates countless millions of readers, should be a source of pride to you.

My coauthor, Frances Spatz Leighton, author of more than thirty books, says, "Your best defense to protect yourself in dealing with agents and editors is to be like a toasted marshmallow, crisp and tough on the outside, while maintaining your warmth and softness on the inside—the softness that gave you the sensitivity to understand your material."

A brutally realistic note on the subject of why a writer needs an agent was struck by the late John Cushman. He himself had been on both sides of the negotiating table—first as an editor at several publishing houses and then as a literary agent. As quoted by *Literary Agents of North America, 1984-85,* Cushman frankly admitted, "As an editor, I was hired to help authors make their books better, and at the same time to take financial advantage of them."

While Cushman's views may have seemed a little harsh, they didn't prevent editors and publishers from liking him even while he was protecting his clients from them. For one, James O'Shea Wade, an editor and former publisher, used to meet Cushman every Friday afternoon, without fail, at the Harvard Club for drinks and exchanges of information on the latest wizardry in the publishing world.

When I called Jim Wade to reminisce about John Cushman, he told me a story about another editor-turned-agent with whom he had dealt, Knox Burger. Burger loyally represented New York Police Lieutenant William J. Caunitz for years through many rejections, hanging on and offering him editorial guidance as Caunitz continued working on his novel of inside stories about police life. Burger sold it to Wade, originally for a small down payment, with more to come when it was finished. When the publishing company with which Wade was associated dissolved, Wade remained interested, and brought it with him when he joined Crown Publishers. Wade's judgment was vindicated. After he did additional editorial work with Caunitz, Crown published the novel and it sold over 40,000 copies in hard cover. It also got a $300,000 reprint deal from Bantam for paperback rights. It has sold over 1,000,000 copies. The title: *One Police Plaza*. And another writing star was born.

So you see, often when you look into the history of a successful first novel, a literary agent is very much in evidence.

WHAT AN AGENT CAN DO FOR YOU

I agree with John Katzenbach, author of the very successful thriller, *In the Heat of Summer*, who said that if you try to bypass agents and sell the book yourself, you are "increasing the difficulty."

That is true. An agent runs interference for the author. An agent knows the likes and dislikes of various publishers and does not waste time, as new novelists frequently do, sending a manuscript to a publisher who has a blind spot for that kind of book. An agent knows editors at the publishing houses, runs into them socially, has lunch with them, and can make a more casual approach sometimes to see if interest can be aroused. And the editor or publisher knows that even the most lowly, beginning agent is performing a valuable service— screening out manuscripts and projects not worth considering, a service the publisher would have to pay dearly for if he did it himself.

And then comes the money game. A new writer may say, "I don't want to look like a money grubber. I just want to get this book published." Well, be happy that agents *are* money oriented. It is their desire, their duty, and to their best interest to get the best deal, the biggest advance that can be worked out with that publisher. Agents know when to hold "auctions," which means send the manuscript to a half-dozen or more publishers and see who makes the best offer by a given date the agent sets.

Also, *before* the book is published, the agent has been busy trying to sell excerpts of the book to magazines who might be interested in that type of story. If the sale is made, the agent must arrange to synchronize the story's publication date in the magazine with the publication date of the book.

After the book is published, the work of the agent continues in that he/she tries to monitor and encourage paperback deals and to make foreign sales. And New York agents usually have connections with Hollywood agents for making a movie or TV sale—or in many instances handle these offers themselves.

It's not easy to get a novel before the TV or movie cameras. In an article in *The New York Times*, "Hollywood and the Novelist—It's a Fickle Romance at Best," Edwin McDowell quoted Judy Hotchkiss, story editor for East Coast production at MGM/United Artists: "The figure we use is that one in fifty fiction books gets optioned for the movies, but only one in two hundred actually gets made into a movie."

This seems a reasonable figure, because if you divide the five thousand books of fiction published each year by two hundred, the result is twenty-five, a credible number, particularly if you count in the TV movies.

At a meeting of the Independent Literary Agents Association in 1985, a panel of producers, scouts for movie companies, story editors, and agents discussed at length the mounting delays and woes connected with getting a novel made into a theatrical motion picture; they agreed that fewer and fewer books are made into general-release movies. The wisdom expresssed by the panel at the end of the meeting was, "If you want to see it in your lifetime, go TV."

AN ADVANCE SUCCESS STORY

As I write this, the current prize for getting the highest advance for hard cover rights to a first novel by a writer with no previously published book was claimed by literary agent Jean Naggar. The inspiring inside story is that Karleen Koen was a Texas housewife who had to *do something* to add stimulation to her life when she quit her job in favor of motherhood. She had studied English literature and developed a passion for the 18th Century, reading many novels set in that period.

Koen's jobs had been a far cry from novel writing or the 18th Century—she had been a reporter for the *Houston Business Journal* and then editor of *Houston Home and Garden*.

For several years, between diapers and dishwashing, Koen toyed with her plot and her characters to see what it would be like for a young girl of fifteen to grow up in England at the time of authors Swift and Defoe and Pope. For research, she read or checked through several hundred books, and only toward the end of her labors, did she make a quick trip to England to take a look at her locales.

The first literary agents Koen approached were not interested in handling the 1,300-page historical novel. Hurt but not discouraged, Koen tried to place the book with a publisher herself and was again turned down. That hurt a little more—by then she had been working on it for four years.

Then she sent a sample of her manuscript to agent Jean Naggar, whom she had read about in *Writer's Digest*. Naggar not only liked it but she knew who might be interested, Kate Medina, who had left Doubleday and was vacationing at home—Westhampton, Long Island—before beginning her new chores as vice president and senior editor at Random House. Agent Naggar got the manuscript to Medina. The result was an advance of $350,000.

Would over a quarter of a million dollars have been paid if Koen had continued acting as her own agent? I find it impossible to believe.

AN ADVANCE IS ONLY
THE BEGINNING

Don't worry if your first book does not command a big advance. If the book is a success, you'll make it up on your next book. Anyway, the advance is only the beginning of possible earnings. If the book is published in hard cover first, there may be a paperback rights sale, movie sale, book club sales, condensation, magazine excerpts, and income from foreign rights. And the number of copies sold makes a difference. As soon as the book has earned back the advance through a royalty on each copy sold, you start to get checks for your royalties on additional sales.

John Katzenbach, mentioned earlier, received a modest advance for his first effort. But he was grateful to Atheneum for publishing it at all, after the turndowns he received. Then the paperback rights were sold for $250,000—a bonanza to be split between author and publisher. On top of that, he received a movie offer.

I will not give you a false picture and say more than a few novels receive an advance big enough to change the author's lifestyle. At this point in literary history, many advances for a first novel on a subject of general interest are in the $5,000-$10,000 range. Historical first novels, which are much longer books, usually receive more, while first romances and other genre novels often get less—$2,500, $3,000, but sometimes $7,000 if you are lucky.

However, successful romance writers, in the long run, can make a lot of money, as witness British author Barbara Cartland, whose books are read here as well as in England, and who can afford to live in a castle.

HANDLING YOUR OWN WORK

Writers of romances don't have to have agents because editors of these books are willing to read unagented works, and the contracts offered to first romance novelists are apt to be pretty standard, agented or not.

Publishers often help budding romance writers learn the formula for a romance book, as was the case with Mary Kilchenstein of Rockville, Maryland, who sent her first effort—*Bed of Roses*, under the byline Jean Faure—to Berkley's romance imprint, Second Chance at Love. It was returned with the comment that the characters were too true to real life and many suggestions on how this could be remedied.

Kilchenstein found it too painful to rewrite her book so she threw the manuscript in a drawer and started a new one, paying close attention to the rules of the road in romance writing. She sent that in. Now came the news that her hero was just not quite "heartwarming" enough. As Kilchenstein told reporter Sheila Moldover, of *The Journal*, a Virginia newspaper, "I added a chapter where they went to the zoo and he bought her cotton candy. Then they went home, and he did the dishes. That made him heartwarming."

Even if your book is not a romance, you may elect to act as your own agent. I know several authors who have had whole careers without an agent, or who only used an agent occasionally. Others get started without an agent, and turn to an agent later. Nancy Dibble, who writes science fiction novels under the name "Ansen Dibell," placed her own early novels, a series entitled *The Rule of One*, with DAW Books, and even managed to sell foreign rights to two additional novels in the series herself. It was only later, when her literary affairs became more complex, that she turned to James Allen at the Virginia Kidd Agency, which has a special interest in science fiction. And in Part II of this book, you'll see that several of the authors profiled started without agents, including one whose first novel was a major best seller.

Sometimes there is a more dramatic reason behind the lack of an agent. You may *have to* do without an agent because of your temperament. I recall that in the 1970s, I had a client whose work I liked and whom I liked as a person. But some friction developed between us and he asked me to help him get another agent.

I called Julian Bach, a successful agent I respect. After I praised the author's talent, Julian asked, "Does he call you several times a week?"

"Daily," I replied.

"Does he call you in the evening when you're having dinner?"

"I'm afraid so."

"Does he call on weekends?"

"Yes."

"How does he act when you're not available?"

"He yells at whoever offers to take a message."

"Well, I guess I won't offer to represent him, though he does sound talented. I have enough difficult clients already."

Though one of the advantages of using an agent is his knowledge of publisher's preferences, you can find some of this information yourself with a little detective work. Look at the "Acknowledgments" page of novels in the general category of yours. Usually these pages are at the beginning, or sometimes at the end, of the novel. Often the author will offer a special "thank you" to his or her editor. Articles in writer's magazines such as *The Writer* or *Writer's Digest* also identify editors' interests. Since editors move around, a good way to learn where they are now is to look in the "Names and Numbers" section of the current edition of *Literary Market Place*, which lists names of people in publishing alphabetically, and tells where to reach them.

Handling your own work, you'll probably spend a lot of time poring over *LMP* and directories such as *Fiction Writer's Market*, listed in the back of this book. Their listings tell what publishers say they are looking for.

A simple kind of market research you can also do is to go to a public library and look up the names of publishers of novels in some way similar to yours. Check the year of the copyright. If you find that particular publishers have done *several* of your kind of book in the last three years, then these publishers are obvious targets for you.

For example, though many publishers publish some mysteries, or an occasional one, Doubleday, St. Martin's Press, Walker, Mysterious Press, Scribner's, and Dodd, Mead consistently turn out mysteries, a few by new writers.

And by looking on the title pages of the books, you may note an editor's name, such as "A Joan Kahn Book." Joan Kahn has had mysteries she edits published by Harper & Row, E.P. Dutton, and now St. Martin's Press. She is a specialist editor of mysteries and has introduced many mystery writers. She has her own "imprint."

Librarians who do buying and book store buyers often know what kinds of books a publisher has been succeeding with lately, so enlist their aid.

Don't forget the book reviews in your local paper, and in *The New York Times Book Review, The New York Review of Books, Los Angeles Times, Chicago Tribune,* and *Washington Post,* among others. And study the ads, because the ads show which books the publishers particularly value, and how they think of them. From the reviews and ads, you can get a reading on which publishers like which kinds of novels. You might even want to subscribe to *Publishers Weekly,* the trade journal of the book publishing industry, or read it in your library to learn inside information about what new publishing companies are being formed. It will also tell you which editors have just moved to new jobs.

If you get discouraged marketing your own work, consider what Robert Oliphant did. Reading in *Publishers Weekly* that Clyde Taylor had just formed a new agency, he wrote a letter suggesting that since Taylor was a new agent and he was a new author, maybe they should work together. Taylor not only placed his novel with a publisher, but interested Reader's Digest Condensed Books in using it as one of their selections. He then arranged for film agent Warren Bayless to place the movie rights. The novel and film were *A Piano For Mrs. Cimino,* with Bette Davis starring in the TV film. Oliphant later wrote a *Publishers Weekly* article about his first novel experiences, in which he called Clyde Taylor "Mr. Laconic" and Warren Bayless "Mr. Warm," a good description of two agents' selling styles.

SHOULD YOU TRY
TO FIND AN AGENT?

In considering this question, ask yourself whether or not you like to have other people handle important financial and sales matters for you. Or do you prefer to handle such matters yourself? Do you take the advice of an investment adviser, or make your own financial decisions? Would you use a real estate agent to sell a piece of property, or try to make the sale yourself? Do you prefer to balance your own checkbook, keeping it up to date? Do you get someone else to do it, or do you postpone doing it at all? In sports, can you take the advice of a coach?

In other words, can you *delegate* important responsibilities to others, or are you so nervous and concerned that things be done exactly as you wish that you prefer to handle important matters yourself?

If you decide you need and want an agent to help you with your writing career, you have to face the fact that finding an agent is sometimes just as hard as finding a publisher. Even though *Literary Agents of North America, 1984-1985 Marketplace* lists over 650 U.S. and Canadian literary agencies, some of these are small operations, some specialized, and some only accept clients by referral. Some just don't accept new clients.

Literary Market Place lists over 200 agents. Another listing can be found in *Writer's Market*, published by F&W Publications, Cincinnati. The Manhattan Consumer Yellow Pages has a listing under the heading, "Literary Agents," of about 100 names, addresses, and phone numbers of agents. About half of these are the principal literary agents of the U.S. Besides these fifty based in New York, a few more major agents are based in Los Angeles, Boston, and Washington. The reason most major book agents are in New York is that that city is the headquarters of most of the trade and mass-market book publishers.

Other sources of lists of literary agents are The Authors Guild, 234 West 44th Street, New York 10036; Society of Authors' Representatives, Inc. (called SAR), P.O. Box 650, Old Chelsea Station, New York 10113 (an association of agents formed in 1928); and Independent Literary Agents Association (called ILAA), c/o Sanford Greenburger Associates, 55 Fifth Avenue, New York 10003. Some book publishers will also supply a list of agents.

Any agent you contact will have his/her own sales methods, often idiosyncratic to the point of eccentricity. Can you face the fact that you will have to rely on an agent to tell you whether or not your work is being submitted, and to which publishers? Can you put up with your agent's personal approach, which may involve his seeming to withhold your work from what you regard as major publishers? Can you let your agent decide whether your work is more suitable for paperback or hard cover? Can you take it when your agent holds out for a higher advance royalty guarantee, possibly killing an already good deal? Can you bear to wait while your agent haggles with the publisher over small details of the contract? And can you trust an agent to collect your money, deduct a 10, 15, or 20 percent commission—agents vary in the commissions they charge—and promptly send you the rest?

Whether you are looking for an agent or publisher, you have two appropriate ways to approach them—through referrals or through queries.

REFERRALS

With either agents or publishers, good sources of referrals are published authors, lawyers, contacts you make at writers conferences or writers groups, professors of English or creative writing, business people who deal with agents and book publishers, bookstore owners, reviewers, magazine and newspaper editors. Take advantage of whatever opportunity your alertness presents to you.

But don't be surprised if some people are reluctant to refer you to their agents or publisher friends! Having, or knowing, an important agent or publisher is regarded by many as being part of an "inner circle," and traditionally, outsiders are hazed a good deal when they try to break into any established group. It's up to you to think of a way to get around this problem.

QUERIES

Lacking a referral, the next best route, whether you are approaching an agent or a publisher, is to write a query letter. An ideal query is a one-page, single-spaced, typed business letter with short paragraphs that describe your novel, your qualifications, and perhaps, briefly, why you think it will succeed. With this you may, if you wish, include a brief, two- or three-page outline or synopsis of your novel, plus two or three chapters.

The outline can be single- or double-spaced, but as described earlier, the sample chapters *must* be double-spaced. Do date your query letter. *Don't date your outline and sample chapters*—such dates quickly grow stale. Send out the whole thing, *packed flat*. No binder is necessary, but do paperclip the pages of the outline together, so that it won't get mixed up with your manuscript. Enclose a self-addressed stamped envelope (called an SASE) big enough for return of your materials. Mail in a *sturdy* padded envelope, First Class, to one or more agents. Or to one or more publishers. Send the original of your letter, and clear photocopies of your outline and chapters. It is underwhelming to an agent to receive a photocopied letter—I just throw them away.

Multiple submissions of unsolicited queries are perfectly okay, when they are introduced by individually typed letters. If an agent becomes interested, he/she may ask you to withdraw other submissions. One way to do this is to call all the others, and ask them to reply within two or three days, as someone is very interested.

If a publisher asks you to withdraw other copies of a multiple submission, just laugh unless he makes a firm offer.

But if you actually sign up with an agent or publisher, it would be courteous to write immediately to the others to whom you have submitted and request return of your materials—no reason is necessary.

In writing a query letter, remember you are engaged in business correspondence, so be brief. The person receiving it is pressed for time. When you remember that the person you write may get hundreds of queries—most of them unprofessional or illiterate and *very* few even truly worth a reply—you can see why *your* letter must be outstanding.

Make sure your query is typed perfectly, contains no errors of grammar or spelling, and is filled with facts. The reason a written query is better than a telephone call is that it can be passed around to several people. Remember, you are dealing with *book* people—that is, people who prefer the *written* word as the best means of communication. Also, you are a writer, not a professional speaker, so probably you will be able to put your best efforts more easily into a good letter than an oral pitch.

Carol Cartaino, an experienced book editor, told me an anecdote that powerfully illustrates the point that publishing people prefer reading rather than listening. At an editorial meeting, an editor read aloud a detailed report on a book project, and some excerpts from the book itself. Carol found herself, and a couple of others around the table, leaning forward and saying, "Let me see it," even though they had just heard it.

If you decide to try telephone queries, try to be ready to talk. Have notes in front of you. State your name, reason for calling, and the nature of your novel quickly and succinctly. Is your novel a historical romance? Of what period? Does it have a man or woman protagonist? Or is it a family saga? Thriller, mystery, juvenile, literary, or what? Tell these facts right away. Have the title in your notes and on the tip of your tongue—don't be worried about someone stealing your title.

Don't apologize. Don't say, "I know you get a lot of queries, but. . . ." Yours is a business call—one business person calling another with a business proposition that can be worth a lot of money. If the person you reach suggests you send a written query, agree, hang up, and send it immediately, referring to your telephone call and its date to begin the letter. If the agent or publisher says he/she isn't accepting submissions, hang up and try someone else.

Above all, don't be long-winded even if you detect some interest. You are using the valuable business time of the person who takes your call, and people who receive sales calls don't suffer fools gladly. It might help to practice the call first with a friend experienced in sales, or even alone.

Here is an effective query letter from an author in search of an agent:

(On author's letterhead with address and phone number)

May 10, 1983

Collier Associates
875 Avenue of the Americas
New York, New York 10001

Gentlemen:

I am an ex-Marine, a Viet Nam veteran, and an attorney. During the early 1970's I defended Marine drill instructors accused of boot camp brutality. Today, ten years later, the papers still carry stories of DIs charged with training abuses. The questions are always with us:

What kinds of hardship may be justifiably inflicted when molding men to fight and survive in modern guerilla warfare?

Is there a point at which observance of individual rights in training shortchanges our troops in later combat?

Are drill instructors really such monsters?

I have written a novel about one such incident, a court martial of a drill instructor for murder. Against the background of a society that to an ever increasing extent preferred to "make love, not war," I have told the story about people charged with making war and the uncertainty and self doubt that was the legacy of the Viet Nam experience.

Entitled PAYBACKS, my story provides insights into the rigors of Marine boot camp, the tension of night combat, and the natural drama of a trial for a man's life. I have enclosed an outline-synopsis, a summary of the novel, a brief biography, and copies of the first three chapters which introduce the reader to the main characters: Sargeant Markey, the drill instructor charged with murder; Michael Taggart, the defense counsel disillusioned by his own experience in Viet Nam; and Veronica Rasmussen, the cynical reporter so opposed to the American role in Viet Nam. I hope these chapters will make you want to read my entire manuscript.

Sincerely,

Christopher Q. Britton

CQB:njk

Enclosures

When I got this letter from Christopher Britton, together with "outline-synopsis, a summary of the novel, a brief biography, and copies of the first three chapters which introduce the reader to the main characters," I read it immediately. It was clearly and professionally typed. Its first paragraph engaged my interest, establishing the author's qualifications, then flowed into three intriguing questions. Britton immediately followed up, telling in one paragraph a great deal about his novel. He wound up with the title, and a request for a reply.

After finishing the letter, I immediately began to read the enclosures with high hopes. I was not disappointed, and quickly called the author, requesting that he send the whole manuscript, together with more detail about his background. I became his agent. After he did some additional work on the novel, it only took a small number of submissions before I placed it with Donald I. Fine, Inc. *Paybacks* was published in hard cover in May, 1985—about two years after Britton's letter to me—and the hard cover publisher has, at this writing, negotiated a very substantial five-figure paperback deal with Warner Books.

Novelist Christopher Britton's letter also answers a question I frequently hear: "How much sample material should I show?" The answer is, "Enough to introduce the main characters and to get the main story line of the novel underway."

YOUR AGREEMENT WITH AN AGENT

If an agent offers to represent you, he/she will want to be your exclusive agent, usually for some minimum period of time. It is to your advantage to keep this minimum period as short as possible, such as six months, or at most a year, in case you and the agent prove incompatible, or the agent fails to sell and loses interest. Your agent will also want to handle the dramatic and foreign rights to your novel, and its first serial rights. This is reasonable, as the agent invests time and his own expenses (to an agreed extent) in marketing your work.

Some agents use a written agreement; others rely on oral agreements with you. All will want to insert an "Agency Clause" into your contract with a publisher. Here is a typical agency clause:

All sums of money due under this agreement shall be paid to the Author's agent, _____ , 000 Madison Avenue, New York 00000, and receipt of the said _____ shall be a good and valid discharge of such indebtedness, and the said _____ is hereby irrevocably empowered by the Author to act in all matters arising from this agreement. The Author does hereby irrevocably assign and transfer to _____ , and _____ shall retain, the sum equal to ten percent (10%) as an agency coupled with an interest, out of all monies due and payable to and for the account of the Author under this agreement.

My own policy is to have oral agreements with authors I know well and have dealt with over a period of years. With new clients who are strangers before they approach me or I approach them, I use a written agreement. The one I use spells out seven things:

1. I become your exclusive agent for not only your books, but the dramatic rights to your work.

2. The only works of yours I can collect commissions from are those put under contract while I represent you (whether I made the sale, or you made it alone makes no difference—it's just *when* the deal was made that matters)—not things you sold before you engaged me, or after we have parted company.

3. If I sell a book of yours to a publisher, I get to be the agent of it, forever, for dramatic rights and foreign sales. To make dramatic right sales and foreign sales, I can use coagents.

4. Money earned by your work is paid to me, not you. I then deduct my commission, and pay you your share, promptly (which means *after* the check has cleared in my authors' account).

5. If you ask me to make copies of your work, or I order up to twenty books of yours from your publisher, or send you something by Express Mail, or otherwise engage in some unusual expense at your request, you must pay the cost.

6. You can fire me, or I can resign, anytime. Otherwise, the agreement runs on indefinitely. But even if you fire me or I resign, I still get commissions from earnings of agreements made while I was your agent, and still get to handle dramatic and foreign rights to books published under those agreements.

7. I'm not responsible if your work is lost, stolen, or damaged.

Most agents charge either 10 or 15 percent as their commission for U.S. contracts, and 20 percent for foreign contracts. When your agent uses a dramatic rights coagent, your agent and the dramatic rights coagent usually split the 10 or 15 percent commission, so this costs you nothing extra.

How can you tell if your agent is a good one, and honest? I don't think you can tell absolutely—after all, even the most famous and respected people and corporations are sometimes convicted of crimes. But you can ask such questions as how long the agency has been in business, what some of its recent sales have been, who some of the writers it represents are, how money is handled, what publishers it deals with, what organizations it belongs to, and, of course, what the commission is. Don't be put off if you learn the agent is recently established—just ask what the agent did before. He or she may have been an important editor or executive from a good publisher, highly experienced in handling book deals.

If the agent uses a written agreement, you might want to find a lawyer to look at it. Ask the lawyer in advance how much he will charge for this service. Or you might want to show it to an author who uses an agent. Above all, don't hesitate to ask the agent to explain any part of the agreement you don't understand before signing it.

LAWYERS

If you don't use an agent, probably you should get an attorney's advice on a contract offered to you by a book publisher. While, in my opinion, it would be best for you to make the effort to seek out an attorney already experienced in book publishing contracts, finding such an attorney might be hard if you live in a remote place. I called Harriet Pilpel, a New York attorney who is an excellent guide to book publishing agreements. She suggested that the Authors League of America might be helpful. But when Irwin Karp, their counsel, referred me to the late Peter Heggie, their executive director, Heggie told me the League was not prepared to recommend attorneys to nonmembers. He did say, however, that your local attorney can be helpful. And if your local attorney (not you) wants to ask the Authors League for information, either as to specialist names or publishing information, the address is: Authors League of America, 234 West 44th Street, New York 10036, Attn: Executive Director. They will try to be of assistance.

If you get published, you might want to look into Authors League membership.

BOOK CONTRACTS

Your contract with your publisher is such an important document in your life as a writer that I must say if you really want to understand it, without an agent or attorney, or at least an experienced author to guide you, you should get and read book-length treatments of the subject, such as the one in the list of recommended books in the back of this one. Even if you do this, you'll find you only learn some lessons by experience. After many years in the book business, I'm still learning myself.

So what follows is a brief description of book contracts, and a few main points you should watch out for, not a definitive guide.

Typical trade books or mass-market book publishing contracts specify such things as the name of the author (and any pseudonym), the title of the work, its length in number of words, when and in what condition it is to be delivered, how copyright is to be registered (in your name, preferably), the publisher's exclusive and nonexclusive territories, the advance against royalties, the royalties paid (and whether they are paid on the retail price of the book, or "actual cash received" by the publisher—an inferior arrangement), a definition of different kinds of sales for which there will be less royalties, the subsidiary rights granted to the publisher (such as book club and quotation rights) and the division of earnings between author and publisher from these rights, your warranty that the book is original or your property and contains no libel or invasion of privacy of another person or other unlawful matter, when and how often statements and payments are to be rendered to you by the publisher, the time period the publisher has within which it must publish or lose the right to do so, how many free copies you will receive and at what discount you may buy additional copies, an option on your next book, what happens if you fail to deliver a final manuscript or it is unacceptable to the publisher, and provisions for termination (and thus getting back your rights) if the book goes out of print, plus other elements. Publishing agreements vary from about two pages in the Stein & Day agreement to around twenty pages in Simon & Schuster's contract.

As an agent, my philosophy is that you must plan for success. If you have an agent, the agent will probably want to give the publisher only what the publisher actually does well itself. If it is a hard cover publisher, the agent would try to sell hard cover rights only—and retain for you, and sell separately such other rights as paperback, magazine, foreign, dramatic, electronic storage and transmission, etc. Of course, with a first novel, the agent probably would not often be able to actually achieve such a deal. So the agent settles by at least holding back for you first serial, foreign, and movie-TV-dramatic and allied rights, but leaving paperback rights under control of the publisher. The hard cover publisher ordinarily gives you half the paperback earnings. If the book is a success, all or part of the retained rights can be sold separately, often for good sums of money (except that first serial must be sold beforehand).

On the other hand, if you have no agent, *someone* must market these rights—you could try to do it yourself, or you can leave the rights in the hands of the publisher, and let it market them for you—with the provision that it gets a share.

The problems with the latter arrangement are: 1) the publisher will hold your earnings from subsidiary rights until your advance is covered by your earnings, which may be never, so you don't get anything from, say, a subsidiary rights deal for a modest British edition contract; 2) the publisher only pays you twice a year, and even then usually waits several months after the end of a six-month accounting period to do it. This means you can be rich on paper (say the publisher made a giant paperback deal) and not have a cent in your pocket for many months.

You may find ways around these problems, but it may be difficult if you represent yourself. If you do represent yourself, you should probably focus on the obvious—the amount of the advance royalty, and the amount of the royalty paid on each copy sold.

How much you get for an advance royalty is strictly a matter for negotiation. The more the publisher wants your manuscript, the more money you can get—if you hold out. Usually, for paperback genre first novels, the amounts mentioned previously, $2,500 to $7,000, will not be subject to much negotiation, but it never hurts to try. Longer works, like a historical romance or historical novel, certainly should get more—possibly up to $10,000-$15,000 in a routine case, depending on whether the publisher regards it as a potential lead or second-lead title.

Hard cover first novels usually get $5,000-$10,000 or more—sometimes much more—particularly when an agent is involved and is very excited by the novel and editors agree that it is exceptional—witness Karleen Koen's advance of $350,000 cited earlier. You'll just have to try to feel out the situation if you are representing yourself.

The reason the amount of the advance royalties is so important to you is that this is the only money you can be sure of earning from your book contract. The advance should be a "nonreturnable guarantee," and it is the inducement the publisher offers you to sign the contract. Even if the book sells only a few copies, you get to keep this money.

After the book is published, each copy sold should earn, under the contract, a royalty. Ideally, this royalty will be computed as a percentage of the *catalog retail price* of the book. This way of figuring royalties is vastly superior for you to another way—figuring royalties based on a percentage of "actual cash received by the publisher" for each copy. Naturally you would rather get your royalties as a percentage of the retail, rather than the wholesale, price. The publisher will keep an account of the sales of your book, and the royalties earned, in your "royalty account." When the royalties earned equal the advance royalties paid you, the book has "earned out" and all additional royalties earned are yours, after the end of the next accounting period.

For example, suppose your advance was $10,000, and your book is published in hard cover at $20 retail price. If your royalties are 10 percent of the retail price, that is $2 a book. When 5,000 copies are sold, your book will have earned out its advance. When one more copy is sold, the publisher will owe you $2 additional. If 4,000 more are sold, the publisher will owe you $8,000, and your total earnings on the 9,000 copies will be $18,000—$10,000 as advance royalties, and $8,000 as later royalty earnings.

This example is rather simplified. In an actual contract, some of the royalties might be less than 10 percent because the books were sold in Canada at a reduced royalty rate; and some of the royalties might be more, because your contract may provide that you get 12½ percent royalties for all copies sold over the first 5,000. Be sure and study the fine print of royalty provisions!

If the novel seems likely to be published in hard cover first, try to get your publisher to pay royalties of 10 percent of the retail price of each of the first 5,000 copies sold, 12½ percent on the second 5,000, and 15 percent for all copies thereafter.

If it is to be a "trade paperback," probably the royalties will be less: either 6 or 7½ or sometimes 10 percent of the catalog retail price for the first 10,000 or maybe 20,000 copies sold, and possibly some higher royalty for more sold.

If yours is a mass-market paperback original, depending on the company and your bargaining position, you may get anywhere from 4 to 10 percent of the cover price for the first 100,000 or 150,000 copies sold, and an escalation to a higher royalty, or series of escalating royalties, for increasing quantities sold. A typical contract of this sort would pay 6 percent for the first 150,000 copies, 8 percent for the next 150,000, and 10 percent for all over 300,000 copies. Getting that final stage, 10 percent, might come hard.

If you do not have an agent and have no experience with magazine sales, it would probably be better to let the publisher handle the first serial rights. Though some publishers are not ashamed to ask for 50 percent of the money for these rights, you may be able to get them down to 25 percent, or the 10 percent I consider fair.

Unless you have some reason to think you can handle the foreign rights effectively yourself, without an agent you should probably let the publisher handle them, in exchange for a 20 or 25 percent share to the publisher.

I would advise you to retain the movie-TV-dramatic rights in every instance—you can always try to get an agent or lawyer to handle these later if there is any demand for them. If you let the publisher handle them for a 10 or 15 percent share, the publisher would usually just turn them over to an agent in any event.

For your protection, the agreement should include a "bankruptcy" clause that immediately ends your contract if the publisher becomes bankrupt. And there should be a provision that you may end the contract if the book goes out of print and the publisher refuses to reprint it. If possible, you should restrict the rights of the publisher to edit and change the book without your permission, beyond simple copyediting, and you should try to get the right to approve the title of the novel if it is changed.

Any option on your next book should not be much more elaborate than "on terms to be agreed," and the period in which you have the right to submit your next book should begin, at the very least, on the publisher's acceptance of your final manuscript. If possible, strike out any option clause altogether if you think you will be a prolific writer.

Whether you have an agent, or an attorney, or both, read the contract carefully yourself and try to understand it. If you don't, discuss it with your editor. But remember that the deal itself is the most important part of it, not the details. As one publisher with a not-so-perfect contract, but a reputation for running a large advertising campaign for each of his books, remarked, "Authors are paid in dollars, not percentage points." He was pointing out that with his big promotions, the author could make more through big sales, even if the royalty percentages didn't escalate and the publisher kept a sizable share of rights earnings, than if the author had an agented-type contract with another publisher who did little promotion.

SHOULD YOU GO TO A LARGE AGENCY, OR A SMALL ONE?

This is a familiar question. As a person who has sometimes operated alone, and sometimes with a partner or a couple of associates, I only know the small agency scene from the inside. But as an editor I dealt with the largest agencies as well as small ones. The question is deceptive—what you should ask is, "Do I believe my individual agent can do the best possible job for me?" Clyde Taylor, mentioned earlier, first established his own small agency, and later merged it with the large agency, Curtis Brown. Either way, he is as competent as they come. Mel Berger, one of many agents with the giant William Morris Agency, certainly gave strong personal attention to the writers he represents, in my experience with him. Peter Skolnick, with Sanford Greenberger Associates, a sizable outfit, showed determination and finesse in handling a client whose book I bought from him. Irving Lazar might have a small staff, but is a giant in the deals he manages to make with regularity. Dominick Abel runs his small agency so efficiently he can handle many clients effectively.

In reality, the agent can only maximize the profits from the work he/she handles—there is nothing magical about the agent or the size of the agency. What sells is the property—the biggest agent can't sell a piece of junk any better than the beginner can who has just switched from being a rights assistant for a publisher. If you create a great property—your first novel—your agent, large or small, can sell it, and probably, with enough effort, you could, too.

SHOULD YOU PAY A FEE
TO GET AN AGENT TO READ
YOUR FIRST NOVEL?

Some agencies charge a "reading fee," and these fees can vary from a small payment the agent has imposed to keep too many beginners from making submissions to quite substantial amounts. As I have sometimes charged a fee, and sometimes not, I can say that in fact the charging of fees doesn't seem to deter authors from submitting works.

The attraction fee-charging agents have is that they usually, in exchange for the fee, provide some kind of an appraisal or criticism even if they reject the work, and those agents who don't charge a fee might write across a query letter, as I do when I'm in a hurry, "Sorry, not for me," or, "Sounds okay, but not my kind of thing," and stuff it immediately in the return envelope to go back to the author. I consider this better than the alternative, a form rejection slip.

The question that arises is, is criticism bought for a fee worth anything? I have to say that I think it is, and if you can't get a reading any other way, and can afford the fee, it might be worth your while.

The largest agency that charges reading fees—and fees I think of as big enough to make me pause a little—is the Scott Meredith Agency. This agency also mails out solicitations to submit your manuscript for appraisal—my ex-wife received one, so I was able to read it. While I have the impression that there is a certain mass-production efficiency in the way this large agency handles this part of its operation, I also must say that when authors have approached me with their manuscripts, and the critiques they received from Scott Meredith Agency, the reports seemed reasonable and appropriate. As I have only seen a few such critiques, I can't pass any judgment beyond that one.

Scott Meredith is no doubt an important agency that has a number of major fiction writers among its clients, such as Norman Mailer and Margaret Truman. Among the first novelists it discovered and brought to publication was Douglas Reeves, whose *Night Action* was placed with New American Library in the U.S. and Andre Deutsch in Britain, with movie rights to Warner Brothers. And, using the definition of "first novel" as the first novel written by a writer, regardless of what books the writer might have done before, this agency made the biggest deal I have heard of for a first novel when it placed Carl Sagan's *Contact* with Simon & Schuster for a reported guarantee of $2,000,000.

SHOULD YOU PAY AN AGENCY
A FEE FOR EDITORIAL WORK?

If an agency also offers editorial services for a fee, I really don't have firm advice for you. As discussed in the previous chapter, certainly editorial work can sometimes turn an unsalable work into a salable one. What you have to ask yourself is, "Can *this* agent make the difference?"

The question in my mind is whether, in some instances, *anybody*, no matter how well intentioned or well qualified, can truly help—for love or money. Often it is better to start over on a new novel rather than dwell endlessly on trying to improve an old, much rejected one.

I am not against a writer paying for help of various kinds or for the privilege of rubbing shoulders with other writers and people of the publishing world—even if it is only the fee for joining a local writers club. Knowing the isolation many writers face, I believe it is important that they meet creative people as well as editors, publishers, and agents who deal with creative people behind the scenes of publishing.

What are the options open to the lone writer? Dozens of writers conferences are conducted on various campuses around the country—for a reasonable fee, you even live in a college dormitory. Besides the writers clubs and agencies, writers schools and extension courses offer editorial assistance. Surely they could not all remain in existence year after year if they did not fill a need.

Naturally, in such a large clutch, there will be a few bad eggs. It is a *caveat emptor* situation—buyer, beware. So before you send any money, try to check out the organization—maybe with the Better Business Bureau, or at least find out how long it has been in existence. Some writers conferences have been going on successfully for many years.

A final word is to be sure you understand what service is being offered. Real help in getting you published? Or just friendly contacts with writers and editors? Or psychological support? If you want the answer to be "all of the above," you'll probably have to join several groups.

The work of a literary agent—selling and licensing literary rights to literary property, is an esoteric occupation. This was brought home to me convincingly when I was visiting a fashionable summer resort, and at a cocktail party, met a socially prominent dowager. She asked me what I did, and I said I was a literary agent.

"And what, might I ask, is a literary agent?"

"Well, a literary agent sells or licenses rights to literary property, just as a real estate agent sells or licenses rights to real property."

"Hah!" she said. "I don't believe there could *be* such an occupation," and stalked off.

9.

The Publishers and Editors

Authors and agents talk of publishers and publishing houses, but what they are really talking about are the editors—the backstage stars of your show, the persons who hold the fate of your novel in their hands. Yes, they—the editors—check it out with their superiors, and maybe the president of the company himself has a hand in deciding whether or not you get published. But the president usually would not even have seen your manuscript if it weren't for the editor.

"Each editor is a mini-publishing house," one author told me in astonishment, after I had introduced him to a number of editors who were considering his book at the same time. He added, "These people aren't ordinary business representatives of their companies. They are only interested in how my book will look on their lifetime list." And one editor did add his title to *her* list of credits.

Editors are judged by their "track records" of picking good-selling books and attracting and putting under contract books that sell.

Editors may solicit you, if they hear of you, and often are in contact with agents, asking what is new and good.

After the contract is signed, it is the editor who studies your manuscript page by page, asks for clarifications, new twists, and various changes. And it is the editor who decides when the manuscript is ready for publication and for the printer.

It's interesting to know that editors are a comparatively recent development in the publishing business. In the 1920s edition of *The Truth About Publishing*, British publisher Stanley Unwin advised an author, after he had finished his handwritten "fair copy" to take it to a good typist, who would correct it for punctuation, spelling, sentence structure, and grammar—and it would be ready to publish. The "good typist" of the past is the editor of today.

You might encounter two theories of editing: the British and the American. John Beaudouin, formerly editor-in-chief of Reader's Digest Condensed Books and now a publishing consultant, says, "English publishers, by and large, assume that the book is the author's sole creation and it is the publisher's duty to execute and publish it, whereas American publishers are inclined to offer numorous criticisms and suggestions for improvements—to help the author, by their way of thinking, make the book better."

The editors you will meet on these pages, and or have to work with in real life if your novel is put under contract for publication, are not the "hands-off" British, but American book editors—a nosey, opinionated, book-reading breed who think, often with some justice, that only they know what the public wants. Fortunately, they don't *agree* on what the public wants, and since there are a lot of them, you have a fair chance of finding one who thinks he/she knows that *your* novel is what the public wants.

It's a widely held view that editors and publishers are part of some sort of liberal conspiracy, and in fact, many editors are liberal. But there are also some conservative editors and some completely nonpolitical ones.

Many editors are women. So if you are a woman-hater and write a misogynist novel, they won't like it—unless, as happened with Ileene Smith, an editor at Summit Books, one of them regards it as a brilliant book. She was happy to acquire and help Summit publish *Stanley and the Women*, by Kingsley Amis, even though some angry women thought it shouldn't be published because of its depiction of women characters.

It's only practical for an editor or publisher to look for works that appeal to a wide variety of readers—and to avoid turning off whole classes of readers (not to mention reviewers and librarians) as potential buyers of your book.

So for business reasons as well as considerations of common decency, comb your manuscript free of ethnic, religious, and racial slurs and stereotypes. Stereotypes have no place in good writing in any event.

Editors are proud of their place in the literary world and of the budding novelists they have launched. Ellis Amburn is proudest of his 1970s discovery of Belva Plain, whose first novel, *Evergreen*, gave rise to a new sub-genre, the Jewish family saga.

Every book Belva Plain has written has become a best seller but when Amburn met her, she was an unpublished grandmother in New Jersey, married to an ophthalmologist supportive of her struggle with her manuscript.

As Amburn told my coauthor, "In the evenings I was teaching a class in writing and publishing at the New School for Social Research. I asked Belva if she would like to come to class regularly and let me and the class edit her novel in public, so to speak. She was taking an awful chance, but she was a good sport and agreed—and that's how her first book was edited.

"It did not always go smoothly. Once she and I had a furious argument in front of the class about some bit of proposed editing, and the class was distressed. But then one of the students called out, 'Hey, that's part of the process. There's no need for us to get excited.' They laughed and settled down and presumably learned something as Belva and I finally worked it out."

Amburn did not edit Belva Plain's later books because she stayed with Delacorte Press but he moved to G. P. Putnam's Sons.

The publishing world is never at rest. The president and publisher at Putnam's trade books division is Phyllis Grann. She started as a secretary at Doubleday, was an editor at Morrow, then David McKay, and became a senior editor and vice president at Simon & Schuster, where among the notable authors she launched was Mary Higgins Clark with her first novel, *Where Are the Children?*

The climb up the editorial ladder is not always easy. Genevieve Young told me she had to work a number of years as a secretary at Harper & Row before becoming an editor, and editing the best seller, *Love Story*. But once started, she continued successfully at Lippincott, then was a senior editor and executive at Little, Brown, and now is editor-in-chief of the Literary Guild.

Well-known literary agent Georges Borchardt, addressing a group of publishers, commented on the changeable publishing scene by saying, "Each morning before I can conduct business, I must find out where the players are today."

Howard Cady, an "editor's editor" and one of the greats in the publishing world, made ten moves over a forty-eight-year period. By my calculation, Cady stayed an average of three-and-a-half years each at the first nine, including two stints at Doubleday and two at Holt. Then he moved to William Morrow & Co., where he stayed seventeen years, until his semi-retirement. He continues to edit for Morrow on a reduced schedule.

When Howard Cady came to Putnam's in 1957 as editor-in-chief, he learned that the president of that company had been holding *Lolita*, by Vladimir Nabokov, for several months wondering whether or not the company dared publish the novel. Cady was able to persuade Putnam's to publish *Lolita*, which became a major best seller—and was considered very daring at the time.

Every editor remembers the one that got away. Cady was the first editor to encourage, work with, and advise Leon Uris. It's an inside-the-publishing-world story worth telling.

After World War II, Leon Uris had a job with the San Francisco *Call Bulletin* but he was a long way from the writing end. He was, in fact, in charge of around seventy-five newspaper delivery boys. But nights and days off, Uris toiled at writing about the Marines, based on his war experience. As it happened, Howard Cady was in San Francisco, where he had opened a West Coast editorial office for Doubleday.

The top book reviewer of the *San Francisco Chronicle* was Joseph Henry Jackson. Cady knew Jackson well through having edited two of Jackson's own books for Macmillan, his first publishing affiliation. One day Jackson phoned Cady about a young man he had met who seemed to have a great deal of raw talent, judging by some of a manuscript Jackson had seen. Howard Cady told Jackson to send the writer over with the manuscript. Uris hurried to the Doubleday office where he excitedly rushed in and announced to Cady's assistant, Mary Lou Mueller, "I'm yours." At least, that's what she thought he said. Fortunately, Cady, hearing this, came out of his office, and explained that the young man was saying, "I'm Uris."

So began a one-and-a-half year relationship, with long weekly luncheon work sessions in which Cady guided Uris through his first novel. The book reviewer had said the material he saw had "no punctuation, no paragraphs, but showed a marvelous ear for dialogue."

That certainly was true. What also turned out to be true was that Uris had not one but four manuscripts which had to be studied in putting together one good book, *Battle Cry*, published in 1953 and making Uris an instant star.

But Doubleday, New York, declined to publish the novel. Unwilling to waste all the work he had initiated, Cady tried West Coast Random House and Little, Brown reps, who also declined it. Finally, Cady sent it to Ted Purdy at Putnam's. Purdy gave it to Virginia Carrick, to show to her husband Lynn, who was New York editor for Lippincott, a Philadelphia publisher. Lynn Carrick had been a major in the Marine Corps. So, as Cady tells it, "a book submitted by the West Coast editor of Doubleday was bought in New York by Putnam's on the enthusiastic recommendation of an editor for a Philadelphia publisher."

In contrast to Phyllis Grann and Howard Cady, Kathleen Malley reached the top by staying put. She started with Paperback Library as an assistant editor in 1965, and retired twenty-one years later as executive editor and vice president of Warner Books (the successor to Paperback Library). She was also Editor-in-Chief of Popular Library, a Warner imprint. An author whose first Gothic novel she signed in 1965, Dan Ross, was still writing for her. His historical novel *Denver Lady*, written under the pen name of "Clarissa Ross," was published by Warner in 1985.

Mrs. Malley once told me that I was the first agent she ever took to lunch, and that she was very disappointed when I ordered a spritzer rather than a martini, spoiling her notion of agents.

When you, after you are an established author, try to call your agent or editor between noon and 2:30 or even 3 P.M., you may find they are "out to lunch." These luncheons are an important part of doing business in the publishing world. A few editors and agents, however, resist this routine and have a sandwich at their desk during a quick business meeting. If your editor asks you to this unglamorous kind of desk luncheon meeting, don't be insulted—it's just one of the perfectly acceptable publishing styles of behavior. Your next invitation may be different.

Just as Howard Cady courted and edited the talented Leon Uris at long lunch meetings in San Francisco, you may, as an author, find yourself invited to lunch by a publisher. It's a good sign he or she is interested in your book. But don't become bedazzled. I remember the first time I made a multiple submission to publishers back in the 1960s. My client was taken, in turn, by two major editors to very elegant lunches at famous and expensive French restaurants, and later both made an offer. We also had a third offer from an editor who never went to lunch. I suggested we make a deal with one of the three editors, and the author replied, "No, no, make more submissions, so we can have more fancy lunches!" We ended up with the editor who *didn't* wine and dine him.

HOW MUCH OF A NOVEL
DO YOU HAVE TO WRITE
BEFORE SELLING IT?

I firmly advise that you write your whole first novel before a publisher sees it, even if an agent has seen part of it and encouraged you to go on. As editor Ellis Amburn explains it, "The first-time novelist has no track record. That writer had better create the whole story so that I can see how it was handled and how the plot was resolved. Remember that a publisher spends a great deal of money launching a first book, and with that risk, he really must know what he is getting."

But there is always an exception. One agent, Harriet Wasserman, was so impressed with the first hundred pages she had seen of a beginning novelist that she gave it to a particular editor she thought would appreciate it, Jonathan Galassi, at Houghton Mifflin.

Galassi liked what he saw and Houghton drew up a contract which gave author Alice McDermott a $12,500 advance to be paid in three parts—an immediate payment, an installment at the midpoint and the final part when the job was completed. Then Galassi switched to Random House and the budding author had to decide where her loyalty lay, with the editor or the publishing house.

She decided to go with her editor and Houghton's advance was reimbursed. Of course, had Random not gone along with Galassi's desire to guide McDermott through her first book, she would have had no choice but to stick with Houghton and take whatever editor was next assigned her.

HOW DOES A PUBLISHER DECIDE
WHAT TO DO ABOUT YOUR
MANUSCRIPT?

More than half the manuscripts that are offered to trade book publishers come from literary agents or lawyers acting as agents.

Others come in because editors show interest in an author's query. And many are simply sent in unheralded, or are hand-delivered by the author. Such manuscripts are called "over the transom" or "unsolicited" submissions.

"Solicited" manuscripts come from every direction. Sometimes from within the publishing house itself, brought in by someone who has taken an interest in a new writer—an editor, executive, or other employee—salesperson, publicist, clerk, secretary, or even the janitor.

If anyone, such as your attorney, agent, friend, teacher, or mother-in-law—or you yourself through a query—has asked someone at the publishing house whether they want to see your novel, and the person at the publishing house says yes, then your novel becomes a solicited submission.

Solicited submissions receive better treatment than unsolicited ones, in most cases. Unsolicited submissions are often routinely returned unread if the publisher has a policy (to save money) of not considering them. Or they may be turned over for reading and appraisal to a very junior person, such as a recent college graduate taken on for a trial period as an employee. Fortunately, sometimes even if a junior person gives your manuscript a bad report, others such as the editors or editor-in-chief will have second thoughts and might actually glance through the unsolicited submissions to make sure something of real interest is not being overlooked. But you have no assurance of this, because the volume of unsolicited submissions is large, and experience has shown that many are hopeless—obscene, illiterate, unprofessional, racist, incoherent, or colored by such odd religious or philosophical bias as to be of little interest to a large audience. Because of editors' built-in readiness to say no, many possibly okay works are returned after only brief inspection.

To show how accidental and casual the treatment of unsolicited manuscripts can be, I'll tell you a story from my own experience, without revealing the author's identity. When I was a busy editor of hard cover books at Prentice-Hall, a manuscript of a novel came in addressed to me, but by a person I did not know. I presume the would-be author took my name from a directory, such as *Literary Market Place*. I looked at it casually, decided it was unsuitable for hard cover publication, and told my secretary to return it with an individually typed, polite form letter.

But instead of returning it, she began to read it during her lunch hours, and when she finished it, passed it on to another secretary to read. When both had finished it, they approached me and said, "This is good. You shouldn't just send it back with a form letter. If we can't publish it, Oscar, why not at least tell him where to take it?"

More because I appreciated the fine secretarial help I had received than because I respected their literary judgment, I took the manuscript home and read it over a weekend. I realized they were right. It was a perfect paperback original. So I sent it back with a letter suggesting the author take it to a certain paperback publisher, whose headquarters happened to be near where he lived. He did, they published it as a lead book successfully, and sold the British rights also for a goodly sum, of which the author got a share.

Solicited manuscripts are handled by more experienced editors, and the editor who gets your manuscript is now the key person in determining your novel's welcome or expulsion from that publishing house.

Even so, the busy editor might first have someone else read the novel for him and write a brief report. This person might be an assistant editor, or an "outside reader," that is, some freelancer who will read the novel and write a report, or even the editor's spouse. Regardless of whether the report is positive or negative, usually the editor will make at least a brief inspection of the work.

This brief inspection might be to read the first few pages, to read at random in the manuscript, and possibly skip to the end. *Therefore, each page of your work must be excellent,* so that no matter where the editor's eye falls, the work will attract his attention—"hook" him, so he wants to read more.

If the manuscript survives this initial cursory inspection, usually the editor himself will read it carefully—or read as long as it holds his interest.

Again, if your novel survives these tests, the editor will then begin to prepare a case for and against the success of your book. If the case for it is stronger, he will begin to try to interest others in the publishing house in it—the editor-in-chief, the sales manager, the publicity director, the rights director, and so on.

This can be a formal process, in which the editor writes up an elaborate proposal, comparing your novel to best sellers or other successful works, and makes an estimate of sales (or an informed guess based on experience), and pointing out its promotional virtues. He may have to circulate this proposal, get comments from others, and then defend the manuscript in an "editorial conference," that is, a formal meeting of those who have decision power.

Or, in a system used by some other publishers, he may have to get the approval of only one other person, such as the publisher or president of his company. Then the editor is free to go ahead and make an agreed-upon offer to publish—an offer that would include an advance against royalties and contract terms.

Keep in mind that publishers are inundated with manuscripts and have little patience with slipshod work. That is why it is really important to eliminate trivial drawbacks, such as poor spelling, a poor typing job, a dog-eared manuscript, one with too-narrow margins, one that is not double spaced.

Poor spelling means more expensive copyediting and delay while this work is done. Poor typing means the manuscript will not photocopy well to submit to book clubs, and may have to be retyped—expensive and time-consuming. A dog-eared manuscript looks as though other publishers rejected it. Narrow margins or single-spaced format makes it hard to edit.

These drawbacks, plus other doubts, in combination with strong competition from professional-looking manuscripts, may add up to the judgment: "It's too much trouble to publish this work."

But say you make it. You sign with the publisher, the long process of editing and copyediting is behind you, and the book is scheduled for publication.

Is it all clear sailing now on a trip to fame, success, and megabucks? A lot depends on the next step.

WHAT ABOUT PUBLICITY FOR YOUR FIRST NOVEL?

Your publisher may or may not be prepared to spend much time and publicity money on a beginner's work. In the old advertising jargon, he may "run it up the flagpole and see if anyone salutes." If your novel gets a good advance notice in *Kirkus Reports* (a publishing newsletter with advance reviews) and in *Publishers Weekly,* or if a good paperback or book club sale happens, or if book buyers happen to like the jacket and blurb, and a good number of copies are ordered in advance by bookstores, then the publisher may promote vigorously. What he is doing is following the theory of pouring gasoline on an already burning fire. But suppose these good things don't happen right away. What then?

Many writers don't know that there are specialized public relations consultants who can be hired by *writers* to get publicity for a new novel. So, rather than take a chance that you will be disheartened after you are published and get only a few reviews, no advertising, and scattered distribution, you can try to do something about it in advance, and hire someone.

According to Lisl Cade, a New York public relations consultant for authors and publishers who was formerly publicity manager for Harper & Row and director of publicity for W.W. Norton, good reviews are the most important publicity a first novelist can receive, because they can affect your whole career. Other kinds of publicity, such as press stories, radio and TV interviews, and autographing parties, can reinforce the good impression of reviews, but are of less importance in the long run.

No one in the publishing business can promise or accurately predict that you will get *good* reviews. But a skilled public relations person can greatly increase the chance of your getting *many* reviews simply by advocating your novel with letters, press releases, and phone calls. And if you get many reviews, people, including editors, will say for years, "Oh, yes, I heard of that."

For someone like Lisl Cade to help you most effectively, the time to start promoting your book, she says, is several months *before* publication—at least four months before for the actual publicity work, and a couple of months before that for planning and making arrangements. She and most others in this field will only accept author clients if they like the author's work and can envision how they can succeed in publicizing it.

So you may have to shop around. The arrangement is to negotiate a monthly retainer with a publicist for some agreed-upon number of months. In addition to the retainer, expenses must be paid—travel, press kits, photographs of you and your book, many long-distance phone calls by the publicist, postage, and messenger fees. Unless your publisher is cooperative, you may have to buy sets of advance bound proofs from him, and even buy copies of your book beyond what your publisher planned to send out for review.

If your publisher shares your publicist's enthusiasm, he may pick up all these expenses, and do even more than you thought of doing yourself. Naturally, if your publisher *tells you* of the very extensive plans for review mailings, and has helped you secure important advance quotes from famous authors and personalities, and asked you to set aside time for a promotion tour, then you may not have to do anything on your own.

But say the publisher makes no promises, seems to have no promotion plans. Then *your* publicist can do it instead. After getting advance quotes, advance reviews, and initial reactions to your novel, your publicist may be able to secure additional publicity for you, such as radio, TV, and press interviews, and a book tour. To do this, he or she will have to work with you to figure out an angle interesting to the media—an angle connected with your book, but not just based on what's in it. New faces are news. Having a lively personality helps.

Your publicist will look for a real story, not concoct one, to make you newsworthy, a story you might not realize you are carrying with you all the time—such as how you write your Doomsday novel in a fallout shelter. Or you may be able to publicize your mystery story by talking about your adventures on your neighborhood Crime Watch.

Sometimes the publicity story can be very obvious, yet still exciting. When Lisl Cade publicized *Six Days of the Condor* for W.W. Norton, the story was that this first novel by the young James Grady had been retrieved from the "slush pile" by editor Starling Lawrence. It was "from unknown to author of a best seller bought by Robert Redford to be made into a movie." That campaign was so powerfully effective that I bought and read the book myself, and went to the movie.

To publicize *Fields of Fire*, the first novel of the much-decorated Marine Corps hero, James Webb, Patty Neger, then publicity director of Prentice-Hall, arranged a long publicity tour in which Webb discussed the public's neglect of Vietnam veterans. But first she laid the groundwork by circulating good advance quotes from well-known writers, sending out many advance bound proofs, and by telling reviewers she met with that the publisher considered it an important book. Good reviews, the powerful publicity, and good subsidiary rights sales gave the publisher obvious reason to do sizable printings, advertise the book and the first-time author was launched successfully.

Fate helped publicize the first novel *Don't Embarrass the Bureau*, by former FBI agent Bernard F. Conners. The novel was critical of the FBI, and when J. Edgar Hoover died practically on its publication date, the "Today" show invited Conners to appear. In a long interview, he predicted and advocated reforms for the FBI a new director might introduce—women agents, black agents and agents from other minorities, plus relaxed dress codes, among other things.

Often a publisher will devote little or no apparent effort to publicizing a mass-market paperback book. A good cover and big printing is the name of the game instead. When the first novel of Niel Hancock's fantasy quartet, *Circle of Light,* was scheduled to be published, he visited the editor-in-chief of Popular Library, Patrick O'Connor, and said, "I have some ideas. What are your plans to publicize my book?"

O'Connor replied, "I'm glad somebody has plans to publicize it, because we intend simply to publish and distribute it." And that's all they did. But editor Karen Solem (later editorial director of Silhouette Books) had recommended that O'Connor authorize the expense of a famous cover artist. He agreed, and with nothing more than a beautiful cover and wide distribution to introduce the series, *Circle of Light* has become an enduring seller.

If this review of the world of writing, agents, editors, and publishers has seemed unduly depressing, don't despair. Read on and learn how some other novelists, both famous and still striving, got their start. Remember, *they* were first novelists once, too.

Part Two

HOW SEVENTEEN FIRST NOVELISTS BROKE INTO PRINT

10.
They Weren't Always Superstars: How Six Famous Novelists Got Started

Novelists are made, not born. And if you look at the lives of even the most famous of them, you will see that they are *self*-made. When you read the elegantly packaged books of authors who are international celebrities, they may seem seamless and perfect, to adapt the "zipless" phrase from Erica Jong's breakthrough book, *Fear of Flying*.

It's hard to imagine Pulitzer prize-winning James Michener, or Nobel prize-winning William Golding struggling with a first novel. Or to think of the fabulous money-maker Harold Robbins failing before he succeeded, and Stephen King, writer of multiple best sellers, facing rejection slip after rejection slip. Or to remember that sophisticated sex-and-celebrity-book queen Jackie Collins started to write because of her anger at male writers.

Why were they different? Why did *they* become superstars? The answer is superior strategy. They found what they could do and did it again and again. After a quick look at this half dozen whose names to publishers spell money in the bank, we'll examine twelve others.

These twelve have been carefully selected from among the authors I know personally, because their lives and work illustrate the most vital points you need to know in building your own success.

JAMES MICHENER

Winning a Pulitzer prize for your first novel is an auspicious beginning. But James Albert Michener already had a more-than-full lifetime of experience when the Pulitzer jury passed over John Steinbeck's *The Wayward Bus*, Theodore Dreiser's *The Stoic*, Laura Hobson's *Gentleman's Agreement*, Sinclair Lewis's *Kingsblood Royal*, Malcolm Lowry's *Under the Volcano*, and other worthy books written in 1947 and awarded the fiction prize for "a distinguished novel, preferably dealing with American life, by an American author" to an obscure forty-year-old first novelist.

The novel was *Tales of the South Pacific*.

Michener protested modestly that he didn't deserve the Pulitzer, but the judges decreed otherwise. What had so completely captivated them? Originality, a breakthrough in the run of serious war books and books about major battles.

What *Tales of the South Pacific* had was an offbeat view of World War II—how a great war trickles down to small adventures on obscure tropical islands far from the big action, and how it enters the quiet lives of the natives.

Second, it had unique native characters such as Bloody Mary, who sold shrunken heads to make an honest living, and Teta Christian, who claimed to be a descendant of the real "Mr. Christian" who mutinied against Captain Bligh in *Mutiny on the Bounty*.

And finally, it had a great love story—that of an American nurse, Nellie Forbush, who falls in love with a French expatriate planter, only to find that he is still wanted by the police back home for stabbing a man to death, and that he has already sired eight illegitimate children with Tonkinese, Javanese, and Polynesian women.

James Michener's life is a study in breakthroughs that can inspire any writer. He had risen from being a foundling, a throw-away baby raised by a poor woman with a big heart, Mabel Michener, who gave him her name. She also gave him an anchor as he started hitchhiking at an early age, searching, searching, he knew not for whom.

He did not find his real mother but he did find adventure, and the wanderlust never left him. As a kid, he acted as a lookout to catch short-change artists at a carnival. He worked as a fortune teller named "Mitch the Witch." He was a hotel night watchman. At the age of fifteen, he wrote a sports column. He spent one summer traveling with a tent show.

Each job showed him more about the ways of the world and widened his horizons. Once he was arrested for juvenile vagrancy in Georgia. He explained he was not a vagrant but was very busy. He was engaged in seeing the world. When Michener graduated from high school, Swarthmore College did something it had never done before—it granted a four-year scholarship to "a student who showed the greatest promise."

Even after becoming a teacher in private schools in Pennsylvania, Michener could not resist an adventure and he left security behind to travel abroad on a fellowship, seeking out the unusual. He dropped everything again to travel with a troupe of bullfighters in Spain, then joined a group collecting old ballads in the Hebrides. He even served as a chart boy on a Mediterranean coal boat.

Eventually, the fun was over and he returned to the States to further his education and resume teaching. An article he wrote, *The Beginning Teacher*, brought him to the attention of Harvard University and in time, to Macmillan, where he became a textbook editor.

When World War II started, adventure beckoned again but he felt dejected by the title given him—historical officer for a vast area in the Pacific.

Only when he had gotten acquainted with the natives and heard their stories, did the creative juices start to flow, and he never stopped writing again.

He brought the stories back with him after the war and wove them into a book-length manuscript, but Macmillan editors were not too impressed. They reminded Michener that his future lay in his excellent editing of education textbooks. "Don't jeopardize it," they said.

Only when he sold two of his "Tales" to the *Saturday Evening Post*, a major fiction market of the period, did Macmillan agree to publish Michener's stories in book form.

But the company was not moved to put forth a major effort, and the book was printed on leftover, faulty, war-time paper. Chapters did not even rate a new page—they were tacked on at the end of the preceding chapter.

The book made its debut without fanfare, and few took note of it except for one major reviewer, Orville Prescott of *The New York*

Times, who said flatly, *Tales of the South Pacific* was "one of the best works of fiction yet to come out of the war," and predicted that it "will make Mr. Michener famous," because it was "humorous, engrossing and surprisingly moving."

The book didn't become a best seller, and when Michener won the Pulitzer prize the year after its publication, the award, though enormously impressive, seemed the end of the story.

But now fate took another turn, and an actor, Kenneth McKenna, was so impressed with the novel he tried to get a movie studio to produce it as a film. He was told that it was not right for a film, it was "unmanageable." Then McKenna showed it to his brother, stage designer Jo Mielziner—and Mielziner showed it to the celebrated Broadway team of Oscar Hammerstein and composer Richard Rodgers.

A year after receiving the Pulitzer, a version of the book was mounted on Broadway as a musical. The producers called it *South Pacific*, and gave Michener a percentage ownership.

The show ran five years, and the feisty singer-actress Mary Martin, as nurse Nellie Forbush, sang in it such now-classic songs as "I'm Gonna Wash That Man Right Outta My Hair," playing opposite the great baritone, Ezio Pinza, whose role was the island cad, Emile De Becque.

The success of *South Pacific* made Michener financially free to write anything he wanted. But Macmillan declined his next book, so he got on a bus and rode over to Random House. And Random House is still his publisher, some thirty books and a number of number one best-selling novels and movies later.

And he did not forget Swarthmore's gift to him. In September, 1984, Michener returned the $2,000 scholarship with a little bonus— $2,000,000, saying, "That's a thousand to one, just about the financial value of a good liberal arts education."

Something else should be said about Michener. He has not changed. His ability to make friends and his interest in everything and everyone still draws people to him, so that they are not overawed by his status as a multimillionaire author. My coauthor, who met and had a short talk with Michener at the National Press Club in Washington, came away singing his praises. Though I've only been in touch with him by letters, I have a warm feeling about him, too, just from these brief contacts.

What can a beginning novelist learn from James Michener's career? The first and most important lesson is: Don't let anyone stop you from a writing career. The second is that if your work doesn't initially make it in one medium, try another. When his first novel was rejected, Michener sold a portion of it to a magazine—and the magazine's acceptance of his work made his publisher reconsider, and go ahead. A third lesson is that even if your first novel is not published in an attractive edition, it can succeed anyway. It's your *words* that sell. Fourth, sometimes a first work can compete successfully with the works of the best established authors of the time.

Finally, an initial result is not necessarily the final result. *Tales of the South Pacific* was not a best seller, but the musical *South Pacific* brought Michener a great deal of money.

He became one of the most successful authors of our time, and over and over, has compressed information and characters from a large geographical area like the South Pacific into a novel. He did it again with the Chesapeake, with Hawaii, with Poland, with Texas.

Compression is his winning strategy.

WILLIAM GOLDING

A breakthrough to superstardom does not have to be the result of extraordinary vigor prevailing over a difficult beginning, as with James Michener. It can come from developing a highly original train of thought—from waiting to write until you have a first-rate idea and have developed the power to express it well. William Golding's breakthrough was to give a new twist to an old subject. The problems of castaways had already been brilliantly and successfully used in such works as the eighteenth-century classic, *Robinson Crusoe*, by Daniel Defoe, and the more recent popular classic, *The Swiss Family Robinson*, by Johann Wyss. Defoe and Wyss, though they dealt extensively and in absorbing detail with the problems and dangers of being marooned, wrote hopeful books of the triumph of the human spirit over difficulty.

Golding thought about this problem further, and turned it into a modern fable: What happens if things *don't* go so well for some of the castaways? What if the result is not inspiring, but grotesque? Might not this experience bring out the *worst* in human nature, rather than the best?

In contrast to many writers who tried other careers, Golding, who received the Nobel Prize for literature in 1983 for his whole body of work, seems to have been destined to write. He wrote his "first novel" at twelve and loved to quote its opening line, "I was born in the Duchy of Cornwall on the eleventh of October, 1792, of rich but honest parents." He once laughingly called it a standard he was unable to maintain.

Young William turned next to poetry and even before he graduated from Brasenose College, Oxford, with a degree in English literature, he had seen a collection of poems published by Macmillan, the British publisher.

His first job as a settlement house worker was what started him thinking about children and their problems in a way that would eventually surface in his first novel, the great best seller, *Lord of the Flies*.

Next he tried his hand at teaching English and philosophy. He gained practice writing for the theater—he wrote, produced, and acted in London's equivalent of New York's off-off Broadway. And when he finally wrote his first novel, he was ready.

Published in 1954, *Lord of the Flies* starts out as an innocent tale of a group of English schoolboys marooned on a desert island. At first everything they do is civilized and admirable—setting up a democratic government and a compassionate court system.

But as the plot progresses, they regress to savages, painting their bodies with war paint and waging battles that lead to death.

The message of the novel, an allegory of human progress, is that civilization is only skin deep, and is ever in danger of being worn off by adversity. That message is a long way from *The Swiss Family Robinson*.

So Golding's strategy shows that imagination and thought can transmute mundane experience—observing young people in a settlement house—into a glittering novel about all human beings, in a faraway setting that exists only in the mind of the novelist.

STEPHEN KING

Stephen King was not crowned the king of horror stories with his first manuscript. He survived the pain of having four novels and about sixty short stories shot down before he was finally anointed and given the keys to the kingdom of his chosen genre. *Then* riches were heaped at his feet.

His is a story of persistence, energy, and narrow specialization. He built towering success on a very small foundation: A collection of paperback fantasy-horror novels was almost the only thing of value left behind when his father, a sailor, left home when Stephen was three. These influenced the boy at a tender age, so it became natural to try to write in this genre.

There was no hint of a writing career in King's early jobs as janitor, mill hand, and laundry worker. But he did get a scholarship, and graduated in 1970 with a B.S. from the University of Maine. When he settled into a serious job, it was as a teacher on the high school level for a private school in Maine.

King became more closely allied with the world of creative writing when he married a poet, Tabitha Spruce, the following year. King started writing at a furious pace, not stopping even though short story after short story—and his novels—were turned down.

Finally, in 1974, Doubleday accepted one of his novels, *Carrie*. It only took one book to make King famous. *Carrie*, a horror story about a girl with frightening telekinetic power, was made into a movie. And since 1974, top-selling books have been pouring out at a prodigious rate just as though King were still trying to get started—*Cujo, The Stand, Dance Macabre, The Talisman* (with Peter Straub), *Christine, Salem's Lot, The Shining, The Dead Zone, Firestarter, Night Shift, Skeleton Crew, Pet Sematary*, and others like *Thinner*, written under the pen name of "Richard Bachman."

More than once King has had several books on *The New York Times* best seller list simultaneously, and as I write this in early 1986, he has three books on the best-seller lists. According to Edwin McDowell of the *Times*, three of King's books, *Skeleton Crew, Thinner*, and *The Talisman* were among the top ten fiction best sellers of 1985 in paperback and hard cover.

What's his secret? I think it is that he works hard and fast. To King, this work record doesn't seem prodigious. To him, it's just the natural speed at which he works and it only seems unusual, he says, "to someone who doesn't write as much as I do." So far he has stuck to his chosen narrow field of specialization, still building on the foundation of his modest inheritance—that paperback collection of fantasy-horror books left by his father.

The success of Stephen King shows that you can succeed by contributing to a body of existing literature that you admire.

HAROLD ROBBINS

Harold Robbins has been rich and he has been poor. And he was a millionaire the first time when he was only twenty. But it wasn't from his writings—it was from his own finance business. That was in 1936. By 1939, when he was twenty-three, he had lost everything and was starting at the bottom again, this time in the motion picture business.

Robbins was used to hardship. He had been adopted by a family named Rubin, whose name he used until he rechristened himself. He had, from an early age, earned his living on the streets of New York as a runner for bookies, interspersed with legitimate jobs such as short-order cook and grocery clerk.

In 1940, after his fall, Robbins took what he could get—the lowly job of shipping clerk for Universal Pictures. He was determined to climb to the top again. By 1942, he had become executive director of budgeting and planning. He wasn't happy. He saw all those stories being made into movies and none of them were his. With no particular background or training, except possibly a close scrutiny of the works of his favorite writer, John Steinbeck, Harold Robbins, in 1948, "sat down at the piano," wondering who would laugh.

Nobody laughed, though some cried, and critics cheered Robbins's first novel, *Never Love a Stranger*, as marking the birth of a serious writer. One went so far as to call the book the *"Les Miserables* of New York." And what was in it? Everything he could remember about the sordid world he had known as a kid—hustlers, pimps, bookies, racketeers, and his own life as an orphan. He had even given the hero his own birth name—Francis Kane.

Knopf, which had taken a chance on the thirty-two-year-old beginner, was vindicated the following year when Robbins came up with an even greater winner, *The Dream Merchants*. Robbins quickly became a phenomenon in the literary world—a man who has never had a failed book. Of his first thirteen, each sold more than a half million copies in its first year and many, such as *The Carpetbaggers* and *The Adventurers*, were made into movies.

Robbins again became a millionaire and a multimillionaire, this time holding on to his riches long enough to have everything he wanted, like a home in Cannes, France.

He takes his celebrity casually, protesting that he is only a story-teller and that he leaves the deep thinking, message-writing to other men. But for all of that, it still remains true that his first novel was a passionate outcry about his youth, and he is still writing about what he knows: the world of money and power.

ERICA JONG

Erica Jong made the transition from a minor poet, wife, outspo-ken feminist, and former English teacher to author of a best seller, *Fear of Flying*. It made her an instant celebrity. How did she do it? By writing what she saw as the truth about upper-middle-class life as she had experienced it. Her father was an importer, her mother a de-signer working with ceramics. She knew the world of the psychia-trist—her husband was a child psychiatrist. She knew marriage problems—she had come through one divorce before marrying Allan Jong.

When *Fear of Flying* was published, critics argued whether women were buying it for its study of a marriage, or because it was a switch in soft porn or erotic writing—written from the female rather than the male point of view. Soon after the novel was published, I re-member vacationing on a tropical island.

Every day, next to me on the beach sat a respectable, prosperous-looking middle-aged New York couple. The wife was reading *Fear of Flying*. She would read a while, laughing, and then she would get up and pace back and forth a bit. "It's too much," she would say. Or sometimes she would shake her head and say, "How could she, it's awful!" But soon she would go back to reading. The book must have struck a truthful chord in that reader's experience—it must have been more truth than poetry.

Erica Jong, like Grace Metalious in *Peyton Place* before her, was telling it as she saw it—but much more could be said in the 1970s. And Jong has continued telling it like it is with *How to Save Your Own Life* and the brilliant *Fanny: The True History of the Adventures of Fan-ny Hackabout-Jones Comprising her Life at Lymeworth, her Initia-tion as a Witch, her Travels with Merry Men, her Life in a Brothel, her London High Life, Her Slaving Voyage, her Life as a Female Pyrate, her eventual Unravelling of her Destiny, et cetera.*

But isn't *Fanny* far afield from what she knew? No, I don't think so. It is a feminist book, a woman's reply to the classic of male-viewpoint pornography, *Fanny Hill*. Erica Jong fell under the spell of 18th century literature as a student at Barnard College, when she took a course under the scholar James L. Clifford. As part of that course, she had written a paper in imitation of Alexander Pope. Her study of Pope was not wasted. In her book, Fanny meets the famous author, and is stunned to see that in the literary world, a small hunchback can be a giant of literature.

With her own writing, Erica Jong has proved once again that a poet can achieve a giant success, this time in the world of fiction, by the witty use of truth.

JACKIE COLLINS

Jackie Collins is another female writer among the newer galaxy of literary stars to deal in the erotic. But her field and fame lie in writing about Hollywood—its sex and sin, its flash and trash and glitz.

My coauthor, Fran Leighton, met her in Washington, D.C., when Collins was on a promotional tour for her book, *Lucky.*

Collins told reporters frankly that she had originally chosen her theme because of her anger at Harold Robbins. She was sick and tired, she said, of what Harold Robbins did to women. He made them weak. His men were strong and had only to look at a woman to get her "to fall backwards into bed with him." She said, "I decided to do for women what Robbins had done for men." In Collins's books, women are the strong characters and *women* decide who will jump into bed with them. "My women are the aggressors," she said.

Her theme of aggressive women demanding a lot from life and getting it has made her a multimillionaire. Book after book has found a spot on the best seller list as well as in movies and TV miniseries— *Hollywood Wives, The Bitch,* and *The Stud.*

The sister of movie and TV star Joan Collins, Jackie, too, tried her hand at acting but regarded herself as "an out-of-work writer" rather than an actress. But even as she started writing her first book, back in the '60s, she did not aspire to be a literary writer. "I'm a street writer," she says. "I write the way people talk, the way they think." As she tells it, she was politely invited to leave school when she was fifteen and she never went back. She left her home in London and came to Hollywood to stay with her sister.

Her first novel, *The World is Full of Married Men,* raised enough eyebrows to assure that her second book, whatever it was, would also be published. That book was *The Stud* and sister Joan, needing a starring vehicle to help her lagging career, chose it. (Joan also starred in *The Bitch*.) But Jackie did not become a writing star overnight. Her apprenticeship was a long one—spent jotting down conversations overheard in restaurants such as Ma Maison and at parties where would-be starlets sit around in jacuzzis to wait for the best offer and where guests are served cocaine on silver platters.

No, Collins was not a prodigy, writing her first novel as soon as she was kicked out of school. She didn't write it until she was twenty-five and she still gets her material the same way, listening in on conversations or making the most of the latest gossip her friends keep her posted on by phone. If she ever wrote a nonfiction book about Hollywood, she says, no one would believe it. That's because it would have to include such stories as the one told her by the son of a famous movie star, who learned about sex looking out his bedroom window, watching his parents and their guests play "change partners" at a poolside party.

So, commercial as her novels may seem, the truth is that commerce is secondary. She has discovered a way to write tellingly about what she knows best and is most interested in—and tell it the only way it can be told fully—in fiction.

Jackie Collins is a true successor to Jacqueline Susann, author of guess-who celebrity fiction such as *The Valley of the Dolls*. About Susann, one of her publishers once told me he thought her books succeeded because, "My wife says reading them is like listening in on a party line." Jackie Collins has added sight to sound.

11.

Writing About What You Know

1. FROM BOOKKEEPER TO NOVELIST:
Steven Linakis, author of *In the Spring the War Ended*

"Readers of Catch-22 *may find this a superior novel."*
Eliot Fremont-Smith, The New York Times

"And it's a powerful enough book to cause much more of an agonizing reappraisal of our war effort than that earlier conversation piece, The Caine Mutiny, *which by comparison reads like, and has the effect of, a polite literary exercise."*
Samuel I. Bellman, Los Angeles Times

"As important as any novel I've read about the way it was in World War II."
Lester Goran, Chicago Tribune

"Makes Norman Mailer sound like Louisa May Alcott."
Albuquerque Tribune

"Best first novel of the season."

Richard Kluger

With the proceeds earned by his first novel, Steven Linakis, graduate of Hell's Kitchen, school dropout, and self-taught bookkeeper for a hardware firm, bought, among other things, a $6,000 Yamaha nine-foot concert grand piano with genuine ivory keys; a $15,000 stereo system which included Bozac concert grand speakers and Marantz-9 amplifiers; a four-bedroom ranch house on an acre of Long Island, complete with lawn sprinkler system; two new cars; and a mink coat and other furs and clothes for his wife.

How did Steven Linakis (pronounced "Lynn KNOCK iss") come to write such a money-making work the first time out? By living it first during and after World War II, then brooding on it for fifteen years, and finally, being goaded and pushed by his enterprising and talent-nurturing aunt into actually getting started.

I remember my first meeting with Linakis well. It was in the summer of 1963 and I was a beginning literary agent, working out of my apartment on East 72nd Street in New York. The telephone rang. An imperious voice trumpeted, "Os-kar! This is Madame Callas. My nephew is writing a novel. I have arranged for him to bring his work to you on Monday afternoon at 2. Goodbye!" Bang went the telephone. I didn't know how to reach her to call her back. And I had to think that perhaps I should look over her nephew's novel. After all, Evangelia Callas had already shepherded the operatic talent of two daughters, one of them Maria Callas.

Steven Linakis was delivered into the world in 1923 by a midwife at Bellevue Hospital in New York City. When he was five, his father and mother separated, and he didn't see his father again for more than fifteen years. His mother supported them by beading dresses—artistic but laborious work. Much of his childhood was spent at 434 West. "Fifty-Toid" Street, as his Irish streetmates used to say.

The streets of this part of New York, called Hell's Kitchen, were a hard school. Most of his male contemporaries who made it to adult life went to prison, except for a few who went into the Army. Young Steven managed to stay clear of the law. Some of the time he lived with his aunt, Evangelia Callas, and played games with her daughters, Maria and Jackie. In his fourth book, *Diva, The Life and Death of Maria Callas,* he wrote that living with the young Maria Callas had its hazards:

I seriously doubt that Maria knew or sensed that her mother had preferred to have a boy when she was born. She did believe herself to be a fat, ugly duckling, and thought that Jackie was preferred over her, which may have been why she was so assertive, precocious, competitive, and even a bit of a tomboy.

Once when we were both about twelve years old, Maria said it was her turn on roller skates. I made the mistake of telling her it was my turn. She knocked me over, yanking the skates right off my feet. The corner of my mouth was split open and later I had to have three stitches. She wasn't in the least sorry. It had been my own fault. It had been her turn.

Another time, I had fallen off a backyard fence. She let me lay there and wouldn't do anything, although I knew my arm was broken. I had to promise not to say it was her fault. I would have promised her anything, and I had to swear it before she went to get her mother.

After grade school, Steven attended Chelsea Vocational High School until he was seventeen. In retrospect, he regards only one day of his high school career as valuable—that was a day when a school teacher "rapped about life." He then went to, and dropped out of, the High School for Aviation Training, on Manhattan's east side, where he received training in the workings of "obsolete 600 horsepower Consolidated engines."

After leaving school, trying to do some writing ("Toilet seat writing: as long as no one knocked on the door") and holding down manual labor jobs outside New York City, he was drafted into the Army during World War II when he was nineteen.

It was during his sojourn in the U.S. Army and its aftermath that he gained the bookworthy experiences that many years later led to this conversation with his aunt:

"Is it a nice love story?"

"Don't know if you can call World War II a love story," I said.

She was very interested and whenever she called after that she would ask how the book was progressing.

"Oh, it's coming fine," I would say. "Keeps me awfully busy." From the sound of it I had roughed out a 500-page manuscript. I got quite good at talking about the book, when I hadn't committed even a single word to paper.

After basic training in the Army, Steven Linakis was sent to the Firth of Clyde in Scotland, then to the south of England, near Bournemouth.

On D-Day, he was part of the invasion of France, landing at 6:15 A.M. on Omaha Beach, "Dog Red," as part of the First Division, 16th Infantry. Describing his experience, he said, "Parts of people were all over you from explosions. I thought I was wounded—was in a state of shock. I think some of our own stuff was hitting us. Our planes bombed three miles inland. The German defenders were just a home guard unit—their first line outfit was on maneuvers. We were stuck on the beach a long time anyway."

Then, from June until September, he and his outfit "walked, crawled and drove across France—I never got laid once." They reached Belgium September 7, and he believes his unit was the first to invade Germany.

At the battle of Hurtgen Forest ("Statswald was the actual name of the woods," he remembers), his unit had 70 percent casualties. The protagonist of *In the Spring the War Ended*, Nicholas Leonidas, remembers Hurtgen in a flashback:

. . .when I heard that patient screaming, then those hard cracks of lightning, and Johnny talking about the Hurtgen, in my mind I'd been back to the last assault on the Hurtgen after the kraut had finished us. Then it hadn't been that patient screaming, but Lt. Miller and that was after we'd been lost and running, and the tall fir trees were all down, shattered and splintered white. The kraut mail had kept coming in and all the forest exploded behind us, yellow and red, and everything stank of high explosives and the dead.

We'd made it to the clearing all right when they hit us again. Only it wasn't the kraut this time. Our own heavy mortar was falling in a tight pattern, spreading phosphorus, white and hissing. It hit me like a hot iron, scalding. Then Miller screamed and we both were screaming.

Miller tried to stand on his knees after he'd been hit. I rolled in the mud, while Miller still screamed, and then the mortaring just stopped. Then you really heard him. All of him smoking, his face blistering, and him screaming, and his eyes trying to see. I tried to push him down into the mud. He jerked away from me. Going on one knee and then the other, he kept trying to get up, screaming all the time. I'd never heard a man scream like that.

I had to sit on him to work the morphine. I tried his, but it was too shaky. The pain shriveled me and I broke the needle. Then I tried mine. I got it into him all right, but it didn't do any good. I yelled for the medics. There weren't any medics. A squad of infantry came through. They got us to battalion aid. All the time Lieutenant Miller was screaming that they should shoot him. He had the stink of a burned tire. He was blind all right and his face was black with red blisters. It took several medics to hold him down and cut his clothes off.

A medic said to me "Are you hit?" I said I didn't know.

"Wrap him up," said another. "He's going into shock."

"He is like hell," said the first.

"Are you all right?" asked another. I said I didn't know.

On the floor, somebody pulled the heavy cartridge belt and webbing away and yanked off my coat. Somebody else was cutting away the field jacket and pants.

"Look at that," said the first medic. "Like a million cigarette holes, right down to his longjohns. The mud cut off the oxygen."

Steven Linakis was sent from a field hospital to a base hospital, and after he had recovered partially from his wounds, on Armistice Day—the day commemorating the end of World War I—1944, he went AWOL, personally ending his own participation in combat in World War II.

Initially, wandering around in rear areas, he was horrified and furious at seeing five-gallon jerricans of gasoline being sold to the black market, while battlefield vehicles were stalled for lack of fuel.

But as he gained experience in hiding out and adopting disguises, he began to participate in the black market himself to finance his fugitive life. He stole and sold trucks, jeeps, coffee, shoes, parts. He took part in a scam involving confiscation of food stamps worth millions and ended up with $5,000. He stole parachutes from airports—from B-56s, B-50s—and found that stealing from American planes at British-protected bases was easiest, as the British guards didn't seem, he thought, to care what happened so long as their own planes were left alone. A parachute could be sold, for its silk, for from five thousand to fourteen thousand Belgian francs, then worth forty-four to the dollar.

He was apprehended at least a dozen times by the M.P.'s, and escaped—once from Mannheim prison, a medieval fortress complete with moat. Of the fifteen who made the breakout attempt with him, seven were killed. He was in Paris Detention Barracks, in prison garb—maroon O.D.'s and yellow helmet liner. He was severely beaten by M.P.'s several times, and the atrocities he later described in his novel were either experienced or witnessed. He says the conditions in the prisons were worse than those of "the real war."

In retrospect he says that "criminality is very strange—you can justify anything."

For a year, he lived this life on the run, behind the lines in France and Belgium, from November, 1944 to November, 1945. When he was caught at Liege, after becoming one of the most wanted men in Europe, a whole M.P. platoon was sent to escort him, manacled hand and foot, to prison. For thirty days, he was kept in solitary confinement, handcuffed, at a site near Waterloo. The M.P.'s who caught him were given, he heard, ninety-day furloughs as rewards—rewards, he believes, sanctioned by orders from General Eisenhower.

At his trial on a general courts-martial procedure, on Valentine's Day, 1946, Linakis was "charged with every military offense in the book, except rape and treason—including murder, which I never committed."

He felt lucky with his sentence of twelve years in prison. He knew some sentenced to twenty years for being AWOL for two months. While at Paris Detention Barracks, he had seen Private Eddie Slovik escorted out on the way to being shot for desertion under fire. Linakis attended his own trial shackled hand and foot, and guarded by two M.P.'s armed with Thompson sub-machine guns.

In the Spring the War Ended is a fictionalized, picaresque, but often true account of his adventures (and things he saw and learned) while AWOL, coupled with flashbacks of actual battle experiences. This fact was unknown to me when I was the book's original agent, and to his publishers—he only revealed it in an interview with a UPI reporter well after the book was published.

What were the changes that transformed Steven Linakis from a twenty-one-year-old AWOL soldier, sentenced to twelve years in prison, to a novelist praised by major media, published in eight countries?

The first of these changes came about in Lewisburg Federal Penitentiary, in Lewisburg, Pennsylvania. That's when, on Friday the 13th of September, 1946, Linakis and two hundred other general military prisoners arrived in New York on a "Liberty" ship after a sixteen-day trip from Hamburg. It was the first time he had seen the

U.S. in more than three years. The prisoners were taken to Ft. Hamilton, and Linakis was given a dishonorable discharge from the Army. All his decorations were removed from his record: the Silver Star, three Purple Hearts, four Battle Stars, and the Arrowhead for D-Day.

Guarded by a line of M.P.'s with machine guns, they were escorted to Lewisburg and turned over to the prison authorities.

Lewisburg seemed a paradise after what they had been through. When the prisoners arrived, its great hall of a dining room had the melody "Claire de Lune" playing over loudspeakers. They were given plates, and the plates were piled high with spaghetti. "Take all you want," they were told.

"We ate like animals," Steven Linakis recalls.

In Lewisburg, he met some notable inmates: the Lustig brothers, of Longchamps, serving time for tax evasion; Steve Menna and other members of organized crime (it was at Lewisburg that he first heard the then-code word, "Family," to refer to those in organized crime), and Serge Rubinstein, a Wall Street financier in for draft dodging, whom he protected from prison fights.

After six months of depression and inaction came the second change. He decided to try to use his time in prison to make something of himself, and began to read. Before going to prison, his reading tastes ran to adventure stories, such as those published in *Airways* magazine. Now he tackled *Studs Lonigan*, the three volumes by James T. Farrell; the works of Steinbeck, Hemingway, and most impressive to him, the work of John Dos Passos—*Three Soldiers, The U.S.A.* He did not like Hemingway's work at first, but came to appreciate it after he began to write himself.

The third change he owed to public-spirited university people. He studied with a group of tutors from Bucknell, who came to the prison. Steven took classes in writing from an English major. His early efforts, which he submitted to magazines, were rejected. But he got detailed responses, mostly encouraging. Actually, he was not himself convinced he was a writer, because what he was reading was so much better than what he wrote. He initially chose subjects far afield from prison, or what he had experienced; for example, he wrote a story about India, based on a *Time* magazine article. When you are in prison, he says, you want to escape by writing about faraway things.

But occasionally he wrote about the war, and some of his work was published in the prison magazine, *Periscope*. He had a run-in with an associate warden about his war stories. The warden said, "Don't write about the horrible things in war."

"I wrote reams," he says, "and still have a 300-page handwritten manuscript I wrote then." His own characterization of his writing at that time is that "the description was good but the dialogue was wooden." He also began to play the piano—two rooms at Lewisburg had uprights, with another piano in the auditorium—though he had "two bum fingers from shrapnel."

By the time Linakis left prison, his life had new meaning through a "marvelous concentration of learning."

He was paroled from Lewisburg and returned to New York. When he visited West 53rd Street, he was "amused at how small and dirty it all was—the five room railroad flat." He got a job in a zipper factory, and rose to foreman. He didn't like factory work, and sold vacuum cleaners for six months, was a foreman at a plastics factory, and a deliveryman for the David Schumacher company. He met and courted his first wife, and was humiliated when he had to take her to meet his parole officer to get permission to get married. They were married in 1951, and nine years later, with no children, were divorced.

During this time he stopped writing, and began to study the piano, taking five years of formal instruction at the Greenwich School of Music. I believe his study of music is another change that helped him develop as a novelist. In many instances talents don't seem to come singly, but are many and varied in creative people. In Linakis's case, he is a professional writer, quite a good piano player, and has still another talent I discovered in an embarrassing way when I visited him at his Long Island ranch house after the success of his first novel.

Soon after I arrived, I became increasingly aware of a beautiful painting on the wall of his living room. As I had been a professional painter for fifteen years before going into the book business, and had particularly admired the work of Vincent van Gogh, I became very nervous as I realized that what I saw before me was a *painting*, not a reproduction. The brush and palette knife strokes were those of van Gogh. The size of the painting was exactly right. It *was* a van Gogh! I knew by then of Linakis's criminal record and his prison sentence. I became very nervous. He had always been scrupulously honest with me, and I also knew that at his job as a bookkeeper for Mutual Electricity and Machine Co. he had been trusted to make the company's bank deposits and withdrawals. But this was a *real* van Gogh!

Trying to keep calm, I said, "That is a very fine van Gogh you have there."

He replied, "Yes, I got it from the Metropolitan."

That was where I had seen it!

"How did you get it out?" I ventured.

"Oh, I stole it," he replied.

"How?" I asked, my worst fears confirmed.

"A little bit at a time," he replied. "They wouldn't let me copy it in the museum same size, so I went and examined a little part of it each time, and came home and duplicated it on a same size canvas."

I believe that Linakis developed his extraordinary total recall—a skill that helps him write excellent dialogue (and that helped him copy the van Gogh exactly) partly through his musical training.

While he was still a bookkeeper, he noticed a newspaper story about his aunt, Evangelia Callas, being employed to help in a store that had been newly opened by the Gabors, and got back in touch with her. She was then writing her own memoirs, published as *My Daughter Maria Callas* in 1960, with the help of a ghost writer.

I was destined to meet Linakis through Madame Callas. As a salesman for her publisher, I was assisting with her book's publicity. We liked each other immediately, though I have to admit I was a little intimidated by her. She was a natural matchmaker, and when she learned that I was married, she was somewhat thwarted as to how she could return the hard effort I was putting into making her book a success. But as I wrote earlier, she finally did match me, when I became an agent, with her writer-nephew Steven.

As Linakis records it with light and satirical pizazz in *Diva:*

> One afternoon, she called and said she had marvelous news. A marvelous man, a marvelous friend of hers, was extremely interested in my book. I caught the name of Oscar Collier, but I wasn't sure whether he was a publisher or a literary agent. She told me to join her on the East Seventies that Monday afternoon to meet him, and, of course, to bring the manuscript.
>
> Here it was a Friday. I was hung. I'm sure Litza told him I had a 500-page manuscript that was sheer genius. I couldn't very well go empty-handed. So over the weekend I typed out twenty-six pages, which weren't half bad, but I didn't think they were all that good either. Still, it came easily enough. Maria had her traumas. I had mine: World War II.
>
> I suppose I was curious about this Collier. He turned out to

be a literary agent who, very impressively, was handling people like James T. Farrell. Collier was tall and . . . soft-spoken. He gushed a bit when he greeted my aunt, but he didn't seem all that interested when I was introduced to him. I could just imagine what was going through his mind. Every aunt considers her nephew talented, and Collier was going to have to go through that bore. I was amused by it all.

Collier was a little cold when he asked me how much MS I had.

"What?" I asked.

"Manuscript," he said curtly.

"Oh," I said. "I've roughed out about five hundred. But I only brought a sample, mainly not to waste your time and to see whether or not I had it."

He took my address and phone number, saying he would get back to me as soon as he read it. Then he was happily talking to Litza again.

Before I ever got home, Collier had called. When I returned his call, the first thing he said to me was, "How much more of this do you have?"

"Why?"

"It's not bad. Quite good, in fact. If the rest is like this, I can sell it tomorrow."

"You kidding me?"

He wasn't in the business of kidding anyone, and he wanted to know when he could see the rest of the MS, amending that by saying, "Manuscript."

The hell of it was that out of a downright lie that grew, I became an author, a rather perverse way to contributing oneself to literature.

So the fourth change that occurred in Linakis's life is that he was pushed by a nurturing family member into realizing one of his dreams. I was sorry to learn, from Steven Linakis, that his flamboyant, fascinating "Litza" died in Greece in August, 1982, at age eighty. We should all be lucky enough to have such a relative!

At the end of the phone call Linakis described above, he told me that he needed time to polish his manuscript, and that he would be back in touch with me in a few months.

He began to get up at 2:30 or 3:30 in the morning and write until 6:30 a.m. He commuted to work for an hour and a half, worked eight hours, and commuted home for another hour and a half. He participated in family life with his second wife and children somehow while writing more on weekends. Altogether, it took him fourteen months to write a seven-hundred-page manuscript, using a space-and-a-half between lines. The 315,000-word novel started with VE Day, and ended as the protagonist, Nick Leonidas, was being taken from Brussels to be shipped back to prison in the U.S.

When it was partly finished, he showed me a sizable portion, together with a terribly written outline of the rest, and I began to show it to publishers: Pocket Books, Scribner's, Viking, Knopf. At Knopf, Ashbel Green replied that it really was a Putnam's book.

I recommended that Linakis have it read and criticized by a freelance editor, Darrell Husted, who gave him a report and analysis. The comments made by the editors who saw the novel, and by Darrell Husted, were probably the fifth change that helped him become a published novelist—he proved willing and able to take professional advice.

I submitted the manuscript to Peter Israel, then editor-in-chief of G.P. Putnam's Sons, after having described Linakis to him at lunch. Israel rejected it, sending a long, well-thought-out letter of criticism explaining why he was rejecting it.

Linakis enrolled himself in a class Israel was holding at Putnam's, for a $75 fee, in order to get to know more about the editor's ideas. He gained confidence in Peter Israel from the sessions, and began to feel that Israel was the one person he needed. So he started a correspondence, replying point by point to the criticisms Israel had made in his rejection letter. He didn't just take no for an answer.

After some back and forth, his new agent, James Seligmann, to whom I had sent him after closing my agency to take a job as head of a small general trade book publisher, negotiated a contract with G.P. Putnam's Sons. The contract was for a $2,500 advance against royalties, payable $500 on signing, $1,000 on completion of a first draft, and $1,000 on acceptance of a final draft.

He submitted small sections of the novel to Israel through his agent as they were completed. He describes Israel's editing as "do-it-yourself editing," though Israel did correct his grammar. There would be indications of "awk" (awkward, section to be rewritten), "cut?" (suggestion to delete), and "Let's talk" (leading to discussions of what Linakis had meant to say, and was it necessary and desirable?). He had worked now more than fourteen months on the novel, the last six with Peter Israel. With the advance money, he bought furniture, and a color TV.

The manuscript was slimmed down from seven hundred 450-word pages to 376 manuscript pages—which came out as 346 book pages. "When it comes to shortening," Linakis says, "Hemingway is a good teacher." Steve's hardest work was on the dialogue. He began to listen closely to what people were saying and how they said it—their cadence. The dialogue, he says, must reflect your feeling, plus what the character is saying. It is necessary to interpret, rather than quote. "You have to make your characters smarter or dumber than life; you have to feel it, and know when it is good by the sense and flavor. Musical training helps." At times his drafts got too Hemingway-esque, and then he drew on his observations of how Steinbeck and Dos Passos wrote.

Linakis believes that much of the power of his novel came from his anger. But he couldn't write it while angry. He had to *recall* his anger coolly, analytically, and think of what really happened, from both sides. Above all, he says, the novelist must read, and study how other writers achieved effects like the ones he wants.

Peter Israel recommended the novel to movie producers and foreign publishers, even though Putnam's, as is usual in agented contracts, didn't control those rights. James Seligmann took on a co-agent to help him handle movie rights, and used his coagents abroad to negotiate foreign rights contracts. Peter Israel generated interest in others by calling the book "one of the best of the three thousand first novels that have crossed my desk."

Putnam's auctioned paperback reprint rights, and Dell won at $49,500. Book clubs turned down the novel because of the strong language. *Man Magazine* ran a piece of it as a first-serial-rights sale. Foreign editions were published in France, Holland, Germany, England (hard and soft cover), Sweden, Denmark, Spain, and Japan. It was a best seller in Holland, and earned royalties well beyond its advance.

Larry Turman, producer of *The Graduate*, optioned movie rights, with $35,000 paid on the option, vs. $200,000 purchase price. Though the film was never made, Linakis realized over $75,000 in option money and a settlement, and earned $500 a week plus expenses for quite a period when Turman brought him out to Hollywood to try to write a new screenplay after the one by William Goldman didn't fly. Linakis didn't care for Goldman's version of his novel. He said, "I felt like a bird came into my house, took everything I owned, then shit on my grand piano." Turman warned Linakis that "Doing a screenplay of your own novel is more painful than doing an appendectomy on yourself."

Peter Israel left Putnam's shortly after *In the Spring the War Ended* was published. (He is now back at Putnam's as president of The Putnam Publishing Group, a combine of G.P. Putnam's Sons, Coward-McCann, Berkley, Ace, Charter, Jove, Perigee, Tempo, Grosset & Dunlap, Platt & Munk, and various other divisions and imprints, and no longer edits, he told me.) Putnam's took out a full page ad in *The New York Times Book Review* and a small ad in the daily *Times* for the book. It received many glorious reviews, except for severe pannings in *Time* and *Library Journal*. Hard-cover sales were in the six to seven thousand range. The Dell paperback reprint was moderately successful, and several years later, Popular Library reprinted it in still another edition. Altogether, he estimates he made over $200,000 in 1960s money from his first novel.

Steven Linakis offered some reflections on writing: "Write about what you know—cheat from it, but use it as a base. You must hit a nerve for the best of writing.

"What is a novel? A piece of yourself—but just a piece—not the whole picture. A novel is the tip of the iceberg. Never give it all away.

"A story must have structure. If you find repetition in your writing, cut it away, but leave some if it works. Put it all in at first, then trim it away. You can't see the whole story until the whole thing is written—then you can see the structure. Put it away to cool, then see what you have got.

"Start with what's interesting to you—others will believe your story better if you are interested in your material.

"Fiction is more truthful than nonfiction. Nonfiction has trouble with lawyers. Fiction is nonfiction, nonfiction is fiction today.

"Today's publishers have a fashion industry mentality. The old Scribner's-Maxwell Perkins world doesn't exist any longer. Books are pieces of goods that will sell. Nobody cares about art anymore—but it sneaks in once in a while anyway.

"Procrastination and delay are castrating.

"Agents did help me, but most are cold bastards and not very smart.

"The effect of my success was to turn my life topsy-turvy and I have some regrets. It caused family problems. Writing is a lonely, unsure existence. Writing is the easy part, though—the problems you have to deal with are the reviewers and the industry. I have been dissuaded from a number of books. But if you stick to it, it can work."

Beginning novelists can learn many lessons from the experiences of Steven Linakis. To me, the actions that contributed most to his success were: He acquired a marvelous concentration of learning through reading good novelists. He developed his ear and memory by studying music. He allowed himself to be pushed into action by a nurturing, interested person. He proved willing and able to take professional advice. And he didn't take no for an answer—probably the most important lesson any budding creative person can learn.

2. FROM SPOOK TO SPY NOVELIST:
George O'Toole, author of *An Agent on the Other Side*

George O'Toole writes about the CIA with authority: he served .as an intelligence officer in that organization for three years before leaving to devote full time to writing. He is an expert on the use of computers in intelligence work. His other interests include parapsychology, which has long absorbed him; cryptography (he has invented a cryptographic device); and flying light aircraft. "But," he says, "some of my most interesting accomplishments are, unfortunately, classified.

Flap copy from the hard cover edition

George O'Toole, who later changed his writer's name to "G.J.A. O'Toole," had the opposite task as a novelist from that of Steven Linakis. Linakis wrote a picaresque autobiographical novel which was a rearrangement and development of his direct experiences. He had to select from those experiences, enhance them in a true-to-life but powerful way, and arrange them into a plot.

O'Toole, who had been an intelligence officer for the Central Intelligence Agency for a few years of his career, had signed, casually, when he joined, a form agreeing for all time to show the Agency anything he wrote that might even remotely be about the CIA or things he had learned while working there, and not to include materials the CIA forbade.

Up to the time his first novel was published, 1973, there had been no court case testing this agreement, and he had actually forgotten he had signed it. Nevertheless, since his novel was about a fictitious CIA operation, he decided he had better show it to the Agency, to make sure he had not inadvertently revealed material the CIA wanted to keep secret. This decision turned out to be a good idea, because later, in a court case on *The CIA and the Cult of Intelligence*, by Victor Marchetti, the courts affirmed that the pledge he, Marchetti, and others had signed was enforceable by law.

He sent his manuscript to the Agency through a friend who was still working there, and it came back without any requests for changes or deletions, though, he said, "I was intrigued by the paper-clips that had been left attached to certain pages."

So George O'Toole's task was to write a novel that wasn't true in any way, shape, or form—a work that was truly fiction, and contained only such facts about the CIA and the "spook" world as were known from previously published material—yet still would seem to an outsider true to life and very revealing of inside information.

In an "Author's Note" inserted at the end of the novel, he says, "*An Agent on the Other Side* is a lie. Lying, however, like most human endeavors, can be done either poorly or well. Inspector Spinka gives us his two criteria for a good lie: it must contain many elements which are true, and it must include something so improbable that it seems it could not have been invented. In that sense, I have tried to make the story a good lie." However, he concludes this three-page author's note by adding, "Things, after all, are often not what they seem to be," and thereby leaves the reader freshly tantalized. Is there truth, after all, in the novel? This is a proper final note.

O'Toole got the idea for his novel in 1970, when he read a Soviet paper on parapsychology that said the Reds encouraged psychic research. He began to wonder how the psychic could be used in an espionage operation—to hoodwink the other side.

He had also become interested in the situation in Czechoslovakia when, after ending his CIA service, he published a paper in *Computers and Automation* that had mentioned, in his biographical sketch at the end, that he had been with the CIA. He received a letter and a request for a reprint from a Czech correspondent, and later an invitation to visit Czechoslovakia. From friends he learned that the person who wrote to him was working for Czech or Soviet intelligence agencies, so he decided to decline the invitation.

Because of these events, he began to follow the news about Czechoslovakia, and studied the Soviet invasion of that country with close attention. The invasion happened during the period he would have been there had he accepted the invitation.

He wove these two themes into his novel, looking around for possible characters. At the time, he was working for a company that made educational films, so he chose a person from that industry for his protagonist. He then devised characters based loosely on people he had met in the CIA, being careful that the resemblances to real people were not close enough to be "actionable." He based his main female character, a medium who received messages from "the other side," on his reading about a famous woman medium, altered in personality and appearance to fit into his developing novel.

He selected the idea of the CIA becoming involved with mediums as something highly unlikely to have actually happened—but since it was known that the Soviets were experimenting with parapsychology, the idea was credible enough to use in a thriller. Here, from the book jacket, is his publisher's description of the novel:

> A superthriller, involving the CIA, international intrigue, the use of psychic power for conveying messages from a dead man.
>
> In the summer of 1968, on the eve of the Soviet invasion of Czechoslovakia, a lovely young woman with psychic powers approaches the CIA and claims to be in touch with the spirit of a dead Russian spy. As evidence she offers the detailed secret Soviet invasion plans.
>
> But there's a hitch. The CIA learns that another medium in Prague, a celebrated one, has been selling identical information to West Germany. And it could only have come from the same dead spy! To unravel this strange web, the CIA taps John Sorel, a young filmmaker, who starts his investigation under cover of his work in films. Overnight he finds himself involved in a plot complicated by internal, doubledealing double agents, murder, and strange occurrences in the world of the occult on both sides of the Atlantic, including a spine-chilling seance in a Bohemian castle.
>
> The inside view of the CIA at work in this exciting tale is fascinating and perhaps only partially fictional.

To write this first novel, George O'Toole took a six-month leave of absence from his work, and lived on accumulated savings. After finishing it, he queried six publishers, writing a long—"too long," he says now—letter addressed to the "Editor-in-Chief." The novel was rejected by Burroughs Mitchell at Scribner's, Hal Scharlett at Doubleday, John Willey at William Morrow, William Targ at Putnam's, and editors at Walker & Co. and Dutton.

After reading an article in a writer's magazine on how unsolicited manuscripts are only published "once in a while," he decided he must find an agent. He secured the list of agents who are members of the Society of Authors' Representatives (SAR), and began to read *Publishers Weekly*. In Paul Nathan's *PW* column on rights and permissions, he read that Seligmann & Collier had handled the first novel—

Don't Embarrass the Bureau—of former FBI agent Bernard F. Conners. O'Toole wrote an inquiry letter to James F. Seligmann. Seligmann passed this letter on to me, as a person more interested in such novels. I wrote away and sent for it, liked it, and arranged to secure five copies for a multiple submission.

Within two weeks, while George O'Toole was attending the Bread Loaf Writer's Conference, Eleanor Rawson of David McKay called and made an offer, which I recommended O'Toole accept. The contract provided that $1,000 would be paid on signing, and since McKay wanted him to work more on the novel, $1,000 on acceptance of one-half the manuscript, and $1,000 on acceptance of the whole work—$3,000 total as an "advance against all earnings." He became something of a hero at Bread Loaf!

One of the pleasures of "writing about what you know" is putting into your novel satirical passages about the world you are describing. O'Toole included in the novel a couple of pages of very funny material about a CIA agent who was a failure, but because of the situation, was pushed on through various stages of his training anyway. He kept failing "Breaking and Entering."

> He had to do that part of the course several times, and became a familiar figure in the Baltimore lockup. Finally, because he was an embarrassment to all concerned, he was permitted to graduate on the strength of a forced entry into a grain warehouse in a tiny Virginia hamlet, and the successful evasion of the town's eighty-year-old constable.
>
> His training record was not scrutinized too closely because a big to-do then being planned had created a great demand for case officers. After a brief vacation he was flown to a secret base in Guatemala to assist in the training of a group of Cuban refugees to land on the southern coast of Cuba. When the invasion was finally launched, Hagarty had the task of coordinating the air support over the Bay of Pigs. . . .

O'Toole's editor called me to complain about the material involving this comic character, Hagarty, and O'Toole's stubborn support of it. I have to admit I defended it vigorously, saying, "After all, where else can you learn about the air support officer at the Bay of Pigs?" McKay left the material in.

The book had only modest sales, and O'Toole says it was not very widely distributed. It received very few reviews. But Dell reprinted it in a paperback edition, and Arthur Barker Ltd. published it in England. It was translated into Italian and published in Italy by Mondadori. Through Seligmann & Collier's dramatic rights coagent, Warren Bayless, a modest movie option was negotiated with screenwriter Joseph Boyd, who paid $1,875 for nine months' option time. Boyd extended the option nine months more for $1,875 additional, after which it lapsed with no movie made and the $25,000 purchase price unpaid.

Altogether, George O'Toole made about $10,000 for six months' work, which was acceptable in 1970s dollars—he had been making about $22,000 a year at other work. And of course the book could make more money still, through new reprints, or a new movie option.

Though he received somewhat higher advances and earnings from his subsequent books: *The Assassination Tapes* (nonfiction), *The Private Sector* (nonfiction), *The Cosgrove Report*, a highly acclaimed novel, *Poor Richard's Game*, a historical novel about spying during the Revolutionary War period, and *The Spanish War*, a history, those later books took much more time to write, and O'Toole believes that on a per-hour basis, and allowing for inflation, his compensation rate for writing has remained pretty constant.

Still, one has to wonder, how did G.J.A. O'Toole, computer expert, former naval air cadet, MENSA member, cryptographer, and one-time CIA intelligence officer, turn to writing for a career?

What has probably made him a professional writer, though he sometimes threatens to give up the occupation, is the same force that made him leave the CIA: "There were no policy differences—I had exhausted the possibilities of my job. I came in to do certain things, and got them done. I didn't want to stay and just mind the store." Small wonder. He is an exceptionally bright person. When he took an intelligence test so he could join MENSA, he was rated as having an I.Q. in the top .001 percent. He has sought work that is interesting enough to stick with, and to date has found it in being a writer.

About writing, he says, "Writing about what you know is knowing about what you write." He likes to write in the morning, and says he works well for a short period of time after sleeping. When he lacks inspiration, he takes a nap. During periods when he wants to work constantly day and night, he alternately writes and naps.

About the necessity of research, even when writing fiction, he says, "I can't expect the reader to suspend disbelief when I can't suspend my own disbelief." Sometimes when he writes he hears "a voice inside speaking it."

12.

Collaborating with an Expert

Nan F. Salerno, author of *Shaman's Daughter*, in collaboration with Professor Rosamond M. Vanderburgh

Summary Report

Title:	Shaman's Daughter
Submissions:	*Twenty-eight by an agent, all rejected* *One by Nan F. Salerno, as arranged by a friend, to Prentice-Hall*
Advance royalty:	*$10,000*
Hard cover sales:	*20,000+ copies*
Reprint rights:	*Dell Books, $137,500 guarantee equally divided between authors and publisher. Used as a Dell lead title, 800,000 first printing.*
Book clubs:	*Book-of-the-Month Club alternate selection; selection of Reader's Digest Condensed Books of Canada*

161

| Foreign rights: | French hard and soft cover editions, Danish edition, serialized in Norwegian magazine |
| Author's earnings: | About $74,000, split 50-50 between the authors |

It all seemed to happen so naturally. A friend called me, said a friend of his had written a good novel; I read it and loved it, recommended it for publication, and everybody else in the publishing house I worked for loved it, too. We did publish it, and it succeeded. Even the title, *Shaman's Daughter*, came from the authors, and nobody even thought of suggesting another.

And listening to Nan Salerno's account of how *Shaman's Daughter* came to be written as a collaboration between her, a writer, and Professor Rosamond M. Vanderburgh, an anthropologist, the collaboration seemed to happen very naturally too. Mrs. Salerno's daughter, Michele, was attending the University of Toronto, and was fascinated by the accounts of Ojibwa Indian life told in Professor Vanderburgh's anthropology lectures. Michele related the stories to her mother and said they ought to be in a book for the general public.

Nan Salerno wanted to write a children's book, and went to see Professor Vanderburgh to arrange to use her material.

But Professor Vanderburgh said, "No, no, that's already been done. What is needed is a novel about the everyday life of Indian women."

So before the visit was over, Nan Salerno and Rosamond Vanderburgh agreed to collaborate on such a novel. They got together occasionally, and wrote and telephoned each other with new ideas and progress reports. Over a two-year period of intermittent work, they produced the novel. Together they constructed the basic plot. Mrs. Salerno did the writing. Professor Vanderburgh supplied information to be woven into the story, sometimes vetoing ideas, incidents, or plot twists Mrs. Salerno added that were not appropriate or authentically representative of the real lives of Indian women of the Ojibwa groups she had lived with and studied.

It's a heart-warming story of two nice people getting together and putting together a good book which naturally succeeded because of its quality. Seems easy as rolling off a log, doesn't it? Quality will tell.

But when you look at the story behind the story, it takes on a greater complexity—an incredible chain of coincidences, extraordinary preparations, the most powerful qualifications, good luck, and determination in face of apparent failure. Of course, without the lyrical beauty of the novel, the coincidences would probably never have happened, so both the story, and the story behind the story, are worth study, especially by a beginning novelist who is looking for good material, and finds that such material might best be acquired through collaborating with an expert in the field.

But first, I'll deal with one of the questions I'm often asked as an editor, literary agent, and publisher: "How do you split monies earned by a collaboration? What's fair?"

Nan Salerno and Rosamond Vanderburgh never troubled themselves over that question. They just assumed from the beginning that it was an equal effort, with earnings, if any, to be split 50-50. As it turned out, their only written agreement was the publisher's contract they both signed, which provided that each would get 50 percent of the author's earnings. I say "author's earnings" because in most book contracts, the "author" is defined as all those who write a book, whether one, two, or more. The 50-50 split is the most usual and ordinary one, easiest to understand and justify when people start out together.

Problems with that arrangement arise when one partner of a collaboration comes into it with a lot of work already done, or when one partner has much more weight or commercial clout than the other. Or when, sometimes, one partner has already spent a lot of money on research or related travel. Or when the project will involve a good deal of expense (copying, typing, or retyping, for example) for one partner and not the other.

The only procedure I can suggest to those deciding on the percentage each partner will get is that each should frankly say at the outset what he or she thinks is deserved, and openly argue for her or his case.

That argument, and the stubbornness of each partner, will determine the final formula. Sometimes it will be 50-50, other times 60-40, 75-25, or an even more disproportionate division.

Another solution, appropriate for a collaboration between a proven professional writer and a person with an obviously valuable story or powerful name, is an adequate and motivating fixed fee—probably split into installments (i.e., so much down, and so much on completion of the job) for the writer, and all remaining earnings for the nonwriter. In this case the nonwriter may strike it rich, or be money out of pocket.

Sometimes it seems appropriate to have two different splits—one of advance royalties, and a second for earnings beyond the advance. I would always recommend that the terms of the collaboration be put in writing, in a plain-English contract understood by each partner, reviewed and approved by an agent or lawyer of each, and signed, even witnessed or notarized.

How did Nan Salerno come to be so well prepared to collaborate with Professor Vanderburgh, when it was the first novel she ever tried to write? Though she suspects she may have had an Indian among her ancestors, she knew little of Indian life before she started *Shaman's Daughter*. The answer may be that her life prepared her to become a novelist.

She began reading at age three. When asked what she read while growing up, she gives the same answer George Bernard Shaw gave when asked what a young girl should read: "Anything I could get my hands on." Her father was an Army ordnance expert, first as a civilian, then, during World War II, as a colonel in the U.S. Army. An only child, she was constantly with her parents, who took her with them wherever they went. If they went to dinner with friends, she was taken along, ate with the adults, and was put to bed on a couch, then awakened for refreshments at midnight before the trip home. She says, "I listened to everything and absorbed much of what was said."

As her parents moved from post to post, she traveled with them to Texas, Virginia, Florida, North Carolina, New Jersey, Indiana, Missouri, and Colorado. She attended eight different schools before she'd finished high school. Asked what she had learned from so many changes, she replied, "How many ways children can be cruel. It wasn't easy but I never regretted it." She had a sense of separateness and independence: "I never came to regard any particular place as home—I have the whole U.S.A. as my home. And I gained a strong sense of the difference of each region."

But I do not doubt that there was strain in all this change and saw a certain tightening of her lips when she talked of it. I am reminded of the report of a psychologist who studied the effects of stress on children. Under the blows of stress, he found, "Some bend and stretch, some shatter, and some resound like a bell." The strong music of *Shaman's Daughter* is, I believe, Nan Salerno's bell note, still resounding.

Nan said she sometimes attended public and sometimes Catholic schools—in the country, and in big cities. When I asked if she were a Catholic, she replied that her mother believed "attending *any* church is better than attending no church. But I came to admire Indian religion while writing *Shaman's Daughter*."

Her father finally settled down to work for a stretch of seven years in Washington, D.C. and she graduated from high school and attended art school there. She had written her first short story by the age of ten, and continued writing, while also becoming fascinated by art.

As she had gone about the country on her family's travels, she had "educated myself by looking." She was a sharp-eyed child who watched the scenery and the people wherever she went, and describes this child's study of adult interaction with environment as "the beginning of my training as a novelist." Her power of observation was further sharpened by her art training. In *Shaman's Daughter* the reader never feels lost. In fact, the sense of place and atmosphere is so powerful and all-pervasive that her way of including it is almost unnoticed (which I would call good technique). The reader can concentrate on the action because he always knows where he is, what it looks like, how it sounds and feels. Only a few times in the novel does Salerno withdraw this penumbra or fringe of integrated sensation—and when she does, she is able to achieve an out-of-time, out-of-place effect that is very impressive, as when she describes the disorientation of a long water journey.

The way Nan Salerno combines setting, sensation, and action is shown in the following passage. Supaya, the heroine of the novel, is twelve, and has been seeking a life-guiding vision for two years. This time, her grandmother tells her, she might succeed, and she has left her house early in the morning.

> Above her a bird called; another answered faintly, and she knew she must hurry to reach the hilltop before dawn. As the trees thinned out, she moved faster and was soon climbing the slope, slipping on the damp, loose stones that rattled under her steps. She felt for footholds and climbed over and around the boulders, pulling herself steadily upward. Gasping for breath, she paused and, tilting back her head, saw the rocky summit silhouetted against the paling night sky and knew she had come too far. Skidding and sliding, she scrambled to her left and down and found the small pocket hidden between the boulders. She sat down on the patch of earth, dizziness momentarily overcoming her. Her pulse throbbed, her forehead was clammy. She had eaten nothing since midday the day before, and felt an empty, nauseating fear. Perhaps she should go back. Perhaps. . . .

Notice the active verb forms of this passage: *called, answered, hurry, reach, thinned, moved, climbing, slipping, rattled, felt, climbed, pulling, gasping, paused, tilting, paling, saw, come, skidding, slipping, scrambled, found, hidden, sank, overcoming, throbbed, eaten, go.* And note at the same time how few adjectives she uses!

Nan Salerno's father asked her, while she was studying art, how she could make a living with it. She investigated the employment opportunities for an artist in Washington, D.C. and decided they were very limited, so she became an English major in college. She attended Wilson Teachers College, American University, and Catholic University in Washington, and then at the University of Wisconsin was awarded a Ph.M. degree (similar to an M.A.). She has taught at American University, the University of Colorado, University of Illinois, and Purdue—English literature, composition, the novel, Shakespeare, poetry. She did not like teaching, saying she regarded the students not as a teacher but as a mother—fascinated and curious about their development or lack of it.

While teaching at Purdue, she met fellow staffer Henry Salerno, who has been a professor of English at the State University of New York at Fredonia for the past fourteen years.

After their marriage, Nan took jobs as divergent as working in a university steno pool to part-time teaching. The Salernos had two children.

Henry Salerno, while teaching at Purdue, started a magazine to publish original plays, called *First Stage.* Nan Salerno was the editor who screened the large number of submissions from all over the world. She managed its actual publication, read proof, and maintained its subscription list. This labor of love was a heavy burden of work, and it continued until the year before she began *Shaman's Daughter.*

During those years she tried writing children's stories, none of which have been published. After *First Stage* ceased publication and her children were grown, she was ready for more writing action.

That was when fate—and daughter Michele—stepped in with an introduction to Professsor Vanderburgh.

Rosamond Moate (her maiden name) was born of a British father who had come to live in Canada, and an American mother who came from Massachusetts. Though her parents lived in the north woods of Quebec, they traveled to Massachusetts for her birth, then returned to their home in Canada. Rosamond Moate chose Canadian citizenship. Later her family moved to Toronto, and when she completed high school there, she had already decided she wanted to study other peoples' cultures.

But in the 1940s such studies were not available in Toronto, so Rosamond came to the states and entered Radcliffe College in 1944 on a scholarship, taking a concentrated course of anthropology and graduating cum laude.

After a year as a research assistant at Harvard, working with Dr. Ernest Hooten, Rosamond went to Northwestern University, where she earned her M.A., writing her thesis on the influence of southern Africans on the cultures north of the Sahara.

Then, after two years at the University of Pennsylvania, she and another graduate student planned to work toward a Ph.D. by doing field work with tribes in Morocco.

But there was trouble between Morocco and the U.S.A. at that time, and the State Department would not approve of two young, single women going there to live.

Rosamond returned to Toronto, where she met Albert Vanderburgh, a young electronics engineer, and married him. He was not enthusiastic about her undertaking foreign travel for her field work, so she looked for anthropological work nearer home.

As it happened, the Southern Ojibwa, who lived around Lake Huron in Canada, had not been studied since the 1930s. While working as a teaching assistant at the University of Toronto in 1965, she began to study them. She had previously worked two years as a curatorial assistant at the Royal Ontario Museum in the Department of Ethnology. In 1967, when the University of Toronto opened its Erindale campus, she joined its faculty, where she has been teaching since, and is an associate professor. She and her husband have two grown children.

Every year since 1965, Professor Vanderburgh has done field work among the Southern Ojibwa, and also library research on them. In addition to some fifteen scholarly publications on anthropological subjects, she has written what was originally conceived as a trade book—the biography of an Ojibwa woman, Verna Johnston, entitled *I Am Nokomis, Too.* It was published in 1977 by a Canadian firm. The book has been widely used as a text for native studies and women's studies.

She wrote it to begin to set the record straight about the lives of Indian women, a subject she believes has been neglected by other anthropologists and writers.

I asked Professor Vanderburgh how she had come so readily to accept the idea of collaborating on a novel about the life of an Indian woman.

She replied that the tradition of anthropologists expressing their knowledge in novels goes back to the turn of the century—1890, to be exact—with the publishing of Bandelier's *The Delight Makers*, a story about the Pueblo Indians of the Southwestern U.S. The novels of Dr. Carleton S. Coon are part of that tradition. What *was* new, she said, was a collaboration by an anthropologist with a lay person. Despite her scholarly credentials, Professor Vanderburgh felt she lacked fiction-writing talent, and it *is* rare for an expert in a scholarly field also to have novel-writing skill. She recommends collaboration to others.

When I further asked how she could trust Nan Salerno, who had no previous credits as a writer, with such an enterprise, she replied that she felt Nan's long work as an editor of plays, her teaching experience, and overall air of competence and sincerity were what convinced her. Once she made the decision to go ahead, she did not question it or have second thoughts.

An important principle in such a collaboration, she believes, is that the expert must not stint in offering information for the writer to study, and the writer must study and absorb everything offered.

So Nan Salerno was able to carry on her research in a deluxe manner, as a student under the tutorship of a highly qualified expert. In effect, Professor Vanderburgh gave her a personalized crash course in the anthropology of the Ojibwa Indians. She offered books, tapes, lectures, photographs, a chance to view Ojibwa objects and artifacts, and a field trip to an Ojibwa reserve.

In about two years, Nan Salerno and Rosamond Vanderburgh had written their novel, and adopted the title suggested by Nan's husband, *Shaman's Daughter*.

They gave it to a literary agent known to Henry Salerno. The agent made twenty-eight submissions with no offer resulting. When Nan Salerno learned that the book had stalled with a major publisher for a number of months while that publisher had a competing novel with similar subject matter scheduled, she withdrew it from the agent, and they mutually agreed to end their association.

Meanwhile, in Ridgewood, New Jersey, where I was then living, my wife one day took our young son, Christopher, to a story-telling session at the local library. There she met Sandra Scarry, who had brought her daughter, Sioban, to the same event. Children and mothers became acquainted and friendly, and eventually I became friends with Sandra's husband John, an assistant professor of English at Hostos College.

The role of John and Sandra Scarry in bringing *Shaman's Daughter* into print is an important one, and the world is better because of people like the Scarrys: the bustling, busy, creative people whose energy is great enough to do their own important work—both John and Sandra teach full time, and John has authored two English textbooks—and still find the time to recognize and encourage the talent of others.

When I think of the Scarrys, I am reminded of the story of a person watching ants. He observed that a few ants in each anthill were much more active than others. These active ants, which he marked with a little daub of colored powder, strayed off the regular ant-highways and nosed into everything around. They took short cuts and long cuts; they climbed blades of grass and twigs, and simply seemed to go everywhere. They discovered new sources of food, started new trails while the other, more orderly ants ploddingly stuck to established paths and food sources. In a cruel experiment, the ant-watcher removed these few active ants from several anthills. In each case, the colony slowed down and eventually died from lack of food.

If you meet people of this sort, treasure them! Be alert for them, because they will enhance your life, and may even further your career.

Nan Salerno, though discouraged by the many rejections encountered by the agent, sent the manuscript of *Shaman's Daughter* to the Scarrys to read. Sandra Scarry read it first and recommended it to her husband. John Scarry was impressed by it, and by Sandra's strong positive reaction. With Nan Salerno's permission, he asked me to read it, with the request that I recommend a new agent.

When I read the novel, I had to admit that several of the scenes made me cry, and others made me laugh with joy. I found that I really cared about what happened to its main character, Supaya, and her family and friends.

When the Salernos came from Fredonia to visit the Scarrys some time in the mid-1970s, I met them.

Nan turned out to be an attractive brunette who laughed easily, yet had a deep undercurrent of seriousness about her, so that her expression changed frequently. I asked her if, instead of sending her book to an agent, I could take it as a submission to Prentice-Hall, where I was then working as a senior editor of trade books.

She agreed. I also asked her to contact her collaborator, and to secure her agreement that Nan would be the member of the team I would work with almost exclusively. I had learned by hard experience that it's better for one member of a collaborating team to act as its spokesperson in dealing with a publisher (or agent, for that matter). Professor Vanderburgh agreed to this procedure.

What happens inside a large- or middle-sized publishing house when a solicited work is submitted to a senior editor? While each house varies, the procedures in the Trade Book Division of Prentice-Hall by which *Shaman's Daughter* was considered are fairly typical of those of larger trade publishers.

As the editor who had brought in the submission, I first told the editor-in-chief, John Kirk, that I had in hand what promised to be a pretty good first novel.

After completing a second reading, I gave the manuscript to Kirk together with a memorandum recommending it, but saying it needed work. I asked Kirk to be its second reader, as he was an experienced fiction editor with a strong interest in finding new works of merit. Had he been very busy at the time, or primarily interested in other forms of literature than novels, I would have sought other opinions instead, either in house, or from outside readers.

He read it quickly and reacted very positively, though he agreed that it needed editorial sharpening. He promised to help with the editing, and offered some good insights on points needing attention. He gave me permission to write and circulate a proposal that the company make an offer to publish the manuscript.

Using the form the company used for that purpose, I wrote up the proposal that Prentice-Hall publish the work. I described the authors' qualifications, briefly described the content of the manuscript, projected the market for the book and what readers it might appeal to, found out sales of similar books recently issued by other publishers, estimated minimum and maximum sales, and guessed at possible subsidiary rights sales.

The proposal and the manuscript were then circulated to the marketing director, the sales department, the publicity director, the head of production, and the subsidiary rights director. Each wrote comments on the proposal form—estimates of sales by the marketing director and sales department; estimates of review potential and other publicity by the publicity director; estimates by the production department of the cost of manufacturing it as a hard cover book at different levels of initial and reprint printing quantities; and estimates of likely book club, reprint rights, serial, and foreign sales by the subsidiary rights department. As I was, by then, intensely interested in the novel, I handed the proposal and manuscript personally to each person who would comment on it, and made a little speech to each praising the manuscript and urging that it be read promptly.

They all loved it! They found it good enough to read to the end, which assured me the book had broad appeal.

Armed with these positive indicators, I returned the manuscript and completed proposal form to the editor-in-chief. After conferring with the president of the division, he gave me written authorization to offer a $10,000 advance royalty to the authors, and negotiate a contract along terms we agreed on. We decided to offer a favorable contract, similar to what would be negotiated by an agent, as we hoped the authors, particularly Nan Salerno, would become significant writers, and would want to stay with our publishing house if their book succeeded.

The authors accepted the offer, and signed the contract. Part of the advance royalty was paid on signing, and the rest was to be paid when the authors completed revisions to the publisher's satisfaction.

The editor-in-chief and I made a number of editorial suggestions—none major—to tighten the narration of the story and maintain suspense in key sections. As I edited each portion of the manuscript, I sent it with a longish letter to Nan Salerno explaining the reasons for the proposed changes.

Before I began, however, I had a phone conversation with Nan that may shed some light on the editor-author relationship. I told her that an editor, in making suggestions, was not a hostile critic putting down an author, but was rather more like a friend conspiring with the author for the book's greatest possible success; also, that the author should feel free to reject any of the suggestions made, and argue freely in favor of, and thus explain to the editor, the original version, as expressions of the author's insights and intentions.

Without this understanding, it would be impossible for the editor to express his/her possible ignorance, insensitivity, and even ineptitude to the author, just as the author had exposed her views and insights, and possible failings in submitting the draft manuscript. In addition to being a very experienced reader and student of the structure and appeal of books in general, the editor is a stand-in for those who will later buy and read the book. As such, he/she treasures his/her ignorance as well as experience, because no reader has a perfect preparation for a particular book, and what confuses or fails with the editor may well confuse and fail with the ultimate consumers, the readers of the book who determine its success or failure.

The editor, usually a person who has chosen the profession out of a love of reading, is first and foremost a *reader*, a consumer of books. For a novelist to have a successful dialogue, the necessary give-and-take, with his or her editor, the novelist must first regard the editor as a reader or fan, and ignore the notion of the editor's power over the writer's business success. The relationship, to be successful, must be one between equals. Editors *must* find, and get along with, many types of authors. And unless you, the author, are interested in self-publishing—a rough road for a first novelist—you must work with an editor at a publishing house. Just remember the equation has two sides, separated by an equals sign, and you'll find it easier.

In the case of *Shaman's Daughter*, the editor-author relationship went smoothly, and Nan Salerno promptly revised the manuscript, keeping in mind the ideas expressed by me and by John Kirk, but using them in her own way—in fact, improving on our suggestions many times.

Her relationship with the book's copy editor (the editor whose job it is to correct English usage and spelling, smoke out inconsistencies and omissions, find cliches, etc.) was a little tense at times, as Salerno herself was a former editor and English instructor, but quibbles about commas were resolved, as were other small points of style. Most publishers are willing to allow a novelist more latitude of style than would be granted a nonfiction author.

When the book reached the next stage, being set in type, Prentice-Hall ordered 100 "BOM's"—page proofs of the book bound with a paper cover. These were sent to other authors, anthropologists, bookstore buyers, book clubs, paperback reprinters, and major reviewers who need plenty of advance notice of what a publisher regards as a "big book."

The mailing produced some favorable comments from other authors. Two of these comments—one from Anna Lee Waldo, author of the best seller *Sacajawea*, and one from anthropologist and author Dr. Carleton S. Coon, were selected to be printed on the back of the book's jacket.

Dwight Myers, one of Prentice-Hall's most active and influential salespeople and an expert on writings about American Indians, helped assemble the list of those to receive the bound proofs. The editorial department was delighted with his active help, as he had great influence with the other salespeople who had to distribute the book to bookstores and book jobbers. Authors are often distressed to discover that publishers have to sell their books to their own salesmen!

As the question of how to deal with a publisher's sales force is eventually faced by every published author, I will interject here some pointers on this important subject. The key principle is: Cultivate the publisher's salespeople in a friendly, positive, but not overly demanding way.

The best thing you can do for them is to provide them with information: the names of bookstore people you know, local authors or critics who admire your work, business people who might make bulk purchases of your work for special purposes, interviewers who might want to invite you to appear on radio or TV, and librarians who are your friends and supporters.

But don't push the salespeople too hard, or they will begin to duck you and stop returning your calls. Remember they have a long list of other books to sell, too. And keep in mind that they must obey the orders of their superiors about what to push. If your book is not in a key store, remember that there could be a very good reason why the store isn't handling your book.

For example, the store might not have paid its bills to the publisher, and hence not be able to get credit from the publisher. Or, if the store is part of a chain of stores, buying is probably done centrally, and the local salesperson might not be able to influence whether or not the branch handles your book. If a bookstore clerk, buyer, or owner says, "Oh, that salesman never calls on me" or "She visited but never mentioned your book," stay cool, and say, "Then why don't you order it from your wholesaler? They probably have it."

In my experience—and I've been a publisher's salesman and sales manager—publishers *never* refuse to sell to a credit-worthy bookstore, so *if* the salespeople in fact didn't call, it was probably for a sound reason. And a bookstore owner can always get a book in stock if he or she really wants to do so. There is no advantage to you in getting involved in problems between a publisher and a bookstore.

If your friends say, "I went to three stores and nobody had your book," investigate. But be skeptical—they might not want to put out the money to buy a copy.

All of that said, I will admit now that publishers often do an abysmal job of distributing a first novel, or any book. A famous author of nonfiction best sellers told me that one of America's largest and best known publishers only sold slightly more than a thousand copies each of his first three books, all novels. That's the kind of business publishing is, and the possibility of such results is one of the hazards of authorship.

If friends or relatives really want to help, then they should go into bookstores and ask for copies of the book. If the store has it, fine. If the store doesn't have it, they can ask the store to order a copy for them, thus calling it to the store's attention in the most positive way possible. It is particularly good for the friend or relative to bring in a good review, and say, pointing to the review, "Do you have this book? I'd like to buy one."

In the case of *Shaman's Daughter*, published in 1979, the sales department had some positive news to help their people place the book in bookstores: the jacket quotes, the fact that Book-of-the-Month Club selected the book as an alternate (and in Canada, that Reader's Digest Condensed Books of Canada would use it as a selection), and that a major sale of reprint rights had been arranged.

Prentice-Hall's subsidiary rights director, John Nelson, had touted the book to paperback publishers, and before publication, had staged an auction of paperback reprint rights. Dell Books made a "floor bid with topping privileges" for a substantial sum, which was accepted by Prentice-Hall. This meant that Dell would have the right to make the last bid in the auction, and if its last bid exceeded everybody else's by 10 percent, Dell would get the reprint rights to the book. The highest bid made by another publisher was $125,000, and Dell chose to top it, so Dell acquired the book for an advance royalty guarantee of $137,500, an excellent reprint deal for a first novel.

The sales department was able to impress bookstore buyers with this display of confidence in the book's commercial potential.

Prentice-Hall of Canada was delighted to have a good book coauthored by a Canadian to add to its list, and pushed the book in that country.

On the negative side, the price of the book, $12.50 for a 404-page, 6"x9" hard cover, proved a little too high for major rental libraries. And review coverage, while largely positive, was not as widespread as all had hoped. *The New York Times Book Review* and the daily *Times* did not review the book.

But over 20,000 hard cover copies were placed in bookstores, and a year later, Dell Books did an 800,000-copy first printing of its mass-market paperback edition when it used the book as a "lead" in one of its months of promotion. Nan Salerno and Rosamond Vanderburgh appeared on some radio and TV shows, did some bookstore appearances, some lectures, and each got a good deal of local publicity.

While neither all of Prentice-Hall's 20,000 + hard covers, or Dell's 800,000 paperbacks were sold, and the book did not become a best seller, a good time was had by all.

Nan Salerno wrote a second novel published by Prentice-Hall and is at work on a third book. Professor Vanderburgh was able to take much-desired time off for some research.

What can a hopeful beginning novelist learn from Nan Salerno's and Rosamond Vanderburgh's experiences with *Shaman's Daughter?* Here are some of the main points I see:

A writer and an expert can collaborate successfully to create a work of fiction.

The key to a successful collaboration is to draw an agreement that carefully defines the duties, responsibilities, and rewards of each partner—and to stick to it.

When marketing the manuscript that results from the collaboration, it is better to designate one of the collaborators to represent the partnership in dealing with a publisher, though each partner should of course have the right to approve or veto any deal made.

Don't give up hope if an agent fails to sell your work. Keep trying on your own, or with another agent, or through a friend.

When your editor offers suggestions about your work, regard him or her as a friend and collaborator, not as a know-it-all critic.

Look around you to see if any of your acquaintances has good contacts or is a natural putter-together of people—and ask that person to read your work and help you find a publisher.

Sometimes things turn out all right! And all because two children met at story hour. And then . . . and then . . . and then. . . .

13.

Genre Novelists

1. AN INTELLECTUAL WRITES A ROMANCE:
Russell Kirk, author of the Gothick Romance,
Old House of Fear

Down the street a quondam factory serves as Kirk's offices
and repository of the 10,000 books of his library. Here he
writes his columns for newspapers and magazines, his books
of history and biography, his essays on education and politics,
and, between times, his ghost tales and his Romances. In
addition to his written work, Kirk travels for lectures and
debates on university campuses, radio, and television, both in
America and abroad.

Don Herron, The Romantist, No. 3, 1979

The publication of Russell Kirk's first novel, *Old House of Fear*,
and its critical and commercial success, opened a dam that produced a

flood of gothic novels in the 1960s, 1970s and which continues in the 1980s.

The novel was published in 1961 by Fleet Publishing Corporation, a small publisher in New York. It had been acquired by Robert Hunter, an editor of conservative leanings, and when Hunter left Fleet, I inherited it. My editing consisted of the remark, "The beginning is a little slow," and Russell Kirk reworked it. We published a small hard cover edition with a terrible dust jacket, and sent out more than three hundred review copies. This review mailing, plus inclusion of the book in some announcement ads aimed at the book trade, was its only initial promotion.

A flood of rave reviews followed. Some quotes from them were put on the jacket of the second edition:

> *"We follow him with dazed and delighted attention from the first muffled cry to the final midnight scream."*
>
> The New Yorker

> *"Lovingly and thrillingly executed."*
>
> *Anthony Boucher*
> The New York Times Book Review

> *"A singularly beguiling book."*
>
> *New York* Herald Tribune

> *"An unblushing Gothic tale and a good one."*
>
> Saturday Review

> *"It is terrifying, ingeniously constructed, and truly Gothic."*
>
> National Review

> *"No one need be either a cold-out addict of whodunits or an antiquarian to become utterly absorbed in what I confidently assert is the most exciting, thrilling, blood-curdling adventure mystery of the year—Old House of Fear."*
>
> *Lewis F. Ball*
> Richmond-Times Dispatch

Around 10,000 hard cover copies were sold, and Avon issued a succession of a dozen large paperback printings for about ten years after. The American Library Association chose *Old House of Fear* as one of the half-dozen best books of 1961 for young adults, and transcribed it on tape for listeners at the ALA display at the New York World's Fair. Detective Book Club used it as a selection.

Show magazine published a condensed version. Gollanz published a British edition, and the whole novel was read serially over the BBC. Het Spectrum published a Dutch edition. And Fleet republished a more attractive hard cover edition in 1965, which was reviewed by the *Wall Street Journal* and some other places that had missed it the first time around.

A memorandum about the book Russell Kirk had prepared for me records, "He intended—and in the judgment of reviewers, achieved—a *tour de force*, deliberately reviving a mode of fiction nearly forgotten, the Gothic romance. His success was promptly followed by what Nathaniel Hawthorne (another strong influence upon Kirk) called 'a damned mob of scribbling women,' imitating him. One publisher suggested that Kirk write for his firm another Gothic novel—but ascribe it to a feminine pseudonym, most of the readers of such books being women who identify themselves as much with the presumed authoress as with the romance's heroine. Kirk declined this offer, but suggested to his fiancée, the beautiful Annette, that she write such a romance, with his assistance; she too declined."

Though other historians might have other comments on the reasons for the success of the gothic novel in American paperback publishing, I believe Kirk has a good point. When *Old House of Fear* was published, it was classified as a mystery novel, as the "gothic" category didn't exist. Russell Kirk, by writing a good novel, unleashed an industry.

A "gothic" novel has come to be defined as a work much like Russell Kirk's: An attractive young woman is somehow confined in an old house, and is menaced there by an awful and interesting villain with sleazy confederates. An admirable hero, who gets involved because of some respectable business mission, rescues her, but not before many terrifying complications. The villain gets his just deserts. The attraction of the novels lies in the delicious thrills produced by the menacing machinations of the ingenious and clever villains.

Originally no sex scenes were included in this genre. As an editor told John M. Kimbro, the "Kathryn Kimbrough" who wrote *The House on Windswept Ridge*, the heroine needs to be "squeaky clean." In his next gothic, Kimbro had his heroine take a bath, and afterwards, she says, "I feel squeaky clean." Eventually sex crept in, and today, some gothics include sex scenes.

How did Russell Kirk, influential conservative thinker and old-fashioned man of letters, come to write a "Gothick Romance"? He has written of his intellectual development:

Mine was not an Enlightened mind, I was now aware: it was a Gothic mind, medieval in its temper and structure. I did not love cold harmony and perfect regularity of organization; what I sought was variety, mystery, tradition, the venerable, the awful. I despised sophisters and calculators; I was groping for faith, honor, and prescriptive loyalties. I would have given any number of neo-classical pediments for one poor battered gargoyle.

He says he was influenced in his romance by Walter Scott and Robert Louis Stevenson—though he did not take any particular books of theirs as models. His wide reading of nineteenth-century ghostly tales also is reflected in *Old House of Fear*. Although some reviewers tried to find political motives in the novel, he says he only intended to "arouse dreadful joy; the few political references were meant simply to amuse the reader."

The novel was written mainly for Kirk's own amusement, and for his "kith and kin." He wrote the book at night while living in an old hotel. The source came from Kirk's experiences during visits to Scotland. The setting, the island of Carnglass, is a composite of two islands in the Inner Hebrides. Kirk spent a month in Eigg in 1949. Major Gair, a character in the second chapter, was taken from life—a mysterious man "nocturnally in St. Andrews about 1951." Various other episodes and scenes "reflect Scottish castles the author knew well, among them the Fife houses of Dellie and Earlshall." Years later, wandering in the big island of Mull, Kirk visited Duart Castle, and "found it amazingly like *Old House of Fear*. Even the guide at Duart, a beautiful red-haired girl, small and charming, was astoundingly like the Mary of the romance!"

Russell Kirk's other books of fiction, interspersed in a long list of nonfiction works, include a collection of ghost stories, *The Surly Sullen Bell*, *A Creature of the Twilight*, and *Lord of the Hollow Dark*. Though the supernatural is an element of most of his fiction, he follows the gothic tradition of having apparently supernatural happenings turn out, in the end, to have been natural events—thereby safely returning the reader from his "bucket seat of suspense" back to the ordinary world at the end of the story.

What can you learn from Russell Kirk's adventure in writing a first-rate suspense novel "in unblushing line of direct descent from *The Castle of Otranto*," and thereby spawning a new literary industry? Mostly that a "genre" novel can be, with labor and love, as good as any other novel, even in the view of the most exacting critics.

Kirk's remarks about his fiction-writing methods, taken from his nonfictional *Decadence and Renewal in Higher Education*, offer insight into an important power a writer needs to write effective novels, namely, the development of pictorial imagery:

> When I write fiction, I do not commence with a well-concerted formal plot. Rather, there occur in my imagination certain images, little scenes, snatches of conversation, strong lines of prose. I patch together these fragments, retaining and embellishing the sound images, discarding the unsound, finding a continuity to join them. Presently I have a coherent narration, with some point to it. Unless one has this sort of pictorial imagery—Walter Scott had it to a high degree—he will never become a writer of good fiction, whatever may be said of expository prose.

2. TWO FANTASY NOVELISTS:
Karen Brush, author of *The Pig, the Prince and the Unicorn,* and Niel Hancock, author of *Circle of Light*

August 7, 1984

John Douglas
Senior Editor
Avon Books
1790 Broadway
New York 10019

Dear Mr. Douglas:

As arranged by telephone today, here is *QUADROPED* [later published as *The Pig, the Prince and the Unicorn*], a fantasy novel by Karen Brush. This is her first novel, and this is its first submission.

Ms. Brush is a recent graduate of Yale, and is entering Columbia this fall to take an advanced degree in anthropology. She lives in New York, and is from here also. I didn't meet her until after reading the manuscript (she came recommended by another client), but I found her pleasant and amusing to talk to and be with. She has led an adventuresome life with much travel and sport, and knows a lot about geology, skindiving, and animals.

Probably the beginning could stand a little speeding up, but otherwise I found the novel a really good read, and hope you will too.

Sincerely yours,

Oscar Collier

In writing the submission letter above to an editor I knew only slightly, but had previously queried by phone, I tried to engage his interest by stating facts: I reminded him he had asked to see the novel; it was the first submission of a first novel, giving him a chance to discover a new writer. After first making it clear I liked her novel, I painted her as a pleasant person to meet, adventuresome, and hence possibly creative. By saying she came from another client, I was pointing out she had at least a tenuous connection to professional writing. As she was well-educated, her novel would probably be written correctly and typed clearly. And while he might have to do a modest amount of editorial work, I tried to lead him into reading the whole novel by saying I found it enjoyable. This remark also assured him that I had done my agent's work of screening out an unsuitable submission. Since I had already described it by phone, I didn't go into the contents, preferring to let the novel speak for itself.

About nine months later, after receiving a few quick and quiet reminder calls and a couple of brief, newsy letters from me about Karen Brush's activities, John Douglas said he was going to recommend *Quadroped* for publication. Later he said he had authority to make a formal offer, and after getting some sales projections, did so. Karen Brush accepted.

I hadn't pushed John Douglas, because I felt, from our phone coversations, that he liked the work, so I left the timing of an offer up to him. Karen Brush had been just as discreet in her few phone calls to me, inquiring about what was happening.

The idea of writing *Quadroped*, which is well described in her query letter that follows, came to Karen Brush when she was a freshman at Yale. She started to write it in the first person, as narrated by one of the older characters, but quickly abandoned that approach "because it was hard to speak in the voice of an older man." She switched to the third person, and the reader always sees events by staying close to the novel's hero, Quadroped, a young and small white pig who lives in a magical world. She finally finished it as a senior "in a writing seminar taught by Francine DuPlessix Gray, who urged me to submit it for publication."

Quadroped is about 85,000 words long, but Karen Brush says "I wrote it about two hundred times its final length in trying to get it right." She says she did not study books about how to write a novel until after she was finished; her approach was "just to write it."

As a young person, she "lived on Tolkien, C.S. Lewis, Lloyd Alexander's *Book of Three*, and of course, Lang's fairy tales. Also, *The Wizard of Oz*." She could find no better books of fantasy than these!

After she finished her fantasy novel, she had not the slightest idea of what to do next. She inquired of her parents about their circle of friends, and though several of them had published "books on sailing up the Amazon and exploration," none had published a fantasy novel. Her teacher, Francine DuPlessix Gray, a distinguished author, referred her to her own agent, but that agent said she had never sold a fantasy novel, and so didn't have anything to offer. Finally, Karen's father came up with the name of Palm Beach attorney and author Carole Criswell, whom I knew, and Carole gave her my name.

Since one of my clients is a successful fantasy writer, and I enjoy reading fantasy and science fiction novels, I was quite willing to read *Quadroped* after she telephoned me and described it. With it she sent the following submission letter (together with a handwritten note reminding me of our telephone conversation and Carole Criswell's referral), which, except for its length, is a model letter of its type:

July 29, 1984

Mr. Oscar Collier
Collier Associates
875 Sixth Avenue
Room 1003
New York, NY 10001

Dear Mr. Collier:

A thousand years ago the Black Unicorn of Ravenor was imprisoned in Chaos, and a terrible war was resolved. Every hundred years the gateway to Chaos begins to open. It must be locked or the Black Unicorn will escape and the war begin again. The Gate has begun to open . . . and the Key is lost. Heroes from both armies are searching for it.

Quadroped is the unlikely young hero of this story. He is a small white pig upon whose head the Key is accidentally dropped. As the unwilling

Key Bearer, Quadro finds himself struggling for survival as the malevolent Warlords of Ravenor attempt to seize the Key before he can lock the Gate.

Through a series of encounters with the extraordinary leaders of both lands, and their humorous sidekicks, Quadroped demonstrates his innocent ability to always land on his feet and to make friends of his enemies. As his journey progresses, Quadro realizes that his problems can not be solved by locking the Gate. Deprived of its king, the land of Ravenor is dying. Quadroped must choose either to free the Black Unicorn, plunging his homeland into war, or to lock the Gate and allow Ravenor to die. How Quadroped, universally scorned and scolded by his heroic companions, manages to resolve this monumental conflict without sacrificing either side, is the exciting climax of this tale.

Quadroped is a humorous fantasy that maintains a steady counterpoint between magic, science, and ordinary common sense. Its strong visual descriptions make it an ideal subject for illustration or animation. The novel was completed for a writing seminar taught by Francine DuPlessix Gray, who urged me to submit the piece for publication.

I am a cum laude graduate of Yale University with my B.S. in Geology and a strong background in English. I will enter the Ph.D. program in Anthropology at Columbia University in September. I have travelled extensively and my experiences form the background for *Quadroped*. I have explored caves in Australia, studied volcanoes in Iceland, gone on safari in Africa, and gone hot-air ballooning in France. I am a certified SCUBA diver and have made several night dives and participated in two underwater excavations. I have published poetry in *The Poet*, *Backpacker Magazine*, *American Poetry Anthology*, *Yale Alumni Magazine*, and *Poetry Press*.

Sincerely,

Karen A. Brush

I read the novel soon after it arrived, and called with an offer to represent her. She accepted, took a copy of my form of agreement to study, and later rewrote it to exclude her children's books and short stories (which I don't handle ordinarily). Meanwhile, John Douglas's name came to mind, because I had seen references to him in writer's newsletters, and I called him and described the novel. He asked to see it, and we were on our way.

The Avon contract, which arrived about a month after we had made an oral agreement by phone, called for a $2,500 advance against royalties, payable half on signing, and half on Avon's acceptance of a final manuscript—John Douglas had some editorial comments and suggestions for revisions. Karen Brush was somewhat disturbed that the contract provided "The Publisher is authorized, at its sole discretion, to make any editorial changes, deletions, abridgment and condensation whatsoever in the text of said Work. . . ." I was able to say truthfully to her that I had encountered no editorial problems with Avon on books placed with them, but I brought this up with John Douglas, and he agreed that we could insert "in consultation with the Author" in this provision, which assured her.

Time will tell whether we can realize another kind of potential revealed in Karen Brush's submission letter, the use of *The Pig, the Prince and the Unicorn's* "strong visual descriptions [as] an ideal subject for . . . animation."

By way of contrast, here are some brief notes on the experiences of Niel Hancock, author of ten published fantasy novels, with three more under contract. Niel Hancock, who sometimes calls himself T.H.E. Otter, made over thirty submissions of his unfinished four-volume first novel, *Circle of Light*, all of them to editors of juvenile books. He had turned to writing the fantasy after first doing a good deal of other kinds of writing, which he had discarded. Finally, a junior editor of juvenile books at Atheneum Publishers, who liked his novel (and signed her letters to him "Toad") wrote him and said, "This is not a juvenile—you should get an agent and try adult publishers." She recommended James Seligmann, whom she had met through his submissions to her. Seligmann passed the submission to me. Fantasy is not one of his favorite kinds of reading, but he knew I enjoy it.

I happily offered to represent "Otter," who is a truly cheerful, sunny man. Since he had been practically everywhere with his manuscript, I submitted it to one of the few publishers he had never approached: Patrick O'Connor, then editor-in-chief of Popular Library.

O'Connor later told me, "I saw its commercial potential." His judgment proved correct, and Niel Hancock has stayed with Popular Library and now with its present owner, Warner Books, where Patrick O'Connor is again his editor. Popular Library paid a $15,000 advance for the four-volume novel. Hancock's subsequent novels about "Atlanton Earth" followed there, and at Warner Books. They have been attractively packaged as mass-market books, distributed practically everywhere, and more than a million copies sold in the U.S. Now they are coming out in Japan and Germany as well.

Why did it take Niel Hancock more than thirty submissions to find a sympathetic editor who referred him to an agent, and take me *one* submission to place his first quartet of books? The answer lies simply in his original belief that the books were juveniles, which, to me, they weren't. Is there any way he could have avoided this travail? And is there a lesson for you, a beginning novelist, in his story? Probably one way he could have told that the novels were not necessarily juvenile books was from their length—they are longer than most juveniles. When you are trying to break into a particular field, it is important to look at the length of the majority of the books published in that field or genre, and make your first effort no longer than average.

But by persistence Niel Hancock was able to get published anyway, and now he lives and travels on his royalties, surely one of the happiest outcomes of a novelist's career.

3. WRITING NOVELS AS A NEW CAREER:
Arthur Gladstone, author of forty Regency romances

A common idea about a first novel is that it is the work of a young person. But many writers make their debuts as novelists later in life. Here is a real-life example of such a novelist.

In 1973 Arthur Gladstone was a fifty-two-year-old chemical engineer who read in his spare time and occasionally thought of writing some day when he wasn't busy with his hobby of photographing insects. By 1982, just nine years later, the same Arthur Gladstone was a full-time professional writer with forty Regency romances written under four pen names to his credit—novels published by such familiar New York publishers as Berkley, Dell, Fawcett, Jove, Playboy Press, Popular Library, and Pyramid. When interviewed for this book, he was five hundred pages into what may become a major historical novel.

How did he make the transition from chemist in industry to the chemistry of romance? It took a shock and sorrow to get him started writing.

Arthur and his wife, Margaret Sebastian Gladstone, had often read together the works of such authors as Charles Dickens, William Shakespeare, and Jane Austen. In the 1960s, Margaret introduced him to the novels of Georgette Heyer, Regency romance author par excellence. He caught the Regency fever to such a degree that his wife made a remark he was not to remember until much later. "When you retire, you can have a new career of selling your photography and writing Regency romances."

When suddenly, in March, 1973, Margaret died in an automobile accident, a vital part of Arthur Gladstone's life was gone forever. Unable to continue as before, he retired from his job and began to write.

After trying several kinds of writing and being unsatisfied with the results, he remembered his wife's remark about writing Regency romances. He began to work on his first novel, *The Honorable Miss Claredon*, in a style that was a sincere and appreciative imitation of that of Georgette Heyer. Now he had found his niche.

Why was it a good idea, aside from his wife's suggestion, for Arthur Gladstone to write historical novels about the Regency period? The answer is, I believe, that Arthur Gladstone is a gentleman—it's the only word that fully describes this slim, dapper, silver-haired man. Not only does he have and value excellent manners, he also has the coolness and alertness of the gentleman. Always ready to give a light and witty reply, he nevertheless notes and responds to even the slightest discourtesy or aspersion on his honor. His great natural and cultivated pride enables him to get inside the speech and actions of his characters, who are mostly ladies and gentlemen dealing with problems generated by manners and rank.

To help with his writing, Gladstone bought the *Oxford English Dictionary*, which tells when a word was first known to be used in the language, and sought to write only with words and names that had been in active usage in England during the period of his novel. He became an expert on English history between 1780 and 1820—the time of the end of the reign of George III, the Regency, and the beginning of George IV's reign.

The first draft of *The Honorable Miss Claredon* was fifty pages, and was written in the first person. After he was satisfied with it, he showed it to a carefully chosen friend. She suggested that it would be better to write it in the third person, advice he accepted and now believes to have been crucial, as writing in the third person is much more flexible and allows better coverage of characters and events.

The budding novelist soon realized that fifty pages was not a commercial length, and wrote a second draft of 150 pages, expanding his dialogue and development of characters. Still not sure his novel was long enough, he wrote a third draft around 120,000 words long. He decided that the novel was now too long, and cut it to what became the usual length for his novels, 170 to 180 pages, about 70,000 words.

All of this labor was accomplished in three months. After rejections from E. P. Dutton and Harper & Row, Georgette Heyer's publishers—my own observation as an agent is that it is hard to sell an imitation of a master writer to that writer's publishers—he studied writer's guides, and decided to try a paperback publisher. In September, 1973 he sent his manuscript to Pyramid Publications, addressed to no specific editor, but just to the publisher itself.

After two months of silence, he telephoned Pyramid, and was told *The Honorable Miss Claredon* was still under consideration. After another month he called again, and learned the happy news that his first novel had just been accepted for publication. But a contract didn't arrive until March 1974, by which time he had written two more novels. *Miss Claredon* came out in March, 1975.

Meanwhile Jean Glass, his editor at Pyramid, had left, and a new editor called his new novels "slow," though they were essentially written at the same pace as the first one. After trying a couple of other publishers and getting rejections—an editor at Ace praised one of the novels, but said that Ace had a sufficient inventory of Regencies at that time—Arthur Gladstone realized that he took these marketing efforts too personally and decided to find an agent to market his novels for him.

Using a directory as his guide, he began to telephone agents. These calls were not a pleasant experience for a gentleman; the agents he spoke to, he felt, acted as though they would be doing him a favor by representing him, or even reading his novels.

After getting another agent's name from a lawyer friend, instead of phoning, *he wrote a letter to the agency*, and for a change, the agent called *him*. While the telephone is a marvelously convenient instrument of modern life, writers, agents, and publishers are, I find, almost uniformly most at home with the written word. This agent was more receptive, and the only questions asked concerned how well Gladstone knew the history of the Regency period—questions the author welcomed as reasonable and appropriate. He was well prepared to answer. He dropped off his second novel, *The Young Lady From Alton-St. Pancras*. The agent liked it and was able to place it. During the mid-1970s, Regency romances were among the most popular kinds of paperback original books with readers and publishers.

What exactly is a Regency romance? According to Kate Duffy, now editor-in-chief of Worldwide Library who through the years bought and edited several of Arthur Gladstone's novels at various houses, a Regency is a *comedy of manners* set in the Regency period of English history. The motives of the characters and plot twists turn exclusively on the social mores of the period, and not on outside forces as they would in a mystery novel. Kate Duffy likes Arthur Gladstone's novels because he takes full advantage of the period and knows it thoroughly. His characters are consistent throughout his novels—and most important—his novels are not just "bodice-rippers." Gladstone, she pointed out, gives equal weight to his fully depicted male and female characters, as opposed to some Regency romance writers who focus so much on the female characters that the male characters are two-dimensional. She was impressed, too, that he introduces new subject matter, such as the not-quite-gentlemen dealing with a *real* lady, in his *Bow Street Runner*, a novel about the forerunners of the London Metropolitan Police. Perhaps most important of all, Kate Duffy says, "He made me laugh out loud with his wit and humor."

His agent, Lisa Collier of Collier Associates, comments that in spite of his 18th century plots, Arthur Gladstone is very 20th century in his use of computers. Since he often has several book contracts on hand at once for book projects sold from outlines, Gladstone puts on his home computer all their delivery dates and details, such as royalty rates and when royalty reports or other payments are due. Gladstone is just as meticulous in his writing habits. He has a regular writing schedule, and a self-imposed quota of at least five fully finished pages each day. His agent Lisa Collier says that most full-time professional writers she represents have regular working hours and definite writing schedules for completion of an explicit amount of work each day—which confirms my own observation.

Gladstone once told Lisa that many of his best plot ideas came from reading *newspapers of the Regency period*—a tip that she believes could be of help to any writer of historical novels.

Why does Arthur Gladstone write under feminine pen names, and how is he able to get away with this? He first began to use a feminine pen name as a tribute to his wife, who loved Regency romances, and signed his first novels "Margaret SeBastian." But when he found that writing under a female name also helped sales, and began to get more contracts with different publishers, he also started using the names Maggie Gladstone, Lisbet Norcross, and Cilla Whitmore (the latter based on the name of one of his grandmothers). He shows his manuscripts to women readers whose opinions he values, and asks them to point out any use of language or reactions of characters that they consider unsuitable or unlikely to have come from a woman writer, and edits his novels accordingly.

Actually, many historical novels, Regency romances, gothics, and other romances are written by men writing under feminine pseudonyms, so Gladstone's practice is not unusual. He plans to offer his new historical novel, set in America, under his own name.

Gladstone's private life is happy once again. In 1980, when attending a writer's conference in New Jersey, he met Helen Worth, a poet and cookbook author. They married in 1981. Nor has he neglected his hobby—photography of insects. Currently, he and Helen Worth, at their new home in Virginia, are working on a book that combines his photographs and her poems.

What tips and principles does Arthur Gladstone have to offer beginning novelists? The most important, he says, is "Don't offer anything you have written, even to a friend to read, until you are satisfied with it yourself."

He continues, "Don't try to force your characters. Let them develop naturally. I once had to discard fifty or sixty pages of one of my novels because I had tried to force a character into a mold and actions that were not natural to her."

"Avoid contrived solutions," he adds. Gladstone's characters attack knotty and attractive problems, and solve them in ways natural to the characters.

Unlike most writers I have known, he has found showing his work to friends is quite helpful. But he warns that you must choose a *sympathetic* and *honest* person who will give you frank comments, which you should then consider carefully, and *only follow the suggestions you agree with.*

Though he prefers to let the interaction of his characters determine much of the plot, he has been forced by the necessities of the publishing business to sell mostly from outlines in recent years. But now that he is trying a longer novel, he has reverted to writing the whole novel first before trying to sell it.

Originally Gladstone wrote pencil drafts, and then typed his manuscripts. Now, to save time, an important consideration in writing genre books, he composes on the typewriter. He finds that he has become so proficient in setting up surprising situations and imagining the reactions and dialogue of his characters in them that he must exercise self-restraint to keep dialogue a manageable length.

What have been the financial rewards of Arthur Gladstone's first years as a novelist? His advance royalty guarantees have ranged from $2,500 for his first novel to $15,000 for a later one. Almost a million copies of his books have been sold. A number of his novels earned more than their advances, and earned extra money by going into large-print and foreign editions. And some of them may continue to sell for additional years. Novels that go out of print with one publisher can sometimes be sold, several years later, to a new publisher. Since he has written forty novels, it seems likely that the final fruits of this first nine years will exceed half a million dollars, with the largest part of it already paid to him.

Clearly Arthur Gladstone has a great talent as a novelist. But talent alone didn't do it. It took a lifetime of reading books and the shock of his wife's sudden death to push him into realizing, in mid-life, that if he wanted to leave his mark on the world, he had better not delay in getting started as a writer.

Once he began, he did everything right: He worked to perfect his new craft, and quickly developed a regular writing schedule. He chose a genre he liked and that was in demand, Regency romances. He modelled his first novel on the work of an outstanding practitioner of this genre, Georgette Heyer. He immediately tried to market it. Though upset by rejections, he was not deterred. Then by analyzing his problem, he found a compatible agent to sell further work so he could concentrate on writing rather than marketing.

Arthur Gladstone is a good example for a beginning genre novelist to consider. I particularly admire his use of the newspapers of the period, and the *Oxford English Dictionary*, to be sure that the names and places and language of his characters are appropriate to his chosen period. That is the kind of attention to detail that marks a winner in this competitive field.

4. LOVE FOR SALE—WRITING ROMANCES:
**Susan Johnson, author of *Sweet Love, Survive* and
Joan Wolf, author of *Portrait of a Love***

A wide range of difference exists in the way Romance writers handle sex. Here are two samples: the first is much more explicit.

Apollo ran his hands leisurely up her naked back and smiled knowingly, his pleasure infinitely enhanced by hers, pleasantly envisioning many more panting orgasmic cries before he brought himself to climax . . . His hands glided to her narrow waist, lean fingers splayed over her reed-slim slenderness and gently rounded hips. He filled her still, his hardness undiminished; she was impaled on him like a willing sacrifice, her ivory arms, pale against the dark silk of his robe twined around his neck, her head nestled into the hollow of his shoulder. The hands lying on her hips tightened and . . .

from *Sweet Love, Survive*
Susan Johnson

His shoulders came away from the door in a kind of lunge and then he was across the room and holding her in his arms. Isabel closed her eyes and stopped thinking. Her whole life seemed to have narrowed down to this room, this man, this moment. His mouth was hard on hers, his hands moving possessively over her breasts, her waist, her hips. She felt his desire, felt also the unnamable, irresistible force in him that called out so strongly to something in her. Her head was pressed back against his shoulder and his lips left her mouth and moved, searingly, to her exposed throat.

"Isabel," he muttered. "God. Isabel." And suddenly she was swept by fire. Her whole body shuddered and she clung to him fiercely. They almost didn't make it to the bedroom.

"Would you like to go down to look at the beach?" he asked softly a very long time later.

from *Portrait of a Love*
Joan Wolf

Writers have often asked me, "Should I include explicit sex scenes? Are they necessary to sell a novel?" As an agent, I don't feel this question has any one answer. I can't tell a writer what is morally or commercially correct; I am not a legislator or moral leader, and I see all kinds of novels succeed. So my reply is only, "If you want to, or your subject demands it, go ahead. But you don't have to include explicit sex scenes in order to succeed. Don't *force* yourself to write them."

I happen not to like hard-core pornography, so I don't handle it, but I think *Lady Chatterley's Lover*, by D.H. Lawrence, is a romance worth reading.

The comments of two successful writers of historical and contemporary romances, Susan Johnson and Joan Wolf, whose love scenes you just read, may be helpful to a writer trying to decide this matter.

Susan Johnson is a former librarian and now a full-time novelist whose historical romances are published by Playboy Press and its successor, Berkley Publishing Corporation under its Charter imprint. Johnson writes novels which contain delightfully detailed and erotic sex scenes. She says, "My first story dealt with the mutual attraction of a hero and heroine in terms of realistic human sexuality. There's very little sex in romance writing today. The greatest number of romances published are what are termed 'sweet' romances. Then there's the romances labelled 'sensual' and lastly a very small number of 'sexy' romances. Sexy romances aren't easy to write.

"Many writers are uncomfortable writing about sex, others aren't capable of writing a sexy love scene. One sees many love scenes which are awkwardly embarrassing to read. And then, there are the writers who feel they must do the obligatory sex scene so an attempt is made. Both of these last two categories are the greatest turn-off in the world.

"I doubt you'll get too many openly to admit it, with all the 'good girl'-'bad girl' conditioning in our culture, but whatever degree of sensuality readers prefer, they *are* looking for 'amour.' Romances offer a delightful fantasy, removed from mundane reality, where one can immerse oneself in the adventures of an intrepid heroine, a dashing hero. It's sheer entertainment. My characters delight in life, feel each day is to be lived."

Joan Wolf, on the other hand, award-winning author of many contemporary romances, Regencies, and historical romances published by New American Library, resists including explicit sex scenes in her novels. She says, "I don't like to write about explicit sex, so I don't do it in my novels, and they succeed anyway."

Wolf believes women readers want to read about intense relationships, and many writers are deceived into thinking that the only way intense relationships can be described is through sex scenes. She thinks it is not necessary to describe sex in order to show a powerful interrelationship between a man and a woman. Emotion is what romance readers are seeking, she believes, and so long as you provide it in your novels, you don't need to describe sex acts.

To generalize from what these writers are saying, they agree that you should write about what you consider most important, and what you can write about naturally and well. This may mean explicit sex scenes, or it may instead mean intense emotional scenes without a great deal of explicit description. So I would add to my answer above the following caveat: "Only write explicit sex scenes if you believe you can write them well."

Because contemporary romances are very popular, and can be seen in bookstores, on some newsstands, and in supermarkets, many would-be novelists think they might as well join the herd, and write a romance. Actually, this kind of book is just as hard to write as any other novel, and today, maybe harder.

If you decide you want to write a contemporary romance, a good starting point is to buy and read a number of them, and *if you like them*, maybe this is the genre for you. But if you don't, you should probably forget it.

According to an agent who has sold a good many of this genre, if it's romance writing you're after, you should write to the publishers whose books you see and read, and ask for their "tip sheets" that tell the kinds of romances they are currently looking for, and offer writing guidelines. It's really a waste of your time to enter the field unless you follow this procedure, because the needs of the publisher of contemporary romances are constantly changing and evolving.

This agent once sent some current guidelines to a British author she represented. Three years later, the author sent a complete manuscript following one of the guidelines. But by then, the publisher was no longer buying *that* kind of romance. So not only get the guidelines, but get updated copies regularly. And write fast!

Harlequin-Silhouette is the main publisher of such novels, but any paperback publisher might like to see a good romance at the right time. It's up to you to follow this quickly changing field, or find an agent who is interested in romances.

As I mentioned in an earlier chapter, you don't have to have an agent if you are a romance author, as publishers will deal with you directly. But if you prefer to try to get an agent for your first romance, more than a hundred are listed in *Literary Agents of North America 1984-85 Market Place*. These handle "Romances, Women's," or, like Barbara Lowenstein Associates, "Category Romances."

Ilene Fallon of Barbara Lowenstein Associates emphasizes that it is essential to write a query letter to any agent handling romances before making a submission. She says, "Be as specific as possible about what you have written—don't just say you have written a romance." She says that since this field is so rapidly changing, she and other agents interested in romances have had to become highly selective. She suggests that one way to learn what is happening in the romance field is to go to a large chain bookstore, such as B. Dalton or Waldenbooks, look at their stock, and ask to see their lists of good sellers in this field.

The bloom has gone off this category, as too many books have been published in it in the last few years, just as earlier was true of gothic novels and Regency romances. This doesn't mean gothics, Regencies, or contemporary romances aren't being published, but just that editors (and agents) are now highly selective, making it harder to get started.

Anita Diamant, a long-established agent, says that she and her associate, Robin Rue, an author of young adult romances herself and former editor, are still looking at romance queries and manuscripts from romance writer's conferences. But she sees the long-term trend in this kind of writing going downward. Writers with several romance books in print sometimes can't sell new ones. The remedy for these problems, she believes, is to write books of higher quality, or to switch to other genres.

But don't panic. As Erich Segal, author of *Love Story*, remarked in *The New York Times Book Review*, writing about ancient Greek romances, "One respected scholar of the second century A.D. pronounced with certainty that the genre 'would never last.' He was wrong by at least 1,800 years." So if you want to write a romance, be assured that the genre itself will still exist when you do so.

14.

From Businessman to Novelist

**B. H. Friedman, author of *Circles* and
Founding Member of the Fiction Collective**

Friedman, B(ernard) H(arper), writer; b. N.Y.C., July 27, 1926; s. Leonard and Madeline (Uris) F.; m. Abby Noselson, Mar. 6, 1948; children: Jackson, Daisy. B.A., Cornell U., 1948. With Cross & Brown Co., 1949-50; v.p., dir. Uris Bldgs. Corp., N.Y.C., 1950-63; lectr. creative writing Cornell U., 1966-67; staff cons. dir. Fine Arts Work Center, Provincetown, Mass., 1968-82; founding mem. Fiction Collective, 1973—; Adv. council Cornell U. Coll. Arts and Scis., 1968-83, Herbert F. Johnson Mus., 1972—. Author: novel Circles, 1962 (reprinted as I Need to Love, 1963); (with Barbara Guest) monograph Robert Goodnough, 1962; novel Yarborough, 1964; monographs Lee Krasner, 1965; Alfonso Ossorio, 1973, Salvatore Scarpitta, 1977, Myron Stout, 1980;

novels Whispers, 1972; Museum, 1974, Almost A Life, 1975, The Polygamist, 1981; stories Coming Close, 1982; biography Jackson Pollock: Energy Made Visible, 1972; Gertrude Vanderbilt Whitney, 1978; editor: School of New York, 1959; adv. bd.: Cornell Rev., 1977-79; contbr. articles to mags., anthologies and reference vols. in U.S., Eng., Japan. Trustee Am. Fedn. Arts, 1958-64, Whitney Mus. Am. Art, 1961—, Broida Mus., 1983—. Served with USNR, 1944-46. Recipient awards for short stories, including Nelson Algren award, 1983. Club: Century Assn. (N.Y.C.).

—from *Who's Who in America*

One of the most enduring myths in the lore of American artistic life is that an unbridgeable dividing line exists between business and the arts, including literature. B.H. Friedman has succeeded at both, but the power of the myth's possible truth is such that he finally had to succeed at them one at a time—first in business, then as a writer.

When Bob Friedman, as he prefers to be called, decided at thirty-six to abandon his career as a real estate executive at Uris Buildings Corp. (one of the major owners, builders, and lessors of real estate in New York City), in favor of writing, his uncle, head of the company, and mentor of Friedman's business career, was not pleased. As Friedman wrote of it later, his uncle said: "Everything in your life has shaped you for the position you have and the higher one you will have. In writing, what hope of success is there? In five years or ten, you'll surely regret your decision . . ."

I did not meet Friedman until he had written his first book and was struggling to place it. I was not then a literary agent but an editor at a publishing house, as you shall see. But I came to have a special interest in this unusual man and have kept track of him through the years.

His *Coming Close*, written in 1982, answered many of my questions about the man and his thinking, particularly his anxiety about his career change: "I make nervous little jokes to my wife, no one else, about going private."

The tension of doing business by day and writing by night and on weekends is expressed in this passage: "My career in real estate is, in itself, its extra-literary self, a way of attacking my writing. Years ago my uncle said perhaps I should consider writing under a pseudonym. I wish I could do business under a pseudonym."

Now, more than twenty-five years have passed. B.H. Friedman is author of six novels, several nonfiction books, many magazine articles and other writing, and he doesn't regret his decision.

How did Friedman, son of a New York shoe wholesaler, heir-apparent to a substantial portion of New York—a man who, as the character in Freud's joke says, had "a great future behind him"—become a novelist? After years of casual acquaintance with him, study of his work, and a recent interview with him, I have several answers to this question. One of them reminds me of the old New York tale Senator Daniel Moynihan repeated as a speaker at the National Book Award ceremonies at Carnegie Hall.

"A tourist asked a savvy New Yorker, 'How do you get to Carnegie Hall?'

"The New Yorker pondered a moment, then replied, 'Practice, practice, practice!' "

Another answer is that Friedman showed iron determination and persistence in the face of discouragement and rejection. This chapter is the story of that practice and determination, and its result.

Friedman aims at the big leagues in writing: *Coming Close* is sprinkled with such names as Shakespeare, Aristotle, Shelley, Keats, Byron, Rimbaud, Proust, Eliot, Pound, Stevens, Poe, Joyce, Woolf, Yeats, Powell, and Celine. He says the writers who influenced him were Henry James, Evelyn Waugh, Ernest Hemingway, and Marcel Proust.

His interest in contemporary and twentieth century art helped shape his style, and he says his interest in jazz has too. But probably the greatest influence on his writing is the discipline and orderliness he learned in business—how to manage his time.

He says he writes every morning immediately after breakfast, "fully rested, with more time than I need, more blank pages than I can fill. There is no help, as in business, from outside. By lunch I have produced all I can, typically no more than I did in the same number of hours during the years I wrote nights and weekends." But in fact he still uses a secretary to copy his handwritten material, and maintains his writing studio with the neatness of a well-organized office.

Another passage from *Coming Close* tells the key difference between working at home and going to an office: "At home there's always the possibility the decision may be important. At business the important thing is to decide."

After service in the Navy during World War II and graduating from Cornell in 1948, B.H. Friedman came back to New York and took a job managing a building in Greenwich Village. He met a few people in the literary world and began to write. He became a client of

Mavis McIntosh, a well-known literary agent of that period, and after a couple of years, she wrote him a "Dear Bob" letter, saying that while she liked his writing, she was not able to do much with it. He continued to write, and after joining Uris Buildings, began to work uptown. Near his office at 575 Madison Avenue were many art galleries, and he stopped in to see their exhibitions. One of them was the Curt Valentin Gallery. He struck up a friendship with Valentin, a distinguished dealer in modern art. Valentin undertook to help in Friedman's art education, talking to him, lending him books, and discussing what painting and modern art was all about.

Friedman found Valentin, whom he described in a statement published in *Library Journal* as "a character whose business was based on taste," so fascinating that he continued to think of him after Valentin's death.

A year later, "another close friend died, Jackson Pollock. He had, in his work, overthrown everything in painting that had previously been considered good taste (i.e., accepted art). In the two types—not the two particular individuals—I saw an aesthetic conflict, and later, as my ideas became clearer, a conflict between generations. This I tried to dramatize by placing a woman between the two points of view: thus the eternal triangle. My characters began to develop their own wills. The book does not end as I originally planned it to, which was to have the younger generation destroy the elder. The characters, as I have indicated, took over. The destruction of one generation by another became also the creation of one generation by another: reciprocity: beat *and* anti-beat. . . ."

So B.H. Friedman started composition of *Circles* with its main character—and built from there. Since his character was a man of taste, how did he define him? One original and interesting way was to explicitly name the services and products his central character, "Henry Lobelle," used—he flies Air France, he smokes Gitanes in France, Camels in the U.S.A. His shoes are made by Oliver Moore, a British bootmaker in New York. His English bag by Peal was bought at Brooks Brothers in New York. He imports three Picassos, two Braques, two Matisses, two Klees, a Mondrian, a De Staël, a Giacometti sculpture and two by Arp. He buys a Lalique ring to give as a present. He lives on Sutton Place. He drinks Pouilly-Fuissé. He brushes his teeth with a hard Kent toothbrush. He reads *New Art*. He has lemon peel in his martinis. All of these identifications come very soon in *Circles*, starting on the first page of the novel in its published version.

Later, Lobelle is a shown at work, using his impeccable taste: "He lent his taste to the public at 50 to 100%. . . . He had watched a generation shift from jewelry to art: from pearls to Picassos, he had said, from diamonds to Dufys, from rubies to Roualts, from emeralds to Ensors. Lobelle could shift easily from jewels to furs: from mink to Matisse, from sable to Soutine, from beaver to Braque, from leopard to Léger, from ermine to Epstein . . . And from furs to securities: from Monsanto to Mondrian, from Alcoa to Arp, from Merck to Miro, from Kennecott to Klee, from Chrysler to Calder. . . ."

Actually, when I met B.H. Friedman, a lean, tall man, he himself had the clean-cut quality of a Léger painting. But in spite of his store of knowledge and discernment of quality, before Friedman could get his novel to its final salable form, he had to undergo a long apprenticeship: *Circles* was the *fifth* novel he wrote—the others, he told me, are still in the drawer. His first draft of *Circles* was about an art dealer getting involved with a woman artist who wants a show in his gallery. The dealer resists because the show would compromise his taste. The result, Friedman recalls, was too lopsided. Finally, in his third draft, he came up with the manuscript which was the one I saw. But the road that led him to me was indeed a long circle.

While writing *Circles*, B.H. Friedman began to use the contacts he had made as a vice president of Uris Buildings and as manager of 575 Madison Avenue. He submitted the novel to Doubleday through George Hecht, who negotiated Doubleday's lease in the building. It was rejected. Another tenant was Avon Books, then a smaller mass-market paperback firm than it is today. At Avon, he met Charles R. Byrne, editor-in-chief, and others with the company at the time, and showed them *Circles* in its various stages. One of them introduced him to Bonnie Golightly, a writer and former owner of the Park Bookshop on Washington Square. Bonnie Golightly strongly recommended some changes, especially that he abandon his choice of writing the novel entirely in the present tense. He remembers her saying, "You'll never sell it that way. It sounds like stage directions." He took her advice (an excellent suggestion and a crucial decision, in my opinion) and switched to a more conventional way of handling the tenses.

When Charles Byrne left Avon to become editor-in-chief of Macfadden-Bartel Books, a large mass-market paperback publisher of that time, he telephoned me one day at Fleet Publishing Corp., a small general trade hardcover publisher, where I was editor and assistant to the president, to ask if I would read the manuscript. Byrne said he wanted to reprint the book in paperback, and would prefer to see in it hard cover first, so it could get some reviews. As Charles Byrne was the editor who had successfully reprinted the first novels of Nelson Algren, *Never Come Morning*, and Edmund Schidell, *Scratch the Surface*, I immediately agreed. When he added that he would offer $2,000 for a license to reprint the book in paperback after one year ($2,000 was a very satisfactory price for reprint rights to a first novel in 1962), I was doubly interested.

I loved the manuscript from first reading, because I knew its setting and background world, the art scenes of New York City and East Hampton, an art-literary-publishing-society resort near the eastern end of Long Island. I had tried my hand as a professional artist in this area. I believed that Friedman had done a brilliant job of depicting the art and literary scene. The novel reminded me of such works as *The Rock Pool*, by Cyril Connolly, *South Wind*, by Norman Douglas, *Crome Yellow*, the first novel of Aldous Huxley, and some of the works of Evelyn Waugh, Mary McCarthy, and Nathanael West. I also believed that enough people would find this scene of interest to make publishing the novel worthwhile, because it not only appealed as swift-paced, somewhat sensational, sexy fiction, but also had the nonfiction appeal of offering information and opinion about the modern art world.

Though *Circles* had plenty of sexual action in it, the descriptions were discreet and never pornographically explicit or exploitative—they were an integral and necessary part of the plot. I liked the then-advance-guard element of depicting Henry Lobelle's character partly by describing the expensive products he used—pop art was just beginning to emerge at the time.

But best of all, it had a subsidiary rights deal built in. As Bill Adler says in *Inside Publishing*, "Publishers are nice people, but in the final analysis they are only concerned with the bottom line—profit and loss."

When I took the manuscript to George Little, president and owner of Fleet Publishing Corp., (he also owned and operated the tremendously profitable General Features newspaper syndicate), his ears perked up at the mention of Charlie Byrne.

Byrne had several times paid tidy sums for paperback rights to our books, and had made the highest bid, during the Avon days, for *My Thirty Years Backstairs at the White House*, the Fleet best seller by former White House maid Lillian Rogers Parks, in collaboration with my coauthor, Frances Spatz Leighton.

So, I was not at all surprised when George Little, on hearing

Byrne's name, told me, "Well, Oscar, if it's good enough for Charlie Byrne, it ought to be good enough for us."

Fleet made a contract with Friedman, who had no agent, paid him a $2,000 advance royalty, and simultaneously made a contract with Macfadden-Bartel Books licensing paperback rights to them for $2,000.

Before describing the editing of *Circles*, following is a description of the manuscript we received, so you will understand what changes were made.

Part One of the book deals with Amy, the lead female character, in July 1961, and introduces Spike Ross, a young modern American painter who finishes his paintings by shooting through them with a machine gun. Spike and Amy make love. We go with them to the exotic and rich East Hampton party scene and meet a Bentley-driving art collector. They attend a nude bathing party at midnight. Spike, angry with Amy and jealous of the art collector, dumps his machine gun in the ocean.

Part Two, August 1961, introduces Henry Lobelle, worldly fifty-five-year-old dealer in 20th century European art. He returns from Europe to plan his first autumn exhibition, the work of "Foro," an Italian painter whose work consists of neatly painted circles. Lobelle is reunited with Amy and they spend the night together. The second night, they go to a jazz club, and Spike Ross is there. Amy introduces them. Lobelle dislikes Spike and his brash American friends, but Amy invites them to Lobelle's gallery opening of the Foro show. Amy and Lobelle go to bed together again that night, but Amy thinks of Spike afterward.

Part Three describes a day in the life of Lobelle in his gallery. In contrast to Spike and his wild ways, Lobelle is completely organized—his life is built around good taste. He has even picked members of his staff as decorative elements. To me, Part Three is the best part of *Circles*.

Part Four is the opening of the Foro show. After it is well underway, Spike and his friends arrive. Amy is not yet there. Spike is antagonistic and gets into a scuffle with the art collector introduced in Part One. As Spike is being escorted out, he swings at Lobelle and Lobelle pushes him away. He falls against a marble version of "Bird in Flight" by Brancusi, causing it to break in many pieces. Amy arrives just then. Spike asks her to leave with him. She declines, but says she will meet him later. After the show, Amy defends Spike without attacking Lobelle. She leaves alone, goes to a bar, has some drinks, realizes she has had too much, and abruptly leaves to vomit, as the novel ends.

I gave the manuscript to a bright young editor, Marcia Prince (who later, under her married name, Marcia Freedman, became a member of the Knesset in Israel). She suggested a few minor changes and one major one: switch Part One and Part Two, thus starting the novel with Lobelle returning from France, and turning the whole of the East Hampton scene with Spike and Amy into a long flashback. Friedman accepted this recommendation. The resulting novel has balance: the new arrangement is: (1) Lobelle and Amy, (2) Spike and Amy, (3) Lobelle in his gallery, and (4) Lobelle, Spike, and Amy brought together for the climax, which ends with them all apart.

The effect of this change is that Lobelle more thoroughly dominates the novel than before. This did not please Charles Byrne, who reprinted the novel a year later for the paperback mass market under the title *I Need to Love* (a new title supplied by Friedman) with a beautiful semi-nude illustration of Amy on the cover. He had been attracted to the novel for the paperback market primarily because of its sensational original opening of Spike painting with a machine gun, smoking pot, and making love to the waiting Amy, and going on to what turned out to be a rather wild party.

So Friedman's career was possibly inalterably bent toward hard cover publication and more literary novels by his acceptance of a young editor's ideas on form, probably gained during her studies at Bennington.

How did the public receive *Circles* and what did the publisher and author do to push it? Of its twenty-five or more newspaper and magazine reviews, eleven were quite positive. Fortunately for Friedman and his publisher, among newspapers *The New York Times Book Review* and the book section of the *Los Angeles Times* published the most positive reviews, and most of the negative ones were in smaller provincial papers. But the situation was not quite as good among larger magazines: though Friedman himself received nearly a full-page mini-profile in *The New Yorker* that was very positive, Dorothy Parker blasted the book briefly in *Esquire*, and it was roasted for several pages in *Art News* in a review-article written by May Natalie Tabak.

Publicity, in addition to *The New Yorker* piece, included "items" in the nationally syndicated gossip columns of Walter Winchell and Dorothy Kilgallen, both saying that the novel was causing talk in East Hampton and New York. The previously cited *Library Journal* statement by Friedman appeared in its regular roundup of statements by first novelists. Friedman was also interviewed on several radio shows.

Advertisements consisted of inclusion of the book in the publisher's catalog, sent to bookstores, libraries, and reviewers; a flyer sent to major bookstores quoting favorable reviews; inclusion of a brief description and photo of the book in the publisher's announcement ads in trade and library publications; and some small ads, some of *Circles* alone, and some of *Circles* together with other books of the publisher in *The New York Times* and New York *Herald Tribune*, Sunday and Saturday. One ad featured a longish letter from James Michener praising the book.

The fashionable Kootz Gallery of modern art in New York gave, in cooperation with the publisher, a well-attended reception to introduce the book, followed by a large party in the Friedmans' attractive New York brownstone.

Actually, the novel's publication *did* generate a lot of talk, just as Winchell and Kilgallen reported, and much of the talk was by influential tastemakers. While the talk was not all positive, B.H. Friedman was well launched into his career as a novelist.

Martin Levin, in *The New York Times Book Review*, concluded his review of *Circles* by writing, ". . . all of the conflicting currents in this intriguing, original book come together in one edifying explosion."

Ruth B. Solner, in the *Los Angeles Times*, January 24, 1962, wrote, "Contrast between middle age and youth is the real theme, well-handled by means of phrasing and rephrasing the sophisticated dialogue.

"The pace is fast as a young widow tries to lose the image of her late husband in her choice between a dynamic young painter and a worldly, successful middle-aged gallery owner who thinks in terms of 'generations.' Peopled with art critics, buyers, hangers-on, a painter and a socialite sculptor, the novel builds to an exciting climax right out of 'La Dolce Vita.' "

Though *Circles* played well to most of the more sophisticated book critics in the largest cities, and with a select few out-of-towners, it also had to run the gauntlet of provincial and more conservative reviewers.

H.E. Radaty in the Ft. Wayne, Indiana *News Sentinel* said, "If you deleted the martinis, the sex, the pot (marijuana), the sex, the cocktail parties, and the sex, there would be little left in this novel."

The hard cover edition of *Circles* sold somewhere between 3600 and 3700 copies, and the later paperback had a first printing of 110,000 copies. Charles R. Byrne, later a New York literary agent, did not remember how many of these were sold. Friedman's entire earnings from *Circles* to date was the original advance of $2,000.

He went on to sell a second novel, *Yarborough*, to World. He then began to use literary agent Gunther Stuhlmann, who still represents him. Through Betty Prashker, then at Doubleday, he contracted, for $45,000, to write a biography of Gertrude Vanderbilt Whitney.

At about the same time, Friedman and other published writers joined together to form the Fiction Collective, a cooperative group that published the works of its members. The small publisher Ithaca House had already published his prose-poetry novel, *Whispers*, and Fiction Collective published a very fine short novel called *Museum*. Both of these went into second printings, and Viking published his *Almost a Life*. He has written a biography of Jackson Pollock, published by McGraw-Hill, and several monographs on artists.

In 1981 Little Brown published his novel *The Polygamist*, which sold 7500 copies in two printings, received much critical acclaim, and was optioned for the movies for a high sum. He is at work on a novel now about real estate. So his career continues to move along.

Asked to describe his position in American letters, he felt he was a serious and comparatively significant author of his generation—a characterization I consider reasonable, since most of his books are reviewed in publications like *The New York Times Book Review* and *The New Yorker*.

As advice to first novelists, Bob Friedman cited points he made to students when he taught writing at Cornell University. He advised them to learn by writing, and assigned one thousand words a week for the fifteen weeks of the course—less than a page a day, but enough to build momentum. He sees writing as a reinforcement of ambition, and as an activity that strengthens a writer's direction.

Fiction to him is a rearrangement of experience; he believes that even Shakespeare drew from his own experience to depict such emotions as ambition in his characters. The novel is best explained by its root meaning—"new." A novel presents experience in a new way. Originality is being yourself—getting your own voice on a page.

In *Coming Close*, he writes, "I am full of ideas about moving as a metaphor for life, for writing itself. I see it, like writing, as a rearrangement of experience. Each carton is packed with three-dimensional experience, ready to be opened, dusted, replaced, reseen."

Beginning writers of fiction should publish as much as they can in literary magazines, he advises, and portions of his own works have appeared in *Noble Savage, QRL,* and elsewhere. I agree with this observation—book editors read such magazines, and the editors of literary magazines can be important nurturers of talent.

I asked him whether his remark in *Coming Close,* "When I write my anger is dissipated," represented his motivation for writing; he replied that the remark had meaning only in context. His actual motivation for writing, he said, is joy.

What lessons can an aspiring first novelist learn from B.H. Friedman's career? As I see it, even four or five unpublished novels are not too much practice if you are determined to become a writer of quality. Don't be afraid to imitate first-rate writers whose work you admire. But then try to develop your own voice—originality is being yourself. And most important to the theme of this chapter, just because you are a success in business does not mean you cannot become a writer and a good one. In the course of business life be alert to those you meet—one of these contacts may offer entry to a publisher—after all, paper salesmen, printers, lawyers, stock and real estate brokers are everywhere, and they may be doing business with book publishers. Seek advice from experienced writers, and take it if you can. Persist in the face of rejections. Consider editorial suggestions carefully, as taking them may affect your whole career. Write to dissipate anger if necessary, but, if possible, write to express joy.

15.

A Best Seller the First Time Out

Anna Lee Waldo, author of *Sacajawea*

*A 1,000,000 COPY AMERICAN BEST SELLER
8 MONTHS ON THE NEW YORK TIMES LIST!*
—Copy from the cover of the Avon Books revised edition of *Sacajawea*

In the summer of 1974 I was sitting in my New York office when the telephone rang. A woman with a pleasant voice introduced herself as Anna Lee Waldo. Mrs. Waldo had decided that maybe she needed an agent, and though she was calling from her home near St. Louis, she had gotten my name from the New York Yellow Pages. I later learned this was her first call to a literary agent.

She told me that she had written a two-thousand-page novel, and sent it to Avon Books after Avon editor Nancy Coffey had invited her to do so in response to a query letter. That had been in February of the previous year. Now it was August, a year and a half later, and

Avon wasn't calling. In fact, Mrs. Waldo said, Nancy Coffey didn't respond to her letters and phone calls, and she felt desperate. She needed help.

Would I become her agent and look into it.?

My reply probably caused me to lose a great deal of money. Since I had had a couple of unfortunate experiences trying to represent writers whose work I had not read, I replied that I would like to read the novel. As it was about an Indian woman, Sacajawea, and how she accompanied the Lewis and Clark expedition safely across a major part of what later became the western U.S., and I liked the subjects of American Indians and exploration, I said that if I liked the way her manuscript was written, I would offer to represent her. Anna Lee Waldo authorized me to call Avon, and get the manuscript.

I telephoned Nancy Coffey and explained I wanted to come over and pick up the manuscript. Nancy Coffey replied, "Are you her agent?"

"No," I said, "I want to read the manuscript and decide whether or not I want to take it on."

The next day Mrs. Waldo called me again. Nancy Coffey, she said, had telephoned her and offered a contract and $8,000 advance royalties. "Decline it," I said. "If she offers you $8,000, it might be worth more, even much more. Even if you want to make a deal with her, there are the details of the contract to work out—royalty percentages, the foreign and movie rights, the option clause. Tell her to send the manuscript to me."

Waldo replied that it wasn't easy to sell a two-thousand-page manuscript, that she had worked more than ten years on it, and didn't know whether she should take a chance of losing this opportunity. She wanted to think it over.

The next day she called again. She had decided to accept the Avon offer, and not engage me as her agent. Negotiating on her own, she made an agreement with Avon that paid half of $8,500 advance royalties on signing, and half on publication. The advance was against all earnings. Royalties were 4 percent of the retail selling price on the first 150,000 copies sold, 6 percent for 150,000 to 300,000, 8 percent for 300,000 to 500,000, and 10 percent for all sold over 500,000. Subsidiary rights were split 50-50 between author and publisher. These rights included hard cover publication, book club use, serialization, motion picture and allied dramatic rights, British rights, and translation.

Copyright was to be in her name. Avon agreed to publish within twenty-four months "after approval and acceptance of Author's final manuscript." The agreement also included an option on her next book, "on terms to be mutually agreed upon."

Anna Lee Waldo thanked me for my interest in her work, and seemed to ignore my final comment, "At least strike out the option, so that if the book succeeds, you can come to me and we can plan the success of the next one from the beginning."

Two years later, I had turned my agency business over to my daughter and was working, near my home in New Jersey, as a senior editor of trade books for Prentice-Hall. I received another desperate phone call from Mrs. Waldo. After the contract with Avon had been signed, apparently little more had been done—as far as she knew, Avon had not edited the book or scheduled it for publication. Again, Avon wasn't calling.

I pointed out that since twenty-four months had passed, she could move to end the contract, and keep the money Avon had paid her. I urged her to do so, and submit the manuscript to me at Prentice-Hall. I would still like to read it. Or she could get an agent, and tell the agent of my interest.

But Anna Lee Waldo decided to stick with Avon, and, under Nancy Coffey's supervision, an editor was assigned to the book, who did some rewriting, and removed most of the footnotes from the novel. Though it was a novel, Mrs. Waldo had footnoted it extensively with her sources for the great amount of information she had put in about Indian life, Indian medicine, the Lewis and Clark Expedition, geography and geology, and historical background. Avon wanted her to take out the bibliography, but she insisted that it remain.

The novel was retitled *Sacajawea*—the original title had been *From Savage to Saint*—and finally published in April, 1979, more than five years after its February, 1973 submission. It had shrunk from the "698,000 words" described in the contract to the 580,000 or so words in its published form—more than 100,000 words, enough for an ordinary novel, had been taken out. It was, in Nancy Coffey's opinion, the longest paperback novel ever published in its original, 6x9, 1,359 page, two-pound edition. A revised mass-market edition published in 1984 was 1,424 pages, about 630,000 words. Only recently has a slightly longer novel been published in paperback, the Berkley reprint of Helen Hooven Santmyer's . . . *And Ladies of the Club.*

Is *Sacajawea* too long? I don't think so. Anna Lee Waldo can write short as well as long. Here is her one-paragraph summary of the novel, written for the use of movie agent Harry Bloom:

SACAJAWEA
1790's to 1884
Historical Novel
(New York, Avon Books, 1984)
by Anna Lee Waldo

One Paragraph Summary

The story of Sacajawea *is the story of a squaw who became an American heroine by carrying her first-born, infant son to the Pacific Ocean and back with the Lewis and Clark Expedition. She spent the rest of her life as a resident in the frontier town of St. Louis, as a wife of a Comanche brave and as a wanderer to Wind River telling her story and seeking that first-born son in America's great West. As a young girl, she knew savage slavery, rape, abuse, humility, hate, anger, fear, love, anguish, loneliness. As a mature woman, she experienced jealousy, cruelty, respect, glory and true love. She was a cowardly half-breed's woman, a mother among strangers, a warrior's sublime love, a traveler and venerable among her peers, always a talisman for peace.*

Not only does Sacajawea have an epic sweep, but it is the story of the adventures of a genuinely heroic woman. It also encompasses an enormous amount of information on the lives of American Indians, their relationships with whites, and with a black character in the novel, York, in the period of the nineteenth century—America's years of continental expansion.

How did Anna Lee Waldo, a chemist by training and teacher in mid-western colleges, mother of five children, and heretofore author mainly of chemistry articles, come to write a best seller?

About her choice of subject, Anna Lee Waldo said, "It has always been with me. When we were children, one of the games we played was 'Sacajawea.' "

In an interview by Judy Klemesrud in the *New York Times Book Review*, Anna Lee Waldo spoke at length of the inspiration for her book:

Mrs. Waldo . . . said she first became interested in North American Indian lore while growing up in Whitefish, Montana, in the heart of the Lewis and Clark expedition trail. "I used to walk around Whitefish Lake and fantasize I was an Indian girl. . . . I had Ovaltine cans full of spear points, and I hunted, fished, ate bear meat and huckleberries, and learned which plants could be used for medicinal purposes. Some of my classmates at school were Crow and Blackfoot Indians, and my best friend was a Blackfoot girl, Marjorie Heart-butte."

Whitefish is west of Glacier National Park, and this small town is served by the Great Northern Railroad, where Waldo's father worked.

Anna Lee Waldo graduated from the University of Montana at Bozeman and then traveled east to the University of Maryland, where she received a Master of Science degree in organic chemistry, and married Willis Waldo, an inorganic chemist.

She worked first as a chemist for Monsanto, and later did research in leukemia at the Miami Valley Hospital in Dayton, Ohio. Eventually she turned to teaching chemistry at St. Louis Community College—Meramec.

When each of their five children was born, the Waldos gave the infants Indian nicknames: Skookumchuck, A Polliwog, Williwaw, Kloochman, and Hee Hee Tum Tum. By the time *Sacajawea* was published, Mrs. Waldo was fifty-four, and her children ranged in age from sixteen to twenty-five.

Not until her fifth child was born did she decide to write her novel. "My husband, Bill, had great empathy," she recalled. "He never complained about my dislike for housework, about my papers on the floor, and he never picks them up."

The research for the novel became a family project. She, her husband, and children traveled over the Lewis and Clark expedition route three times. Besides the travel, Mrs. Waldo's research took her to libraries, history societies, and people who were experts in Indian lore. "I wrote to universities all over the country—even in Germany. That's where Sacajawea's first-born son spent at least three years," she told an interviewer in *Publishers Weekly*.

In writing her first novel, Waldo learned much more than just what there was to know about her heroine, Sacajawea. She learned much history and the realities of life for a Shoshoni living during the period of transition from tribal independence to domination by the United States.

Had she originally considered writing a nonfiction book about Sacajawea? Waldo replied that there were too many problems. "There were controversies about her life. Did she die at twenty-five, or live to be ninety? There were big gaps in the background, and in the history." By writing the book as a novel, Waldo said, she could continue her childhood game of pretending to be Sacajawea, and fill in the gaps imaginatively.

The research and writing took roughly ten years. She told me it was her "third or fourth draft I submitted to Avon." As the draft she sent to Avon was two thousand pages long, and was rewritten three or four times, that means she typed more than seven thousand pages—two million words—before she had her final manuscript.

About her work habits, she says, "I start in the morning after breakfast and get as much done as I can. After lunch I work until 5. I have a hard time sitting down—every day it's just as hard. Sometimes it takes me forty-five minutes to an hour to get started. I find it helps backtracking and rewriting the last few pages I did the day before." Part of the time while she was writing, she had to teach an early class and wasn't able to start until ten. In other periods, after finishing in the afternoon and having dinner, she taught a chemistry class at night. She continued to teach after her book became a best seller.

During her writing, "when my children came home from school, I would usually be in the middle of typing something creative. They would tiptoe and whisper to me. They could have yelled. I still wouldn't have heard."

When she finished the novel, she sent off query letters to hard cover publishers, "starting with A and continuing to Z. I sent queries one at a time. They wrote back letters showing they weren't interested. None invited me to submit." A Viking Press salesman she met through a local bookstore took the manuscript, and a year later, she went to his house and retrieved it. She does not believe he showed it to Viking.

Finally, Waldo decided to submit it to paperback publishers, and composed a fresh query letter. Starting again with A, she queried Avon first. She got no further down the alphabet. Nancy Coffey at Avon replied to her query, and asked to see the manuscript. Mrs. Waldo packed the manuscript into a 2x3-foot clothing box, and sent it off.

"I know I sound cocky," she later said, "but I never once felt that the book wouldn't be published. There was more than a four-year delay after Avon bought it. I was told Avon took the manuscript apart chapter by chapter and sent it to historians and anthropologists to check its accuracy. I knew they couldn't *lose* the manuscript—it was too big."

Though Anna Lee Waldo was not originally aware of it, Avon, once it had a final manuscript, planned to try to make the book a best seller. Nancy Coffey prevailed on the company to publish it as a trade paperback, priced at $8.95. Reader's copies were shipped in January, 1979, and a poster was shipped with the books when they went to stores. A *Publishers Weekly* story in the spring of 1979 devoted a full page to describing the book and Avon's campaign. At the time of its publication, the book immediately faced the competition of Double-day's already established best seller, *Hanta Yo*, by Ruth Beebe Hill, which was also about American Indians.

Avon asked Anna Lee Waldo to make a publicity tour to promote the book. Mrs. Waldo has been kind enough to let me quote from notes she made about this tour. When she sent them to me, I was amazed to see all of thirty-nine pages—intimate and very human:

> When Avon called about a three-week tour my first thought was: "How can anyone be interested in me? It is *Sacajawea* that ought to fascinate people."
>
> The publicity director of Avon Books, Diane O'Conner Glynn, explained, "People are interested in authors who give them a good read. They want to listen to what you say, ask you questions, and see how you think, what you look like. Avon will handle all details of travel, food, lodging, and promotion itinerary."
>
> My next question was a natural one. "What am I going to wear?" I teach college chemistry and wear jeans, a sweatshirt in winter, T-shirt in summer, under a white lab coat. I couldn't wear that.
>
> I received hints. "Don't wear white or black. Be comfortable. Remember you will have to put on your own make-up for TV. Don't skip meals, you'll need energy."
>
> Living from a suitcase for three weeks in May, a new city each day, I had to find clothes that could be folded and pulled out at a moment's notice and look freshly pressed.
>
> I pulled everything out of my closet and drawers. I wanted to have the smartest, prettiest, sexiest look I'd had in years. None of the old combinations worked. I put the jeans and shirts back in the drawer.
>
> Naturally I went shopping and took my twenty-six-year-old daughter for fashion advice. I bought two shirt-dresses of soft knit cotton, with cap sleeves and graceful gathers across the shoulder, elasticized at the waist. They wouldn't wrinkle. One was the palest yellow, the other apple green. I found another dress, bright red with tiny polka dots, with a deep V-neck, shawl collar and ties gathering the shoulder, made of

the softest kind of cotton knit.

"These are carefree, believe me," said the clerk, ringing up the cash register. "You can wash and hang them to dry overnight. They will look gorgeous next morning."

I found a wonderfully light, superbly comfortable brown sandal with a slight heel, and a white, open-toe sandal. Both had enough of the barefoot feeling to suit me. They would go with dresses or pants. I bought new navy, polyester slacks and an azure blue pair made from light-weight duck, along with a couple of short sleeved, non-wrinkle, cotton shirts, in pastel colors. I couldn't pass by a gauzy, baby-pink shirt, small collared, with cap sleeves and front rows of lacy openwork—called fagoting. Finally I bought an off-white, tailored, nubby weave, acrylic jacket for chilly days. It went well with the dresses and pants. I slipped a pair of beloved jeans into the bottom of my suitcase. I knew if I wore the gauzy shirt, the jacket and sandals with jeans, I'd look dressed-up lots of places.

Each morning I shower and wash my hair, hoping the hair is dry by the time I stand in front of the chemistry lecture hall. I don't take much time with make-up. So, I thought, "If people are going to be interested in what I look like—I should be interested." I assessed my fundamental cosmetic supply: peachy, pressed powder, wild strawberry lip gloss and English Leather Cologne. Right away I saw the stock needed broadening and purchased these additives: super-sheer liquid make-up base, sky-blue eye liner, and a tube of long-lash mascara. With all that could I look terrific?

The publicity tour started in St. Louis, where on May 4, 1979 Mayor Conway proclaimed "Sacajawea Day" and presented Anna Lee Waldo with a parchment scroll memorializing the event. In the afternoon several radio stations and the local KSD-TV interviewed her. She was relieved, because the questions were easy: "How long did it take to write your book?" "Why did you write this book?" "What did your family say?"

At a book launching party, on the riverboat *Tom Sawyer*, which cruised the Mississippi River with media people from New York, St. Louis, St. Charles and Kansas City, she wore the soft green dress, and was careful not to spill "potato salad, spaghetti, Jello, coffee or ice cream. A little champagne jumped out of a glass and sank into the skirt area, but the saleslady told the truth. It washed out easily. My younger son did not recognize me out of blue jeans, until he noticed I was wearing a feather in my hair." Her notes continue:

Monday, May 7th, I faced my responsibility of representing Avon books on a major-city tour. In addition to a suitcase and shoulder bag I carried a flight bag that had a hair-drier and make-up in the bottom. On top was a plastic shopping bag full of duck feathers. I put a feather into each book I autograph. It is appropriate, because I always wear a feather and Saca-jawea means "Bird Woman." Can you imagine Avon's New York PR people shopping for a pound of duck feathers?

Mrs. Waldo toured Chicago, Seattle, Portland, San Francisco. Then in Los Angeles, as had happened in St. Louis, Mayor Bradley proclaimed "Sacajawea Day," and in the council chambers of City Hall, spoke of how he, a black person himself, could identify with the black character in her novel, Ben York.

She spoke before the City Council, which "seemed unreal," she said. Again, she was presented with a parchment copy of the procla- mation. Continuing on to San Diego, she noted:

I had an hour to get to the motel, change to the red dress with white polka dots, white sandals, pin a feather to collar, eat a poached egg, drink orange juice, then do a taped radio inter- view and taped TV interview for "Keen's People."

I carried seven slides of scenes from Lemhi Pass, Fort Bridger, the Wind River Reservation and its elegant, grave memorial to Sacajawea. Sometimes TV people liked to use these slides during an interview.

My longest radio interview was to be taped at a local San Diego university. A graduate student wanted to use the in- terview as part of a master's dissertation in communications. When it was all over she found nothing on the tape. How em- barrassing! She was crestfallen and on the verge of tears.

"How much time do I have?" I asked my contact.

"Thirty minutes before the next interview."

"I can talk twenty minutes on your tape and you can splice in forty minutes of excerpts from Sacajawea that you read later," I suggested.

She brightened. "I'll quote Sacajawea's speech at the Ft. Bridger Treaty, and—oh, thank you—let's start."

She continued on to Salt Lake City, then:

That evening I was in Albuquerque. As the plane opened for debarking I noticed cameramen and reporters bunched together, watching as people moved down the stairs.

"There's a very important person on this flight," I said to myself stretching around to see if I could recognize anyone. At the end of the walkway I spotted a young woman dressed in a beaded buckskin tunic with silver and turquoise around her neck and arms. "How lovely," I whispered. Then I smiled and walked past. She reached out for my hand—cameras clicked.

"Welcome to Albuquerque, Anna Lee Waldo," she said, shaking my hand. It was hard to believe. I was the VIP. This red carpet treatment was for me. She smiled and gave me a hug, saying, "I'm Margret Klass from the Albuquerque Chamber of Commerce." I smiled and my heart thumped when I was handed a small, red banner with the words OF-FICIAL RED CARPET on the center. I still have that banner hanging over my desk.

Then on to Oklahoma City, Denver, Omaha, Kansas City, Chicago again. "Bookstores now generally had *Sacajawea* in stock and it appeared to be selling well. I began to feel important. People said nice things about the book. Before calling it a day, my contact suggested I go to the Marshall Fields Department Store. Their book department did not have *Sacajawea*. In fact, the personnel had not heard of it. That brought me back to reality where I belonged and my head shrank to normal quickly."

After Dallas and Ft. Worth, three weeks of traveling were over, and she was home with her family. Before she was settled back into her old routine, Avon called again, and persuaded her to do another tour "along the Lewis and Clark trail. The tour would not only include plane travel, but also automobile travel and there won't be a contact person in every city," the Avon representative said. "We would like to send your husband with you so he can see about car rentals and keep the media interviews lined up."

Willis Waldo agreed to go. Memories surged of travels with the children along the historic trail; they went to Bismarck, North Dakota; to Billings, Montana; to Great Falls, Montana (where Anna Lee Waldo had been born); to Helena, capital of the state, where she and her husband gathered a box of sagebrush and pine cones to send to "the Manhattan-bound Avon Books people"; then to Missoula, Montana; to Bozeman, Montana; on to Spokane, Washington; to Moscow,

Idaho; to Lewiston, Idaho; to Clarkston and Walla Walla, Washington; to Astoria, Oregon; on again to Vancouver, Washington; Boise, Idaho, and at long last home again to St. Louis.

But her travels weren't over. Avon called and asked Waldo to go to Toronto, to the Canadian Booksellers Convention, where she signed and put a feather in at least a hundred books. "*Sacajawea* was advertised as the number one best seller in Canada. I was impressed. For the first time I met officers of Avon Books." She says, however, she has not to this day met Nancy Coffey.

Eventually many more publicity appearances followed.

The book proved to be an enduring favorite—it was, just as Avon says on the jacket of the 1984 edition, "eight months on *The New York Times* Best Seller List."

In a letter Mrs. Waldo wrote to me in the fall of 1985, she stated, "The latest invoice I have from Avon states that as of 12/31/84, 1,232,000 copies of *Sacajawea* have been printed."

In addition, Avon made agreements with foreign publishers that have resulted in French, German, and Dutch editions.

Meanwhile, Anna Lee Waldo was working on a new manuscript, which she called *Prairie*. It is, again, a historical novel set in the West. She asked me to handle it as her agent, and the reader can probably guess who contracted for it: Nancy Coffey, then editor-in-chief of Berkley Books.

"Like everything Anna Lee writes," Nancy Coffey told me during our talks about the manuscript, "it's a magical book."

This new work was even longer—something over 2,200 manuscript pages. I was able to jam it tightly into five ordinary manuscript boxes. It became a best seller in December, 1986.

As I write, Anna Lee Waldo is researching a third historical novel. I still have not met her in person—only by phone and mail—but I have a photo of her which shows an attractive woman who radiates confidence and good feeling.

What can an aspiring first novelist learn from the extraordinary experience of Anna Lee Waldo? The most important lesson, I think, is that if you take the gamble of trusting a publisher, and stick with that publisher even when things seem to move at a snail's pace, it can sometimes work out very well. Avon Books, represented by their editor Nancy Coffey, was the first publisher interested in Waldo's work, and Waldo stuck with them. And they handsomely, if slowly, rewarded her for that trust by doing everything a publisher can do to turn a giant novel into a giant best seller. Waldo's second novel,

Prairie, has turned out to be another million-copy novel, with a first printing of 500,000 paperback copies and more than 500,000 additional copies for the second, mass market, edition.

So her advice to other writers has the power of experience behind it:

> Never give up. If you feel strongly about your writing, someone will like it and publish it. Take a chance. Get it all out. Don't talk about it too much—your idea can wear thin. Put it all on paper. Don't depend on critics. Your novel must have conflict—man against nature, man against man. Your protagonist must survive conflict.

And you, as an aspiring first novelist, must survive conflict too: competitive ideas floating in your mind about what to write, the tussle for time to write, combat with problems of plot and form, the scuffle of the marketplace, and the struggle within yourself between despair over rejections and elation over creative work successfully completed.

Regardless of the outcome of your first novel's plot, may your personal struggle to write and sell your first novel have as happy an ending as that of Anna Lee Waldo!

Checklist:
Seven Dos and
Seven Don'ts for
First Novelists

Do study and master English grammar, usage, and spelling before completing the final draft of your novel. If you lack these skills, do hire or beg the services of a literate professional writer, teacher, or editor to correct your manuscript, then have it professionally typed.

Do read the works of well-known writers of the kind of novel you want to write.

Do carry a little note pad with you and write down comments you overhear that you may be able to use some day. Or ideas that might otherwise fade away.

Do make your first novel at least 50,000 words long (two hundred double-spaced pages of pica type, using a one-and-one-half inch left margin and a one-inch margin on the other three sides). Try to avoid making it longer than 100,000 words (400 pages), unless it is a historical novel.

Do type with a new, black ribbon so your manuscript will be attractive and will photocopy well. If you have a word processor, use a letter quality printer. Publishers don't like a dot-matrix printer.

Do submit a perfect, plain-paper photocopy of your manuscript, and, no matter what anyone else tells you, retain the original so you can make more copies. That way, you always have a perfect copy yourself. The only alternative is a letter-quality computer printout—one for submitting, and one *already printed* for yourself.

Do put your name, address, and phone number on the title page and cover letter for every submission, whether query or manuscript.

Don't use cliches, stereotypes, or commonplaces.

Don't use anachronisms in a historical novel or any novel: Jesus Christ probably never said, "Gee whiz!"

Don't plagiarize. If you want to borrow or adapt someone else's plot or characters, borrow from classic writers whose work is out of copyright. But even then, don't copy their work exactly; editors are readers.

Don't submit your book without an invitation—send a query first.

Don't call your novel "a fiction novel" or "fictional novel." Those expressions are redundant. Just call it a novel.

Don't expect a reply to your submission or query unless you enclosed a self-addressed, stamped envelope, an "SASE."

Don't stop with one submission. Submit, submit, submit!

Further Reading and Reference

A SHORT LIST OF NOVELS

Which of the current or recently published authors and their novels will endure—say, twenty-five years from now? If you could know that, it might help you. If you could read these books, and get some insight into their enduring qualities and concerns, you might have a little edge over other writers in trying to decide on a strategy of how to express yourself effectively in the form of a first novel.

Rather than hazard such a prediction myself, I have turned to a class of editors and publishers who professionally make such predictions—though for a shorter term—all the time: reprinters, book club editors, and magazine editors. I asked six such people to say what books published in the recent past might still be widely read twenty-five years from now: *Martin Asher*, of the Book-of-the-Month Club, and former editor-in-chief of Pocket Books; *Oscar Dystel*, president and chairman of Bantam Books for many years, and now head of Oscar Dystel and Partners; *Donald I. Fine*, of Donald I. Fine, Inc. and formerly editor-in-chief or officer of other hard cover publishers and of Dell Books; *Anne Freegood*, of Modern Library and editor of Random House; *Gerald Gross*, of Dodd, Mead & Company and formerly editor-in-chief of various paperback publishers; *Robie Macauley*, of Houghton Mifflin Company, and formerly fiction editor of *Playboy* and *Kenyon Review*.

Here are ten authors and their works they suggested might last, be bought, and read twenty-five years from now. You might want to study them.

All the novels of Louis Auchincloss
The Book of Daniel, E.L. Doctorow
Final Payments, Mary Gordon
Catch-22, Joseph Heller
Ridley Walker, Russell Hoban
A Separate Peace, John Knowles
Tar Babies, Toni Morrison
The Young Lions, Irwin Shaw
Mosquito Coast, Paul Theroux
End as a Man, Calder Willingham

OTHER BOOKS AND MAGAZINES YOU
MAY WANT TO READ
OR CONSULT

Theory, How-to, and Surveys

The Art of Fiction: Notes on Craft for Young Writers, John Gardner, Vintage

The Art of the Novel, Henry James, Charles Scribner's Sons, various editions

Aspects of the Novel, E.M. Forster, Harcourt Brace Jovanovich

The Craft of Writing, William Sloane, edited by Julia H. Sloane, W.W. Norton

Editors on Editing, Editor, Gerald Gross, Harper & Row

80 Years of Best Sellers, Alice Payne Hackett and James Henry Burke, R.R. Bowker

Encyclopedia of Western and Frontier Fiction, Editors, Jon Tuska and Vicki Peikarski, McGraw-Hill

How to Get Happily Published, Judith Appelbaum and Nancy Evans, New American Library

How to Write a Romance and Get It Published, Kathryn Falk, Crown

Murder Ink, Dilys Winn, Workman Publishing Company

Novelists on the Novel, Miriam Allott, Columbia University Press

The Realities of Fiction, Nancy Hale, Little, Brown & Co.

The Writing and Selling of Fiction, Paul R. Reynolds, William Morrow

Writing and Selling Science Fiction, Science Fiction Writers of America. Writer's Digest Books

Writing to Sell, Scott Meredith, Harper & Row

Style Guides

The Chicago Manual of Style, University of Chicago Press

Dictionary of Modern English Usage, Henry W. Fowler, Edited by Ernest Gowers, Oxford University Press

The Elements of Style, William Strunk and E.B. White, Macmillan

It Was a Dark and Stormy Night: The Best (?) From the Bulwer-Lytton Contest, Compiled by Scott Rice, Penguin [a diverting how-not-to book on style]

Reference

Oxford English Dictionary, 13 vol., 3 suppl., Oxford University Press

Webster's Third International Dictionary, Unabridged: The Great Library of the English Language, Merriam-Webster

Dictionary of American Slang, Harold Wentworth & Stuart B. Flexner, T.Y. Crowell

Dictionary of Slang and Unconventional English, Eric Partridge, Macmillan

Dictionary of Euphemisms and Other Doubletalk, Hugh Rawson, Crown

Roget's International Thesaurus, T.Y. Crowell

New American Roget's College Thesaurus in Dictionary Form, New American Library

Directories

Contact Book, Celebrity Service, Inc., Biennial

Fiction Writer's Market, Writer's Digest Books, Annual

Literary Agents of North America Marketplace, Author Aid/Research International, Annual

Literary Market Place: The Directory of American Book Publishing, R.R. Bowker, Annual

Manhattan Consumer Yellow Pages, New York Telephone, Annual [see listing, "Literary Agents"]

Writer's Handbook, The Writer, Inc., Publisher, Annual

Writer's Market, Writer's Digest Books, Annual

Contracts and the Law

How to Understand and Negotiate a Book Contract or Magazine Agreement, Richard Balkin, Writer's Digest Books

The Rights of Authors and Artists, Kenneth P. Norwich and Jerry Chasen, Bantam Books

Writer's Legal Guide, Ted Crawford, E.P. Dutton

Magazines

Publishers Weekly, 1180 Avenue of the Americas, New York 10036, Weekly

The Writer, 8 Arlington Street, Boston MA 02116, Monthly

Writer's Digest, 9933 Alliance Road, Cincinnati, OH 45242, Monthly

Acknowledgments

Oscar Collier wishes to thank the following writers for their help or permission to quote their work: Christopher Britton, Karen Brush, J.F. Burke, Clyde Burleson, B.H. Friedman, Arthur Gladstone, Bonnie Golightly, Niel Hancock, Joseph Hansen, Susan Johnson, John Kimbro, Russell Kirk, Steven Linakis, Mark McShane, Robert Oliphant, G.J.A. O'Toole, Nan F. Salerno, Rosamond M. Vanderburgh, Anna Lee Waldo, and Joan Wolf; and the following editors, agents, publishers, and others connected with book publishing for information, opinions, and anecdotes: Martin Asher, Julian Bach, John Beaudouin, Knox Burger, Lisl Cade, Anita Diamant, John Douglas, Kate Duffy, Oscar Dystel, Donald I. Fine, Anne Freegood, Arnold Goodman, Phyllis Grann, Gerald Gross, Peter Heggie, Darrell Husted, Joan Kahn, Irwin Karp, Barbara Lowenstein, Robie Macauley, Kathleen Malley, Scott Meredith, Leona Nevler, Patrick O'Connor, Harriet Pilpel, Hugh Rawson, James F. Seligmann, Oliver Swan, James O. Wade, Ann Hukill Yeager, and Genevieve Young; and for his professional reading of the manuscript, Howard Cady. He wishes particularly to thank the professionals whose encouragement and assistance made completion and publication of this work possible: his daughter and agent, Lisa Collier Cool; manuscript editor Nancy Dibble; managing editor Howard Wells; and Carol Cartaino, editor-in-chief of Writer's Digest Books, whose encouragement, toleration of his delays, and valuable editorial input from his first handwritten outline to final manuscript were essential; and his coauthor, Frances Spatz Leighton, who brought professional zest to its research, writing, and completion.

Frances Spatz Leighton wishes to thank The Library of Congress with its many specialists in each field and its excellent Information Service; George Mason Library of Virginia—especially Alice Mihos; Martin Luther King Library of Washington, D.C.—especially Nineta Rozen and Marian Holt of the History and Biography Division; the Chevy Chase Library of Washington, D.C.—and especially Adel Klalathari; Joyce Engelson; Ellis Amburn; Inga Dean, and Jean Naggar.

Index

Other Books of Interest

General Writing Books
Beginning Writer's Answer Book, edited by Kirk Polking (paper) $12.95
Getting the Words Right: How to Revise, Edit and Rewrite, by Theodore A. Rees Cheney $14.95
How to Get Started in Writing, by Peggy Teeters (paper) $8.95
How to Increase Your Word Power, by the editors of Reader's Digest $19.95
How to Write a Book Proposal, by Michael Larsen $9.95
Just Open a Vein, edited by William Brohaugh $15.95
Pinckert's Practical Grammar, by Robert C. Pinckert $14.95
The 29 Most Common Writing Mistakes & How to Avoid Them, by Judy Delton $9.95
Writer's Block & How to Use It, by Victoria Nelson $14.95
The Writer's Digest Guide to Manuscript Formats, by Buchman & Groves $16.95
Writer's Guide to Research, by Lois Horowitz $9.95
Writer's Market, edited by Glenda Neff $21.95
Nonfiction Writing
Basic Magazine Writing, by Barbara Kevles $16.95
How to Sell Every Magazine Article You Write, by Lisa Collier Cool $14.95
Writing Creative Nonfiction, by Theodore A. Rees Cheney $15.95
Writing Nonfiction that Sells, by Samm Sinclair Baker $14.95
Fiction Writing
Creating Short Fiction, by Damon Knight (paper) $8.95
Fiction is Folks: How to Create Unforgettable Characters, by Robert Newton Peck (paper) $8.95
Fiction Writer's Market, edited by Laurie Henry $18.95
Handbook of Short Story Writing, by Dickson and Smythe (paper) $8.95
Storycrafting, by Paul Darcy Boles (paper) $9.95
Writing the Modern Mystery, by Barbara Norville $15.95
Writing the Novel: From Plot to Print, by Lawrence Block (paper) $8.95
Special Interest Writing Books
The Children's Picture Book: How to Write It, How to Sell It, by Ellen E.M. Roberts (paper) $14.95
Comedy Writing Secrets, by Melvin Helitzer $16.95
The Complete Book of Scriptwriting, by J. Michael Straczynski (paper) $9.95
How to Sell & Re-Sell Your Writing, by Duane Newcomb $10.95
How to Write Tales of Horror, Fantasy & Science Fiction, edited by J.N. Williamson $15.95
How to Write & Sell a Column, by Raskin & Males $10.95
How to Write & Sell Your Personal Experiences, by Lois Duncan (paper) $9.95
Poet's Market, by Judson Jerome $17.95
Writing Short Stories for Young People, by George Edward Stanley $15.95
The Writing Business
A Beginner's Guide to Getting Published, edited by Kirk Polking $10.95
How to Bulletproof Your Manuscript, by Bruce Henderson $9.95
How to Write Irresistible Query Letters, by Lisa Collier Cool $10.95
How You Can Make $25,000 a Year Writing (No Matter Where You Live), by Nancy Edmonds Hanson $15.95
Literary Agents: How to Get & Work with the Right One for You, by Michael Larsen $9.95
Professional Etiquette for Writers, by William Brohaugh $9.95

To order directly from the publisher, include $2.00 postage and handling for 1 book and 50¢ for each additional book. Allow 30 days for delivery.
Writer's Digest Books, Dept. B, 1507 Dana Avenue, Cincinnati, Ohio 45207
Credit card orders call TOLL-FREE
1-800-543-4644 (Outside Ohio)
1-800-551-0884 (Ohio only)
Prices subject to change without notice.

How to Write and Sell Your First Novel. Copyright © 1986 by Oscar Collier and Frances Spatz Leighton. Printed and bound in the United States of America. All rights reserved. No part of this book may be reproduced in any form or by any electronic or mechanical means including information storage and retrieval systems without permission in writing from the publisher, except by a reviewer, who may quote brief passages in a review. Published by Writer's Digest Books, an imprint of F&W Publications, Inc., 1507 Dana Avenue, Cincinnati, Ohio 45207. First edition. Second printing, 1987

Library of Congress Cataloging in Publication Data

Collier, Oscar, 1924-
How to write and sell your first novel.

Bibliography: p.
Includes index.
I. Fiction—Authorship. I. Leighton, Frances Spatz.
II. Title.
PN3365.C64   1986   808'.02   86-11093
ISBN 0-89879-210-X

Design by Joan Jacobus

HOW TO
WRITE
AND SELL
YOUR
FIRST NOVEL

By Oscar Collier
with
Frances Spatz Leighton

Writer's Digest Books

Cincinnati, Ohio